MW01152292

NORTH AMERICA

For Jim Jennings —
Thanks for your support
of ASMI !
Best regards,

NORTH AMERICA
AN INTRODUCTION
Michael M. Brescia and John C. Super

11-15-2014

UTP

University of Toronto Press

© Higher Education University of Toronto Press Incorporated 2009

All rights reserved. The use of any part of this publication reproduced, transmitted in any form or by any means, electronic, mechanical, photocopying, recording, or otherwise, or stored in a retrieval system, without prior written consent of the publisher — or in the case of photocopying, a licence from Access Copyright (Canadian Copyright Licensing Agency), One Yonge Street, Suite 1900, Toronto, Ontario M5E 1E5 — is an infringement of the copyright law.

Library and Archives Canada Cataloguing in Publication

Brescia, Michael M.
     North America: an introduction / Michael M. Brescia, John C Super.

Includes bibliographic references and index.
ISBN 978-0-8020-9675-3

1. North America—History. I. Super, John C., 1944–   II. Title.

E38.B74 2008   970   C2008-904322-7

We welcome comments and suggestions regarding any aspect of our publications — please feel free to

contact us at the addresses below or at customerservice@utphighereducation.com.

North America
10 St. Mary Street, Suite 700, Toronto, Ontario, Canada, M4Y 2W8
2250 Military Road, Tonawanda, NY, USA, 14150
Tel: (416) 978-2239; Fax: (416) 978-4738
email: news@utphighereducation.com

UK, Ireland, and continental Europe
NBN International, Estover Road, Plymouth, UK PL6 7PY
Tel: 44 (0) 1752 202300; Fax: 44 (0) 1752 202330
email: enquiries@nbninternational.com

www.utphighereducation.com

This book is printed on paper containing 100% post-consumer fibre.

Higher Education department of the University of Toronto Press acknowledges the financial support of the Government of Canada through the Book Publishing Industry Development Program (BPIDP) for our publishing activities.

Designed by Daiva Villa, Chris Rowat Design

PRINTED IN CANADA

To Alejandra and Karina, Mom and Dad, with love. M.M.B.

To Sofia and Noelle. J.C.S.

CONTENTS

Preface   ix

A Note on Terminology   xiii

List of Maps   xv

    I   Convergence and Divergence   1

   II   Contours of the Past   15

  III   Regions and Resources   37

  IV   Politics and Power   63

   V   Continental Diplomacy   89

  VI   Indians and Europeans   109

 VII   Immigration   129

VIII   Labor and Class   149

  IX   Trade and Tariffs   167

   X   Church, State, and Society   187

  XI   Structures of the Past   203

Bibliography   217

Index   231

PREFACE

The geographic vastness and historical complexity of North America make it particularly difficult to study as a unit. The many different peoples who have for millennia made their lives in the diverse regions of the continent created unique cultures that at times appear to have little in common. Historians have had difficulty synthesizing this diversity and presenting the North American experience as an integrated whole.

When they have studied North America as an historical region, historians have usually emphasized the Anglo-Saxon record in continental North America. General interpretations of nineteenth- and twentieth-century North American history in particular exclude the Mexican story in the southern reaches of the continent and minimize the recent history of Quebec. The grand narrative tradition not only identified and privileged what were considered unique cultural and environmental traits that helped explain the successes and limitations of each nation, including its apparent political stability, economic prosperity, and social progress but, conversely, also found a place for what was considered backward, inert, dull, or arrogant. Often scholars in Canada, Mexico, and the United States defined their neighbors in ways that revealed more about their own cultural values and political sensibilities than it did about the historical experiences of the peoples they were trying to assess.

This study builds on the premise that the experiences of each country of North America can be better understood in a continental perspective. To be sure, each country has defined, and continues to redefine, the parameters of its national story, adding and omitting nuance and subtlety depending on circumstance. History becomes more intelligible, not to mention more appealing, however, with recognition of shared historical problems and patterns of change and continuity. The mainstream media in each of the three countries of North America tend to offer caricature to their respective audiences, conjuring and transmitting neat and tidy images of Mexicans, Canadians, and Americans that reduce historical complexity to fit a conceptual understanding of North America based on the nation-state. The chapters that follow underscore the similarities and differences in the history of the three countries and suggest how change in one country affected change in another. Broad patterns of change and development are emphasized at the expense of a detailed investigation of institutions or problems in a particular country or time. By placing the North American past in a comparative framework, we draw upon traditional and more recent scholarly efforts within the world history paradigm that seek to interpret the broad sweep of continental history as interconnected processes rather than mutually exclusive variables.

The work alson draws on our own research experiences in Mexico, Canada, and the United States. More importantly, it relies on the vast and sophisticated scholarly literature on the three countries. Works that study historical problems from a binational or trinational perspective were particularly useful. In the former category, we wish to single out Seymour Martin Lipset's *Continental Divide: The Values and Institutions of the United States and Canada* (1989) and William H. Beezley's and Colin M. MacLachlan's *El Gran Pueblo: A History of Greater Mexico* (1994). In the latter category, the efforts of Herbert Eugene Bolton to interpret North America and then the entire sweep of the Americas, especially his essay "Do the Americas Have a Common History?" (1932), convinced us of the value of a continental perspective. Recent works by Anthony DePalma (*Here: A Biography of the New American Continent*, 2001), Wiil Ferguson (*Canadian History for Dummies*, 2nd edition, 2005), Robert Earle and John Wirth (*Identities in North America. The Search for Community*, 1995), and James W. Russell (*After the Fifth Sun: Class and Race in North America*, 1994) provide valuable insights on the social, cultural, and economic history of the continent.

Perhaps we should approach a subject as grand as North America with some trepidation as well as a healthy dose of humor. We are reminded of the opening page of D.H. Lawrence's *Mornings in Mexico*: "We talk so grandly, in capital letters, about Morning in Mexico. All it amounts to is one little individual looking at a bit of sky and trees, then looking down at the page of his exercise book. It is a pity we don't remember this. When books come out with grand titles, like *The Future of America* or *The European Situation* [or *North America: An Introduction*], it's a pity we don't immediately visualize a thin or a fat person, in a chair or in bed, dictating to a bob-haired stenographer or making little marks on paper with a fountain pen" (Lawrence 1930, 9). Or visualize a retired history professor and a tenure-track museum curator and history professor sitting hour after hour in front of a computer (and in the library, on the phone, and via e-mail) trying to make sense out of a rather large and complex subject.

We express our gratitude to friends and colleagues who listened to our points of view and then asked pointed questions: Chuck Adams, Jean-François Bélisle, Richard Eaton, Kenneth Fones-Wolf, Martha Few, Paul Fish, Suzanne Fish, Mark Gaigall, Kevin Gosner, Beth Grindell, Donna Guy, Angelo Joaquin, Vincent Hayes, Ronald Lewis, Hartman Lomawaima, Maurizio Marinelli, Ken Martis, Michal McMahon, the late Michael C. Meyer, Dirk Raat, Michael Riley, Jeffrey Soos, Donley Studlar, and the anonymous reviewers of the manuscript. Our editors, Natalie

Fingerhut and Michael Harrison, have supported this project longer than most others would have done. Their enthusiasm for our approach to North America made the light shine even brighter as we approached the end of the tunnel.

M.M.B. Tucson, Arizona, North America
J.C.S. Morgantown, West Virginia, North America
April 2008

A NOTE ON TERMINOLOGY

Even a cursory glance at the literature on North America published in the twentieth and early twenty-first centuries demonstrates a lack of consensus among historians in Canada, Mexico, and the United States regarding the use of the word "Indian." In the Canadian context, the term collectively describes all the indigenous people who are not Inuit or Métis. The *Constitution Act, 1982*, specifies that Indian peoples are one of three peoples recognized as Aboriginal (the others being the Inuit and the Métis). According to the Indian and Northern Affairs Canada website (http://www.ainc-inac.gc.ca), there are three categories of Indians in Canada: Status Indians (peoples who are entitled to have their names included on the Indian Register and, therefore, enjoy certain rights and benefits under Canadian law); Non-Status Indians (peoples who consider themselves Indians or members of a First Nation but whom the government does not recognize as Indians under the *Indian Act*, either because they are unable to prove their status or have lost their status rights); and Treaty Indians (Status Indians who belong to a First Nation that signed a treaty with the Crown). Generally speaking, "Indian" is considered outdated and offensive, and Canadians employ the term "First Nation" instead of "Indian."

In the United States, historians use "Indian" quite frequently in their work, or they use variations thereof, including American Indian and Amerindian. Often Indians themselves employ the term to reference indigenous people more broadly. Many prefer to identify themselves as members of a particular tribe, however; for example, one might say, "I am Hopi" or "I am Tohono O'Odham." The term "Native American" has become popular in literary and academic circles. College campuses across the United States sponsor "Native American" film festivals and "Native American" poetry readings, while faculty offer interdisciplinary courses on "Native American" culture and society. The use of "Indian" is widespread enough, however, that it is generally accepted and not considered offensive.

In Mexico, "indio" and "indígena" are used interchangeably by a cross-section of society: whites, mestizos, and "indios" themselves. "Indio," in particular, has been part of the lexicon since the sixteenth century, with "naturales" and "gentiles" also being used in specific contexts (legal and cultural) during the colonial period to identify the indigenous population. Language and cultural affinity blend together and remain important markers for many indigenous communities: Zapotec, Tzotzil, Mixtec, Tzeltal, Otomi, Nahuatl, Chontal, etc. While "indio" is used in multiple settings almost everywhere and by everyone in Mexico, the white and mestizo populations also wield the term as an insult in certain social contexts to imply backwardness or a rural upbringing.

Finally, in keeping with current usage, we employ "England" and "English" to refer to the United Kingdom before 1707; after that "Great Britain," "Britain," and "British" are employed. When we refer to language and not the political entity, we use "English."

LIST OF MAPS

Map 1: Polar Projection of North America   13
Map 2: Pre-Columbian North America   19
Map 3: Physical Features of North America   39
Map 4: The U.S.-Mexican War   95
Map 5: Population Densities within NAFTA Countries   183

CHAPTER 1

CONVERGENCE AND DIVERGENCE

On 1 January 1994, the North American Free Trade Agreement (NAFTA) went into effect, signaling the final achievement of a process that had its origins in the early twentieth century. Canada, the United States, and Mexico agreed to lower and eventually eliminate tariffs on most goods. The three countries also created new mechanisms for resolving disputes and for safeguarding the environment. Despite the substantial opposition to NAFTA in all three countries, national governments proclaimed it with enthusiasm and fanfare, arguing that a new era in continental cooperation had been reached.

On the same day that NAFTA was launched, the *Ejército Zapatista de Liberación Nacional* (EZLN) attacked the Mexican government in the southernmost state of Chiapas, undermining visions of commonalities and a new continental community. Taken by surprise, many Mexico watchers had simply forgotten the harsh reality of much of Mexico. Subcomandante Marcos, the leader of the uprising, explained:

> The government has tried to portray Mexico as a First World country … But behind this picture is the real Mexico, the Mexico of the millions of Indians who live in extreme poverty. We have helped to peel off the mask to reveal the real Mexico. We've shown that in Chiapas, the Mexican government and a handful of businesses extract all the wealth … And what do they leave behind? Death and disease … Our uprising was the only way to draw world attention to the poverty and injustices that the indigenous people have been suffering for over 500 years. (Katzenberger 1995, 58)

Here is divergence rather than convergence. The Zapatista uprising bared the fundamental differences between Mexico and the United States and Canada. Mexico was still mired in poverty and oppressive politics, while its northern neighbors had achieved wealth, democracy, and political stability, or at least the appearance of political stability. Events in Canada soon challenged the idea of politics as usual. In 1995, citizens in Quebec went to the polls to vote on a measure that would have given the premier of Quebec the authority to push for sovereignty. The pro-sovereignty faction lost by the narrowest margin, promising that the issue would remain unsettled.

Recent events in Chiapas and Quebec are only two examples of divergent forces at work in North America. Significant foreign policy differences between Ottawa, Mexico City, and Washington, DC, also have stymied efforts at continental cooperation. Canadian and Mexican opposition to the U.S. invasion of Iraq in 2003 is but one glaring example of divergence at the diplomatic level. And stark differences that reflect uneven paths of historical development are found throughout the continent. They are emphasized most frequently in describing the differences between the United States and Mexico, vividly expressed along the Mexican border. Economic data consistently show that Mexico's per capita Gross National Product lags far behind that of the United States and Canada. To make matters worse, Mexico lost ground in the 1980s and 1990s, while the United States and Canada almost doubled their wealth. Wage data confirm the difference. According to U.S. Department of Labor statistics, 2004 hourly compensation costs averaged $23.17 in the United States, $21.42 in Canada, and only $2.50 in Mexico.

Such differences dramatize the uneven, asymmetrical development of North America. Asymmetries also exist within countries and regions. Chiapas, for example, is the poorest state in Mexico, marginalized and distant from the centers of wealth and power. Mexico has dynamic and modern sectors alongside poor and traditional ones. So do Canada and the United States. As examples, at different times in their historical development, Quebec and the Maritimes were in a dependent relationship with the more industrialized and richer province of Ontario, much like Appalachia was in a dependent relationship with the wealthier mid-Atlantic seaboard region in the United States. The asymmetries imply symmetries. Very poor rural laborers, whatever their region or country of residence, share certain characteristics, just as very wealthy financiers have similarities. Asymmetry and symmetry, convergence and divergence—all have been and will continue to be a part of the North American experience.

The Growth of an Idea
The idea of unity and symmetry in American history has deep roots. In this study, America is used in its broad hemispheric sense, including both North and South America, rather than as a synonym for the United States of America, although our primary focus is on the history of the northern reaches of the hemisphere, the continent of North America. Historians long have discussed "American" history as something different from European history. Beginning in the sixteenth century when, from the European point of view, the history of America was still very young, interest was often more in the natural than the historical world. Even the great works of natural history of the period, such as Gonzalo Fernández de Oviedo's *Historia general y natural de las Indias* (written in the second quarter of the sixteenth century but not completely published until 1851-55) took a general, comparative approach to the Americas. The Americas at that time were still called the "Indies," an extension of

Spain and Portugal in the New World. In the seventeenth century, the growing presence of the French and the English led to a more complex rendering of American history as a way of furthering the interests of Europe against America or of one European nation against another. In their musings and theorizing, authors still took an interest in continental and hemispheric themes. William Robertson of Scotland wrote widely read and influential books on the early history of the Americas. In *The History of the Discovery and Settlement of America* (1839), he expressed the exaggerations and generalizations, good and bad, of the age. A simple but elegant phrase describes the grandeur of America: "Nature seems here to have carried on her operations upon a larger scale and with a bolder hand, and to have distinguished the features of this country by a peculiar magnificence" (Robertson 1839, 123). The grandeur of America was a theme much repeated through the centuries.

With the rapid rise of the nation-state in the Americas and Europe in the nineteenth century, national histories swept aside earlier general histories. History as a profession, much more so than geography, was built around the emerging state. And, as expected, historians came to emphasize more the differences, the uniqueness, the special qualities of their respective nation's past instead of the similarities and commonalities with other nations. They often reached far into the past to do so, at times bending the historical record to suit their ideological beliefs. Even the best of the nineteenth-century historians had difficulty looking beyond their borders, except when discussing diplomacy and foreign relations. The Mexico of Lucas Alamán (*Historia de Méjico*, 1849-52) or the United States of George Bancroft (*History of the United States*, 1830s-70s) extolled the special characteristics of the new nations. In the north, the Quebec historian, François-Xavier Garneau, glorified the virtues of the French Canadians, especially their struggles to preserve their domain, in his oft reprinted *Histoire du Canada* (1845-48).

In these works it is possible to see the seeds of twentieth-century trends. Mexico was already plagued by the ideological debates that would flame into revolution after 1910, along with the ever-present fear of the United States that still exists, despite NAFTA. Historians of the United States often articulated haughtiness and a self-righteousness that guided domestic and foreign policy in the twentieth century. In Canada, Quebec nationalism continues to draw inspiration and legitimacy from the historians of earlier days.

A few writers strove for a continental vision. Hubert Howe Bancroft, one of the most prodigious historians of a generation known for exhaustive and wordy histories, is a good example. He published his *Works*—all 39 volumes of them—between 1886-90. Separately they carried titles such as *The Native Races of the North Pacific States of North America*, *Central America*, *History of Mexico*, and a *History of the North Mexican States and Texas*. Bancroft's work at times suffered from the moralizing and racism that was common to late nineteenth-century history, but it was encompassing in conception and scope.

Other examples come from journalists, travelers, and academics who have tried to make sense out of the different paths of development in the Americas. One still worth reading is *South America: Observations and Impressions*, first published in 1912 by James Bryce. Bryce and most of his contemporaries believed that South America began at the Rio Grande. Mexico was Spanish American by virtue of its indigenous populations and patterns of conquest and settlement. Different languages, religions, and social systems divided Spanish America from what he called Teutonic America: "They were, in fact, unlike in everything, except their position in the Western Hemisphere" (Bryce 1923, 495). This attitude hindered twentieth-century attempts to interpret North American history as a whole.

Nineteenth- and early twentieth-century geographers did not have the same problem of the narrow nationalist focus that trapped most historians. They were impressed by the geographic and geological unity of North America: plains, plateaus, and cordilleras (mountain ranges) ran north and south with little regard for political boundaries, giving the continent a coherence that defied political boundaries. Many thought that both the northern and southern borders lacked meaningful geographic barriers. The 49th parallel separating Canada and the United States was perhaps the most artificial of all, but there was little geographic difference to explain the division between Mexico and the United States from Tijuana to El Paso. At that point the Rio Grande, albeit in a very modest way, begins to divide the two countries. States, provinces, and countries were thin plastic veneers covering a structure of solid oak. Geographers recognized this more readily than historians, leading them to observations about the potential unity of North America. André Siegfried, a widely read French observer of North America, put it clearly:

> The Americas seem to have a north-south axis, and also an east-west one. The former is geographic and is the principal one because it results from the very conformation of the continents themselves. It is expressed by the majestic geological folds, by the vertical arrangement of the climatic zones, and the natural trend of commerce. It is even to be seen in the flow of public opinion. One feels that its effects are inevitable, and that, in the end, it will overcome all resistance. (Siegfried 1968, 19)

The resistance to unification also engendered an economic malaise that kept the poorer regions of the hemisphere from developing. Extreme examples of this were the small islands of the Caribbean, where a type of Balkanization existed that prevented political, economic, and social development. Removing political boundaries would reduce the artificial obstacles to growth, or so many thought.

It is possible to see these arguments as an academic diffusion of the Manifest Destiny that had not yet expired in American life. This belief in a divinely led expansion helped to push the United States to the west coast of the continent. Like some juggernaut, the United States had crushed all opposition in its path. By the late nineteenth century, the country was poised to impose its political, economic, and cultural life on new lands. The time period is important to place the interpretations in perspective. The Spanish American War had just been won, and the United States had acquired an empire. Political and economic sentiment for expansion ran high in the country, and the geographic interpretations of development bolstered the undercurrents of Manifest Destiny.

It is just as important to remember the settlement patterns of the time. High and low plains along the borders were almost uninhabited. The agricultural, mining, transportation, and manufacturing industries that revolutionized the U.S.-Mexico border had not yet begun. Most of the southern border was a frontier where few people lived. A late nineteenth-century geographer wrote: "The centers of gravity of the Mexican and Anglo-Saxon republics will always be separated by a distance of at least 1,500 or 1,600 miles, and the intervening space largely consists of arid regions, where the populations must always remain scattered ... Thus Mexico and the United States seem destined to remain distinct ethnological domains" (Reclus 1886-95, Vol. 2, 188). Only visionaries could foretell the growth that would take place in the next 100 years.

Few twentieth-century historians carried the banner of convergence. The most influential was Herbert Eugene Bolton, long a professor of the "History of America" at the University of California, Berkeley. Bolton's fame rests on many contributions, but the most widely cited is the address he gave as president of the American Historical Association at its annual meeting, held in Toronto in 1932, imposingly called "The Epic of Greater America." In the introduction to his talk, Bolton said: "The increasing importance of inter-American relations makes imperative a better understanding by each of the history and the culture of all. A synthetic view is important not alone for its present day political and commercial implications; it is quite as desirable from the standpoint of correct historiography" (Bolton 1964, 68). Bolton did not use geography to buttress his "correct historiography." Instead, he sketched the themes of commonality in the history of America. Most important were similar colonial patterns of development, such as "some vestige of feudalism," mercantilism, slavery, Indian-European relations (although he recognized Spanish and French as opposed to English efforts to Christianize Indians), international conflicts, and independence. Bolton believed that the similarities continued after independence. "In the whole process of national growth and unification in the nineteenth century the outstanding factors were boundless natural resources, foreign immigration, foreign capital, and expanding markets" (Bolton 1964, 92).

There was some historical fallout to what came to be termed the "Bolton Theory." A few adventurous historians led the charge and wrote about the Americas in sweeping terms. Some gave geography the obligatory first chapter; others ignored it all together. When they did emphasize geography, they often did so by describing land as an obstacle to overcome in the course of national expansion, not as a basis for finding regional commonalities. In the end, the Bolton approach faltered, the victim of political boundaries that stood too tall. The history of the Americas idea fell from grace, and there were no North American historians there to catch it.

The exception was the colonial history of North America. Historians continue to use a comparative framework to explain colonization, based on the assumption that the imposition of Europe on America followed broadly parallel patterns of development. Spain, England, and France were different, but the processes of discovery, contact, and colonization offered unifying themes for analysis. Exploration, Indian-European interaction, extractive economies, Atlantic commercial relations, colonial administrations — all and more could be explained through a comparative analysis. Bolton's own *Colonization of North America, 1492-1783* (published in 1920) is an early example of this type of study. The similarities apparently came to an end in the late eighteenth century, either in 1763 with the end of the French and Indian War, or in 1783 when the United States achieved its independence. This approach has its usefulness, but it overemphasizes the influence of European political institutions and minimizes the diversity that continues to characterize the continent, especially in those regions with large indigenous populations. It also minimizes the long history of the continent before the arrival of Europeans.

Discovery

Each phase of North American history is controversial and subject to different interpretations. The words and phrases used to describe historical processes themselves can become controversial, generating debates about hidden meanings. "Discovery" and "New World" are examples of words attacked for harboring Eurocentric points of view. For those who had lived here for millennia, it was not a New World or a time of discovery. "Discovery," in particular, became a much debated term with the approach of the quincentenary of Columbus's first voyage in 1492. The arrival of Europeans, Africans, and Asians after that date did not constitute a discovery as much as an invasion that overwhelmed, modified, and often destroyed what indigenous people had created. Use of the term discovery in this context also minimizes the voyages and settlement of early European peoples in Greenland and Newfoundland and all but ignores the evidence of early contact between Asia and America.

Despite controversies surrounding the use of the term, the concept of discovery has value for understanding the history of North America. Europeans did come to know a new land after 1492. The process of learning about America, its different flora and fauna, its vast spaces, and its many different peoples was a discovery for Europe, and for many Europeans it produced an awe and wonderment over something new and unknown.

Indigenous peoples had their own history of discovering different places in North America. Movement was long a way of life for many people. With the arrival of Europeans, discovery took on a harsher meaning for those trapped by the new labor systems. Forced labor and at times enslavement were a brutal introduction to European culture. But it was not the only one. Indians interacted with Europeans in myriad ways. Only the grossest distortions of the historical record can ignore the emotional, artistic, spiritual, and very human interaction that occurred as the two encountered new languages, thoughts, foods, clothing, and people. It is a mistake to minimize the vitality and resilience of Indians, of their ability to draw from and survive under the new systems.

"Discovery" also applies to the history of later arrivals. Most North Americans today are not descendants of Indians or of the earliest European or African arrivals. They trace their ancestry to the waves of immigration that began in the late eighteenth century and then accelerated in the nineteenth and twentieth centuries. As these millions of people came to North America, they embarked on voyages of personal discovery that changed their lives and those of their descendants. These voyages of discovery entailed traversing and settling distant lands. This process of physically coming to know the land, of roaming, settling, building, expanding, and moving again, gave energy and vitality to life. The vastness of North America absorbed all arrivals. Even today, the traveler in the barren reaches of the Sonoran or Chihuahuan Deserts, or in the boreal forests that stretch across the northern tier of the continent, has a sense of discovery. Indeed, much of this land has witnessed permanent settlement only recently, if at all.

"Discovery" has another meaning. People gradually acquired new identities, first with their local community, then their region, and finally their nation. The discovery of a national identity was a powerful historical force for the three countries of North America in the nineteenth and twentieth centuries. In both the United States and Mexico destructive internal wars challenged the unity of the new nations. In the latter part of the twentieth century the assertion of new identities has challenged the strength of national identities. New ethnic, gender, and regional identities are modifying the course of North American history, and they will continue to influence the way that the past is interpreted.

"Discovery" is useful in still another way. Much of what we know about North America and about ourselves comes from those who searched—and in some cases found—meaning and understanding in the vastness of North America. Accounts of journeys of personal and geographic discovery are so numerous that they defy categorization. Their history reaches back to the conquest of Mexico, when Hernán Cortés wrote his letters to King Charles V and Bernal Díaz del Castillo wrote the *True History of the Conquest of New Spain* (composed in the 1560s, but not published until 1632). Those who followed did the same, chronicling what they saw and did.

The tradition continues, often revealing more about the social and psychological conditions of the twentieth century than about the land. Three of our favorite works of personal discovery set within North America are Jack Kerouac's *On the Road* (1957), the autobiographical novel that came to represent the spontaneity and individualism of the Beat Generation; Wallace Stegner's *Wolf Willow* (1963), a blend of personal experience and history on the upper Great Plains; and Robert M. Pirsig's *Zen and the Art of Motorcycle Maintenance* (1974), a profound and brooding reflection on the meaning of life as a father and son travel across the country on a motorcycle.

Convergence

In the nineteenth century new and powerful forces began to exert influences that surpassed those of earlier times. The steam engine, the railroad, the telegraph and telephone, the increase of commercial agriculture, the rise of the factory, and the beginnings of the industrial city all worked their influence in one way or another from the Yucatán to the Yukon. These convergent forces did not impose unity or uniformity, but they did create some similarities in the path of development.

Other convergent forces helped to integrate North America in the twentieth century. One example is national defense, traditionally a priority for all three countries. To the south, the Mexican-American Commission of Continental Defense increased protection against possible German and Japanese attacks during World War II. After the war, tensions between the United States and the Soviet Union focused attention on the north, where Canada and the United States cooperated in signing the North American Air Defense Agreement in 1957, one of many Canadian-U.S. defense pacts.

More evident in the early twenty-first century than defense issues are economic ones. Capital, technology, and economic organizations are spreading at a rapid pace. NAFTA will only further what had already become reality as economic life fuses North America together. Debates over NAFTA have heightened awareness of other convergent forces. Mexican immigration has been the most controversial, but there has also been widespread attention given to environmental problems. International discussions began with concern over northern waterways and acid rain, then shifted to the extensive pollution of the U.S.-Mexican border. There is now agreement that environmental issues have to be studied in a continental if not hemispheric perspective.

Environmental and economic issues along with political ones bear directly on emerging indigenous objectives. The Zapatista uprising in Mexico exemplifies the interconnections. Reverberations from the uprising spread quickly to the north, especially in Canada, where Ovide Mercredi, head of the Assembly of First Nations, insisted that Canada support the Zapatista demands.

Education is finally responding to the reality of these interconnections. New efforts in the late twentieth and early twenty-first centuries seek to continue to increase cooperation between institutions of higher education in Mexico, the United States, and Canada. Innovative trinational programs and exchanges are already preparing students for the future.

Special mention should be made of the fast moving Canadian-Mexican relationship evident from the 1980s. Both countries, though different in many profound ways, also share commonalities that are leading them to a closer relationship. Diplomats and academics most often stress their export-driven economies, reliance on foreign investment for growth, and foreign policies that often conflict with those of the United States as the basis for a special relationship. A book published in 1996 with the suggestive title *Natural Allies?: Canadian and Mexican Perspectives on International Security* (Klepak 1996) outlines the prospects for future collaboration.

A profusion of new programs and agreements are integrating North America in stronger and more pervasive ways than in the past, creating a new form of continentalism that draws its sustenance from the continuous movement of people, products, and ideas back and forth across borders. This is occurring as part of a wider global movement. Manufacturers, marketers, and pundits, always in search of the telling phrase, now speak of the "borderless consumer," the individual whose behavior is not bound by culture or nation but by global economic and social trends, which are sweeping through North America and the rest of the world.

As a result, political integration is no longer as unthinkable as it was during most of the twentieth century. Nationalism, the dominant political force in all three countries since independence, is waning in the face of increased support for new forms of continental cooperation. Political conditions can change, as the creation of the European Union proves. After World War II, only visionaries could predict the new reality of the end of the twentieth century, a Europe with a common currency that did not require its citizens to have passports to move back and forth across borders. A North American political union, however, remains outside the official rhetoric of continental cooperation in the post-NAFTA world.

Divergence

The movement toward continental integration has its limits. Most North Americans do not yet have a sense of a continental identity, of a shared reality that is affecting their future. Divergent rather than convergent forces preoccupy many, draining attention and energy from continental issues.

In the political realm in particular, divergence seems to reign. Despite new continental organizations, epitomized by NAFTA, basic political contours continue to be strained by local and regional drives for autonomy. It is not nationalism but regionalism that appears as the greatest challenge to a broader North American political organization.

Chiapas and Quebec have already been mentioned as divergent forces. Groups within Chiapas are demanding recognition and support for basic human needs and rights. Quebec is different. Far from being a region exploited and abused by Canada, it is a wealthy, democratic society that has had success in resolving most of its problems, except for the political recognition of its distinct history, culture, and language. Recently, this struggle has been coupled with efforts to project the identity of Quebec beyond Canada. The new continentalism and global economic dynamics have led many in Quebec to envision a much broader role for the province in North America, the Caribbean, and Africa.

In the case of the United States, the only immediate territorial question that could affect the political shape of the country is the status of Puerto Rico. Since its creation in 1952 as an Associated Free State, or Commonwealth, Puerto Rico has had a controversial relationship with the United States. In the late 1990s the question of its future once again became the subject of intense debate. As in the past, voters considered primarily the options of continuation of commonwealth status (or a variation of it), statehood, or independence. In December 1998, they voted "none of the above," which in effect meant a continuation of the status quo.

There are many other movements that contribute to political divergence. The revival of the "South" in the United States, for example, represents a rediscovery and reaffirmation of a cultural and political history long thought dead. The movement is called the Southern League, and it hopes to restore respect for the way of life of the South—its education, religious beliefs, and traditional political autonomy. *The Washington Post* ran a long article on the movement as part of a section with the chilling title of "The Balkanization of North America." The leader of the movement summarized:

> A concern for states' rights, local self-government and regional identity used to be taken for granted everywhere in America. But the United States is no longer, as it once was, a federal union of diverse states and regions. National uniformity is being imposed by the political class that runs Washington, the economic class that owns Wall Street and the cultural class in charge of Hollywood and the Ivy League. (*The Washington Post*, 15 October 1995)

Separatist tendencies at the regional and local level continue to embroil politics in all three countries, exemplifying a particularism that comes and goes in North American history. It might seem paradoxical that they would flourish during a period of heightened continental integration, but the paradox is more apparent than real. Narrowly defined regional political associations have enduring strengths that are often fortified as centralization accelerates. They will not disappear.

Political divergence is only one of the visible forms of particularism that acts as a brake on continental convergence. Demands for recognition of cultural distinctiveness have also grown in recent years. The demands can be local, as in the call for educational support for Ebonics (an African American dialect) in Oakland, California or respect for the distinct form of English spoken by residents of the Sea Islands off the coast of South Carolina. They can also be national, as in Canadian and Mexican efforts to prevent their cultures from being overwhelmed by cultural imports from the United States.

Culture, however defined, is a powerful agent that binds individuals to groups that are not limited by nationality. The "culture wars," versions of which appear in all three countries, speak to the heart of the matter. Ideologies of class, gender, ethnicity, and race can spread far beyond a region or nation and take on continental dimensions. They become forces for both convergence and divergence. Since the passage of NAFTA, both scholarly and popular assessments of North America suggest a move toward seeing the continent as an integral unit despite these seemingly different cultural variables. Certainly more and more policy analysts, as well as academics who have studied the continent, see North America as whole and interconnected rather than as an isolated tripartite of national fragments that occasionally come together for diplomatic niceties. Not everyone agrees, of course, that such assessments accurately reflect historical and contemporary experience. Moreover, popular views and perceptions of what constitutes a North American past and a North American identity vary widely among citizens of Canada, Mexico, and the United States.

North America in the Twenty-first Century
The tragic events of 9/11, as well as the U.S. response to terrorism and the anthrax scare, not to mention SARS in Canada and the profound ebb and flow of Mexican migrants throughout North America, have forced some in the public and private sectors to reconsider the continental dimensions of global phenomena: continental and hemispheric security, the defense of porous borders, the gathering and sharing of intelligence, the rights of workers who cross borders, the availability and distribution of antibiotics, transnational policing, etc. A willingness to historicize these issues beyond the confines of any single nation-state will shape the contours of a broader North American understanding of economic integration and political cooperation, not to mention an appreciation of shared civic values and concerns.

Transnational approaches to the study of world history have shaped the continental sensibility that this study evokes as it seeks to historicize the North American past. Rather than evaluate how each of the three nation-states interacted with one another, which implicitly allows artificially drawn national boundaries to determine the subject of study, we try to integrate a transnational approach to the problem of North America. As Micol Seigel has argued, transnational history examines units that spill over and seep through national borders, units both greater and smaller than the nation-state (Seigel 2005, 63). Tohono O'Odham peoples, for example, have lived in what is today southern Arizona (United States) and northern Sonora (Mexico) for centuries, and they continue to cross over an international boundary that was created in the mid-nineteenth century with neither their input nor consent. The Spanish flu pandemic of 1918-20 failed to stop at the Buffalo, New York-Fort Erie, Ontario border crossing, thus infecting Canadians and Americans of all backgrounds without pausing to determine national identity or citizenship. In the late nineteenth and early twentieth centuries, factory workers and rural laborers demanded just wages and better working conditions from a North American capitalism shaped as much by Wall Street financiers as by upward shifts in global consumption. Convergence and divergence, therefore, are not expressions of contemporary phenomena, as they have deep roots in the continental features of North American history. Neither simply political nor diplomatic, they reveal the complexities of social cohesion, cultural markers, and similar, yet competing, material needs.

What does it all mean? Divergence and convergence will continue to shape North America. It is possible to see a dialectic at work as the currents of convergence trigger the cross-currents of divergence, thus providing a basic structure to the past. There is increasing unity in North America as the forces of convergence continue, but divergent trends will continue to defy the unity. Regional and ethnic identities, for example, continue to shape these divergent cross-currents. Quebec, the U.S. South, and Chiapas all show how a mix of political economy and culture have worked to undermine national aspirations and, in some cases, territorial sovereignty. On the other hand, regionalism can enrich our continental perspective. For example, the international boundary that separates the United States and Canada, or that separates Mexico and the United States, has drawn people in search of economic security and social mobility. Over the long haul, a "borderlands" sensibility has developed that reflects issues and concerns germane to these border regions, such as the environment, immigration, or the flow of illegal narcotics.

In some ways, the lives of ordinary "borderlanders" provide the bone marrow of our continental framework. They come together to identify common interests and shared concerns, while at the same time they seek to bridge differences in order to find solutions that benefit multiple constituencies and entities without regard to national borders. These citizens of North America, residing where the international border divides as well as unites, show us what is happening "on the ground" in terms of clean air and water, the flow of illegal drugs and its accompanying violence, immigration, investment capital, trade, and security.

By evaluating the global processes that have forged continental convergence as well as divergence, we can transcend the conceptual limitations of viewing the North American past as the purview of any one nation-state. A polar projection of North America, as seen in Map 1, expresses the geographical unity that has influenced our approach. As we gaze upon the map, however, our trained eyes, almost intuitively, try to draw the national borders that separate the three countries. School curricula in Canada, Mexico, and the United States are developed, in part, to reflect national aspirations and concerns, and to impart patriotic understandings of the past, all of which work to mold our geographical consciousness. This book's comparative framework asks its readers, therefore, to evaluate the history of North America, not as a series of unrelated and unique culture boxes or political systems, but rather as a complex of historical, geographical, and cultural features that often have transcended political borders. As historian Thomas Bender has argued, "Whatever the

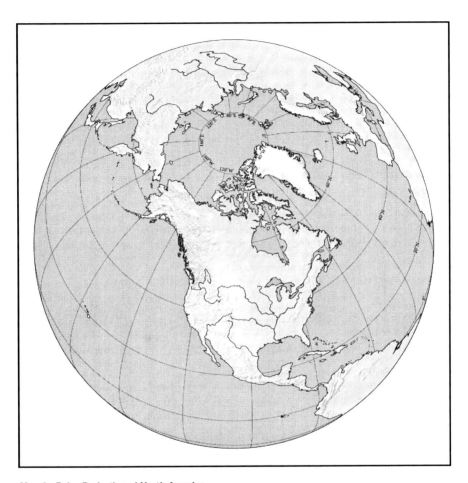

Map 1. Polar Projection of North America.
From Map Central-Website by Bedford/St. Martin's. Copyright © 2002 by Bedford/St. Martin's.
Reproduced by permission of Bedford/St. Martin's.

distinctive position of the United States today [or in our case, the United States, Canada, and Mexico], it remains nonetheless only one global province interconnected with and interdependent with every other. The history of the United States [or Canada and Mexico] is but one history among histories" (Bender 2006, 8).

Instead of employing a chronological narrative to discuss such a large unit of study, we have opted instead for a thematic approach that integrates historical change and continuity. The intellectual communion that binds historians of all stripes is found in our efforts to explain change over time. Chronology, therefore, plays an important role in our assessment of North American history, as we have tried to discern political, economic, social, and even cultural events, spaces, structures, and patterns that speak to the whole while remaining sensitive to the regional, national, and international contexts that gave them shape. We seek comparison and contrast as a way to assess those structures and patterns, and as previously mentioned, the field of transnational history has informed our thematic approach. In the vein of such scholars as Micol Seigel and Ian Tyrrell, we recognize that transnational history treats the nation-state as one among a wide range of phenomena to be studied and that a thematic approach fashioned by comparative methodology may obscure more than it elucidates if all we include in our analysis is a rehash of nationalist historiography (Seigel 2005, 65; Tyrrell 1991, 1035).

We examine and flesh out the history of North America through nine themes: basic periodization, or how historians divide up time to explain historical change; geography and natural resources; political structures and party politics; foreign policy and diplomacy; the relationship between Indians and Europeans; the ebb and flow of immigrants; big labor and social class; an assessment of how trade and tariffs have worked together to forge and stymie continental integration; and the role of organized religion and popular religiosity in North America. In our conclusion, we identify two bedrock features of the North American past that have fashioned the historical trajectory of the continent and anticipate what tomorrow might bring for North America in light of the contradictions rendered by economic integration, which includes the multidirectional movement of peoples, goods, and capital shaped by the continental dimensions of globalization, writ large and small on our historical canvass.

CHAPTER 2

CONTOURS OF THE PAST

The panorama of North American history stretches from the arrival of the first migrants from Asia millennia ago to the rapidly changing society of today. Vast in chronological scope and for the most part hidden from view, the continent's story is difficult to summarize. One way to do so is to emphasize the key shifts and turns that mark the past, the silhouette of the human experience that outlines the main contours of North American history. As this chapter demonstrates, it is all too easy to assume that the three major nation-states of North America have always existed in the same form and shape that they have today. Nationalist and patriotic under-standings of the past, coupled with regional nuance and circumstance, were part and parcel of the historical sensibility imparted in Mexican, U.S., and Canadian schools in the twentieth century.

As a result, the nation-states that today occupy the North American continent are seen as natural entities that have existed since time immemorial when, in fact, they are fairly recent creations that speak to specific historical contexts. While the political and social structures of multiple pre-Columbian Indian societies brokered European colonization, for example, and colonial institutions and political culture influenced subsequent efforts to create nations independent of European control, present-day Mexico, Canada, and the United States were not inevitable, preordained entities.

Historical Periods
Historical periods are the basic building blocks that help to understand change through time. Benchmarks of the past, the periods suggest that there are discrete, identifiable chronological entities that have characteristics different from earlier and later periods. Thus the "Civil War and Reconstruction" in the United States, the "Porfiriato" in Mexico, and "Confederation" in Canada have defining attributes that distinguish them from other nineteenth-century periods.

The periods represent historical reality as well as perceptions of that reality. History blends the past and the study of the past, leading to continual reinterpreta-tions of what is known. The past does not change, but different perceptions and points of view change the way that it appears. Much as the sand and rock formations of the Painted Desert in Arizona appear to change in color as sun and clouds move across them, the past appears to change when viewed from different points of view.

Since evidence and the types of questions asked influence the study of the past, most periodization schemes are subject to debate and disagreement. Demographic studies might emphasize rates and stages of change differently than do political, technological, or cultural studies. The problems expand the more geographically encompassing the attempts at periodization. Despite the difficulties, efforts at periodization are rewarding and provide one way of attempting to generalize about the complexity of North American history.

First Steps

At the most basic level, two periods delineate the history of North America. The first, chronologically vast and daunting in its complexity, includes the history of indigenous peoples from their earliest arrival to the sixteenth century. The second, often influenced by the first, entails the history of all peoples in North America from the arrival of Europeans to the present. Studies of North American history are increasingly attentive to the first period, but all too often they still see it simply as a prelude to the second rather than one that has its own complexity, interest, and beauty.

It is difficult to date with precision the events and processes of early North American history. Recent genetic and linguistic studies suggest the possibility of multiple migrations from different places in Asia to the Americas. There also are theories that suggest the first Americans sailed on make-shift rafts from islands in the Pacific Ocean. The land bridge theory, however, continues to shape archaeological research. Estimates of the time of the first migrations across the land bridge between Siberia and Alaska place it during the Pleistocene Age, about 30,000 to 40,000 years ago. The experiences and thoughts of the first Americans during this long early period, at times referred to as the Paleo-Indian Period, will forever be lost. Their existence is noted only by the faintest tracks. Projectile points like the Clovis (11,000 BC) and the Folsom (10,000 BC) speak of hunting cultures, always on the move in search of game. Only gradually did these people occupy the continent, moving together in families and then in small bands. By 9,000 BC, they had reached Tepexpan in central Mexico. The stream continued, and immigrants continued to arrive in the north, probably as late as 4000 BC. In other words, some early Americans were much earlier than others.

Archaic Period

During the Archaic Period, often referred to as the Neolithic Age, beginning very roughly about 6,000 to 8,000 years ago, new developments began to alter the face of some regions of North America. The central achievement was the domestication of plants. Here again the process was slow, almost imperceptible to those involved. The genius of early generations only revealed itself slowly, finally emerging in agricultural systems that transformed life for future generations. Maize was the engine of change. The first domesticated cobs were tiny, only the size of a finger tip, but the harvests were plentiful, enough to support an increasing population. Along with maize were beans, chiles, tomatoes, squash, cotton, and other plants that provided food and fiber. The elaboration of the first basic tools and storage vessels accompanied agriculture and gave birth to pottery and basketry. Increasing food supplies permitted the concentration of people, leading to permanent settlements and the founding of larger communities. Within these communities increasing complexity of life created specialization of activities. During the Archaic Period, some regions moved ahead quickly, creating patterns of life only dimly reminiscent of the Paleo-Indian cultures, while others, isolated from the main patterns of change, followed the ancient ways of hunting and gathering.

Classic Periods

Nowhere did the foundations laid during the Archaic Period lead to more rapid cultural change than in Mesoamerica, a cultural area including central and southern Mexico and stretching south into Guatemala and Honduras. Mesoamerican agricultural surpluses freed many for cultural pursuits, setting the stage for architectural and artistic achievements remarkable in their grandeur and complexity. During the Pre-Classic or Formative Period, the seeds planted around 1,150 BC by the Olmec at La Venta, followed by the Maya along the Gulf of Campeche and in the Yucatán Peninsula, blossomed into temples, pyramids, plazas, and cities. The Mayan sites that dominated the central area were remarkable testimony to the creativity of early people. Between 250 AD and 900 AD, known to archaeologists as the Classic Period, great cities rose up in the tropical lowlands. Palenque, Uxmal, and Bonampak are three that today still display much of their grandeur. With mathematical precision and an eye toward the stars, the Maya developed writing, calendars, and architectural wonders. To the west in the highlands of south central Mexico, the city of Monte Albán emerged, beautiful with its broad courtyards framed against the rugged skyline. To the north was the magnificent city of Teotihuacán, the fabled "home of the gods," with its monumental pyramids of the Sun and the Moon linked by a long causeway. These and dozens of other cities were much like the jade so dear to their residents, deeply hued with layers of intense beauty and enchanting to those who beheld them. All came to an end around 900 AD, about the same time that Charlemagne was creating his European empire. While archaeologists and historians continue to debate the causes of Classic Period decline, it is reasonable to suggest that a combination of factors facilitated the end of its urban city-states: population and environmental stress, social unrest, increased warfare, and quite possibly external intrusion. These factors aggravated the political and social instability that had plagued Classic Mexico after 800 AD.

The Post Classic was still a time of intense cultural, political, and economic activity in Mesoamerica, first dramatized by the emergence of the Toltecs, often stereotyped as aggressive and warlike. With their political center in Tula just north of Mexico City, they established a political hegemony that extended far into the Yucatán. The city of Chichén Itzá with its colonnades of stone warriors testifies to the widespread influence of Toltec culture.

The Aztecs inherited the Toltec ambition of creating a political empire. After an inauspicious beginning as a small group wandering in the deserts of the north, the Aztecs found a home in the central valley of Mexico sometime in the thirteenth century. Through warfare and diplomacy they gradually created a political confederation that grew rapidly under Moctezuma I and Moctezuma II. By 1500 Aztec military dominance girded a vast tribute system that brought food, clothing, and precious stones and feathers from much of Mesoamerica. This was a complex world of priests and warriors, peasants and artisans, teachers and judges, artists and domestic servants, all living according to carefully crafted rules. Its center was Tenochtitlán, a grand city of perhaps 250,000 residents that sprawled along the lakes of the Valley of Mexico.

No other country in North America has felt the influence of the indigenous past as much as Mexico. As the authors of the leading textbook on Mexican history have stated so eloquently, there is in Mexican society a pervasive awareness of antiquity, for the indigenous presence is everywhere to be found there (Meyer, Sherman, and Deeds 2007, 3). More nationalist interpretations of Mexico find the origins of the nation in the Aztecs or in the Toltecs before them. From this perspective, the Spanish conquest interrupted the course of Mexican history; it did not start it. Since the conquest, the indigenous past has influenced each generation, at times quietly, at other times violently. Apt metaphors are the twin volcanoes—Popocatépetl, "Smoking Mountain," and Iztaccíhuatl, "Sleeping Woman," husband and wife in Aztec mythology—that still stand watch over Mexico City just as they did over Tenochtitlán. Usually dormant, they at times grumble and stir, especially Popocatéptl, spilling fire and ash over the domains that they guard.

Other Areas

North of central Mexico most of the traces of the distant past are less marked by monumental architecture and urban traditions. In the southwest of the United States the Anasazi and their descendants etched out cliff dwellings and the Pueblo built multi-storied buildings of adobe. In the Ohio and Mississippi River valleys large mounds remain from the building efforts of early cultures. One of the largest population centers in the region was Cahokia, a city near modern St. Louis that may have had a population of 40,000 around 1200 AD. Most people, however, lived in small villages, making their homes in makeshift structures of skin or wood that deteriorated with time and leaving only pieces of pottery, tools, weapons, and language

Map 2. Pre-Columbian North America.
From *Mexico and the United States: Ambivalent Vistas* by W. Dirk Raat. Copyright © 2004 The University of Georgia Press. Reproduced by permission of The University of Georgia Press.

as traces of life. The carefully wrought social, economic, and political systems of the past are forgotten or poorly understood, but this should not obscure that growth and change took place.

Each of the main cultural areas in North America, from the Arctic in the far north to the woodlands in the northeast and the coastal west, experienced broad patterns of change, evolving through early, middle, and late Archaic periods, though not in any uniform order. Labels of the more recent past vary from region to region, but again none of them suggest a level of development comparable to that in Mesoamerica. Finally, it is worth mentioning that the terms prehistory and proto-history are often used to describe the period before the arrival of Europeans. To the historian, these are particularly objectionable since they imply an artificial break in the historical continuum. There is only history. Regardless of whether humans had writing and lived in large cities or were illiterate and wandered in small bands across the desert, their experiences were a part of history, not of prehistory.

Contact and Conquest
Spaniards led the expansion of Europe and accelerated the pace of change every-where. From Veracruz in 1519 under the leadership of Hernán Cortés they marched to the Aztec capital of Tenochtitlán and eventually orchestrated a 75-day siege that pummeled and starved the Aztecs into submission. In 1521 Tenochtitlán fell and the course of North American history changed forever. While previous cultures, even the powerful military ones of the Toltecs and Aztecs, had expanded gradually, Spaniards burst forth like a furious summer storm on the landscape, affecting every-thing in their path.

The energy of Spain during the conquest had few equals. Perhaps the followers of Ghengis Khan riding out of the steppes of Asia or the new believers of Islam march-ing across North Africa and then up the Iberian peninsula match up. Spaniards quickly penetrated the heart of the continent, transforming life as they went. Within 20 years after the fall of Tenochtitlán they had reached modern-day Kansas state. By land and by sea they came, claiming all before them in the name of God and King. The result was the subjugation of peoples, the building of cities, the exploitation of land and mines, and the transformation of culture.

Slower and more tentative than the Spaniards, the French and English finally established their presence in the early seventeenth century. The first efforts of the French under Jacques Cartier in the 1530s gradually gained momentum and led to the establishment of a permanent trading post in 1608 under Samuel de Champlain. The small and isolated settlement became Quebec City. A year earlier the English had built a small fort on the James River, naming it Jamestown. In 1620, a religious community known as the Puritans founded Plymouth, one of the best known of the early North American settlements. The Dutch followed soon after, founding New Amsterdam on Manhattan Island in New York in 1625. None of these events had the same cataclysmic reverberations that the overthrow of Tenochtitlán had in the pre-vious century. There was little in the way of "conquest" as these later arrivals built small forts and compounds. The reason was simple. They encountered no dense Indian populations to subjugate, no empires to overthrow, no easy riches to plunder. The history of North America north of central Mexico would forever be different because of these conditions.

Colonialism
The arrival of Europeans signaled the onset of the long colonial period, a time when Spain, England, France, and, to a lesser extent, Holland created administrative enti-ties that ruled the new lands for the benefit of the home countries. Efforts to extend royal authority over the newly settled lands limited the ambitions of the early colonists, creating tensions that lasted for centuries. Here the political history of the main colonies displayed many similarities. The centralizing drives of Europe butted against the aspirations of colonists and eventually led to the dissolution of empires. But this was still far in the future.

Great political struggles were only a part of the process as Europe tried to remake North America in its image. Carried out by a mix of private initiative and public support, colonialism encompassed the transfer and adaptation of European society to an unfamiliar and often hostile land. It is hard to reduce this process to a few abstractions, but its main lines are clear. Political bureaucracies responded to local and European needs; workers and entrepreneurs exploited natural resources and built production and exchange networks; religious institutions offered solace and reached out to new populations; and everywhere men and women, whether single or married, young or old, struggled to survive and create better lives for themselves.

As a part of colonialism, cultures collided, fractured, and mended. At the most general level, Europeans, Indians, and Africans interacted, creating the context for daily life. But this is too simple. Europeans came from different backgrounds and traditions, as did Indians and Africans. General ethnic or racial labels do little to convey the texture of colonial life and the many interacting and competing goals that drove individuals, groups, and nations. Out of this interaction emerged the main power relationships of the colonial period, but they did so at different times and places. The final outcome was not preordained, and in some areas only came about after years of struggle.

Squeezing this activity into specific blocks of time requires a stretch of the imag-ination, but it is useful to have some sense of the chronological rhythm of develop-ment. In Mexico, shortly after the central highlands had fallen to Spanish control in the 1520s and 1530s, expeditions struck out in search of new empires and wealth. Along the way they established the outposts of the Spanish empire, eventually founding Santa Fe in New Mexico in 1609. Following this formative period, the colony, in some ways already mature, experienced elaboration and increasing complexity during the seventeenth century, a period often referred to as the Baroque, or the period of intense religious, cultural, and political expression fashioned by the Spanish participation in the Catholic Reformation. Two brief examples illustrate quite nicely the Baroque Age in Mexico.

Despite his illegitimate birth, Juan de Palafox y Mendoza, son of a Spanish nobleman, rose quickly through the ranks of the ecclesiastical and Crown bureaucracies and was appointed visitor-general of New Spain and bishop of the Diocese of Puebla in 1640. After proposing to the Spanish king a series of political and economic reforms designed to root out corruption and ensure administrative efficiency, Palafox went about implementing the reforms of the Council of Trent, which was Catholic Europe's institutional response to the Protestant Reformation in the sixteenth century. These reforms had languished in Mexico for almost a century despite royal support to implement them. In order to activate the Tridentine decrees related to the education and formation of young men into priests, for example, Palafox donated his personal library of 5,000 volumes to the city of Puebla in 1646, making it the first public library in North America. Housed today in Puebla's Casa de la Cultura (House of Culture), the Biblioteca Palafoxiana, with its ornate wooden bookcases in the Baroque style, contains over 50,000 books, manuscripts, and printed matter. It remains the only colonial-era library in Mexico that maintains its original collection.

Juana Ramírez de Asbaje, more commonly known as Sor Juana Inés de la Cruz, was perhaps the most prodigious intellectual that the Mexican Baroque produced. Also born out of wedlock, Juana came from a family of small landholders of modest means in central Mexico. She, too, glided easily through the many different social spaces that marked colonial society, earning the admiration of the upper classes, including the wife of the viceroy. Ultimately, Juana chose to join a female religious order, entering the convent in 1669. Often called the Tenth Muse or the Mexican Phoenix, Sor Juana Inés wrote poetry, essays, and plays that combined a deep religiosity with critical social commentary. Even today Mexican schoolchildren memorize the first lines of her famous *Sátira filosófica* (*Philosophical Satire*), which critiqued the patriarchal structures that had subordinated women in colonial Mexico: *Hombres necios que acusáis a la mujer sin razón, sin ver que sois la ocasión de lo mismo que culpáis* (Silly men, who wrongly accuse women, oblivious that it is you who occasion what you criticize).

By the middle of the eighteenth century the Baroque gave way to political reform, economic growth, and territorial expansion. It was followed by a period known as the Bourbon Reforms, a label inspired by the reforms initiated by the Spanish King Charles III (ruled 1759-88). On the eve of Mexican independence from Spain in the early nineteenth century, the population of New Spain was approximately 6 million.

To the north, the formative period of the English colonies was longer and slower than in New Spain. From 1607 to 1732, 13 Atlantic seaboard colonies took shape from Georgia in the south to New Hampshire in the north, some of them commercial enterprises such as Virginia, others proprietary (colonies actually granted to one or more persons), such as Maryland, and others directly under Crown control. With a population of perhaps 1 million in the 1750s, these colonies developed religious, economic, and political institutions of great complexity. While the core of the English experience remained in the original 13 colonies, trade and war led to expansion in the Hudson Bay region, Newfoundland, and Nova Scotia in the early eighteenth century, fueled more by London-based entrepreneurs than by simply being an outgrowth of the original colonies.

New France was always more isolated and marginal than New Spain and the English colonies. Control remained under the commercial *Compagnie des Cent Associés* (Company of One Hundred Associates) from its formation in 1627 until 1663, when an intendant representing royal authority arrived with broad administrative, judicial, and military power. Growth took place, but the population remained small, only about 12,000 in 1688. Nevertheless, the desire to expand excited many, best illustrated by René-Robert Cavelier de La Salle, who reached the mouth of the Mississippi River in 1682 and claimed the entire river basin for King Louis XIV. Subsequent efforts led to a string of settlements that culminated in the settlement of New Orleans in 1718. New France at the time was a giant arc stretching from the Gulf of St. Lawrence to the Gulf of Mexico, an enormous area almost equal in size to that claimed by New Spain but sustained by a population of only about 65,000 in the late 1750s.

The Making of Nations
Political events in the middle of the eighteenth century began to move faster in Europe and in North America. France and England went to war once again, and the conflict erupted in North America as the French and Indian War, more fully discussed in Chapter 5. The result was the beginning of the end of colonial rule. France lost New France to the British after the war, a change often referred to as the "conquest" in Quebec history. Soon the British had problems of their own. Political frustrations in the seaboard colonies were vented against the Sugar and Stamp Acts and other measures aimed at increasing revenue from them. A crucial element of the political mix of the 1770s was the *Quebec Act* of 1774, which expanded the territory of Quebec deep into the region between the Ohio and Mississippi Rivers. While the act mollifed the fears of residents of Quebec, it inflamed many in the seaboard colonies, furthering political uncertainty.

Colonists responded to the growing unrest by convening the First Continental Congress in 1774, which quickly hardened opposition to English rule. Violence broke out again in 1775, and this led to the Second Continental Congress and the preparation for war. The final break came with the Declaration of Independence

(4 July 1776), the most cited document in North American history. "We hold these truths to be self-evident, that all men are created equal, that they are endowed by their Creator with certain unalienable Rights, that among these are Life, Liberty and the pursuit of Happiness" are words that continue to enjoy political resonance. The Revolutionary War lasted until 1781, with the final peace treaty coming in 1783. The aspirations of the new nation were formalized in the Constitution of the United States in 1787.

To the north, British dominance continued. If anything, the revolution in the United States strengthened the English-speaking colonists' allegiance to Great Britain (hereafter, Britain). Loyalists (supporters of Britain) went north during and after the revolution, criticizing the rebellion in the south and advocating allegiance to the Crown. The continental impulse, therefore, had many rhythms. Standard history textbooks in the United States tend to overlook how many colonists found meaning and benefit in the political framework and cultural values of British colonialism in North America. Resentment continued to smolder until it erupted once again in the War of 1812 between the United States and Britain, fought mainly over commercial rights in the Atlantic world. The United States mounted a feeble offensive in Canada, hoping to defeat the British and generate enthusiasm for annexation. The offensive failed on both counts, but the United States did free itself of further threats from Britain. After the war, English Canada remained within the British world, politically and culturally.

Mexico was influenced by the success of the United States but had to await events in Europe to strike for independence. Napoleon's forces invaded Spain in 1808 and broke the link between Spain and Spanish America, which led to Father Miguel Hidalgo y Costilla's revolt against Spanish rule in 1810. His Indian army threatened to dismantle the social pyramid that had governed the colony since the sixteenth century, provoking a strong enough reaction that its early efforts achieved little. Other champions of independence rose up to struggle unsuccesfully against Spanish rule. When independence finally came in 1821 it was a conservative reaction against a liberal government in Spain. Agustín de Iturbide, the leader of the movement, actually declared himself emperor. For a brief time, the Empire of Mexico joined the British Empire in controlling most of North America.

Mexico struggled much more than the United States as it sought to create a stable political system. There was little agreement on who should rule, let alone how to rule, which fostered powerful ideological and regional conflicts. Unlike in the north, the seeds of representative democracy had not been sown deeply in Mexico. Just as troubling, Mexico lost Texas to the onslaught of Anglo settlers and then much of its northwest to the United States before the century was half over. As Mexico shrank, the United States grew; Canada, still a colony of the British Empire, also entered a period of rapid growth.

The primary threat to political stability in Canada was mild in comparison to that in Mexico. In 1837 rebellions broke out in Lower (Quebec) and Upper (Ontario) Canada, driven in large measure by hostility to the concentration of power in the hands of small groups of merchants, financiers, and administrators. Referred to as the Chateau Clique in Quebec and the Family Compact in Ontario, these groups became entrenched in the early nineteenth century and warded off reforms that threatened their power. The rebellions, never widespread, led to the famous *Durham Report* (1839) that recommended political reform and the union of Upper and Lower Canada. Though emphasized in most interpretations of Canadian history, the rebellions lacked the disruptive force of the waves of violence that swept across Mexico and eventually the United States.

Mid-Century Challenges

All three countries experienced fundamental shifts in the middle years of the century that provide keys to understanding their subsequent development. Mexico experienced a terrible civil war from 1858 to 1861, often called the War of the Reform or the Three Years' War, that further weakened the nation and eased the French invasion in 1862. Despite Mexican heroics that halted the initial French attack of 5 May 1862, by the following year France was firmly entrenched, and in 1864 Napoleon III imposed the Hapsburg Ferdinand Maximilian as the emperor on a hastily created Mexican throne. Resistance to the invasion continued and finally found success in 1867 when Maximilian was executed. Mexico had achieved independence again, but the cost had been high. Almost a decade of violence left the country exhausted, financially destitute, and plagued by extreme political factionalism.

Deep differences also led to violence in the United States as the North (the Union) faced the South (the Confederacy) in the Civil War. Fought over slavery and states' rights, the war began with an attack on Fort Sumter, South Carolina, on 12 April 1861 and continued until the peace at Appomattox, Virginia, on 9 April 1865. In between, battle after battle was fought at Bull Run, Antietam, Vicksburg, Gettysburg, and hundreds of other sites. Estimates of casualties (close to a million) run as high as 40 per cent of the combatants. The United States had been maintained but at an enormous cost. After the war, Reconstruction, a difficult period lasting from 1865 to 1877, sought to rebuild the nation by imposing a new political life on the South.

Canada experienced change as well but in a far different way. Negotiations, not revolutionary unheavals, led to Canada officially becoming the Dominion of Canada in 1867, a country still constitutionally tied to Britain. The *British North America Act* (renamed the *Constitution Act, 1867*, in 1982) spelled out the terms of Canada's new political system and its relationship with the mother country. The Dominion of Canada was born out of compromise and diplomacy, not violence and rejection of the mother country. As a result, Canada remained closely allied with Britain, embracing the British monarchy as its own and displaying a more pronounced European political orientation than either the United States or Mexico.

Canada did suffer two threats to its sovereignty, neither as wrenching as the civil wars in Mexico or in the United States. In 1869 Louis Riel led an uprising of Métis (mixed-blood peoples of Indian and European descent) in the Red River area of what would become Manitoba. Increased economic competition and westward immigration, hastened by the building of railroads, threatened the Métis, who hoped to create an independent nation to maintain their way of life. The uprising was short-lived but not the reputation of Riel who became a defender of the rights of the Métis and a hero in French Canada. In 1885 he led another rebellion, known as the North-West Rebellion, which cost some 200 lives before it was settled and he was hanged. This was the last violent internal threat to the territorial integrity of Canada.

Growth

Deep social and economic changes accompanied the political reconfigurations. The second half of the nineteenth century was especially dramatic as all three countries entered periods of transition from primarily rural agricultural societies to urban industrial ones, hallmarks of the modern period of their histories. New forces of modernization set in motion people, goods, and services, evident in a westward movement in the United States and Canada and a northward one in Mexico. Space filled rapidly with ranches and towns and cities as all three countries overran their frontiers.

The United States experienced the most rapid changes in its social and economic arrangements. As the geographic frontier came to an end, a new urban society emerged. Cities, larger and more complex and unwieldy than anything seen before, imposed their power over the countryside. Chicago expressed the dynamism and energy of the new cities more than any other urban center in North America. From an insignificant frontier outpost in 1830, Chicago rose to dominate the new midwest. Its population grew to 1 million inhabitants by 1890 and soared to 2 million 20 years later. Its growth was fueled by the completion of a transcontinental railroad, when the Central Pacific and the Union Pacific were joined at Promontory Point, Utah, in 1869. The railroads made Chicago the linchpin in a continental transportation system, at least until 1881 when Kansas City was connected by rail to California.

Chicago was raw power, untamed and ambitious. Its size and wealth and influence overshadowed its competitors. Canada had its Winnipeg, Mexico its Monterrey, both exceptionally powerful in their regions, but it was Chicago that expressed most clearly the changes affecting the continent in the late nineteenth century.

Population increases helped to drive the expansion. All three countries benefited from natural increases in population and from immigration, but the United States experienced the largest population changes of all. At the beginning of the nineteenth century, the United States (5,308,483) and Mexico (5,837,000) had roughly equal populations, a short-lived situation as the United States entered a period of rapid, sustained population growth. By the middle decades of the nineteenth century, the U.S.

population (31,443,321) dwarfed its continental neighbors (Mexico with 8,105,443 and Canada with 3,229,633) and guaranteed its economic and political hegemony.

Imperialism

Beginning in the 1880s, a new foreign policy sought to extend U.S. corporate capitalism and economic culture. The culmination came in 1898 with the Spanish American War and the occupation of Cuba and the Philippines. As the twentieth century began, the United States was an imperial power, flush with the spoils of victory and ready to turn more attention to the Caribbean and Central America.

This new direction veered sharply from what occurred in Canada and Mexico, where neither country had the population or resources to settle its lands as quickly and extensively as the United States. Mexico, after a tumultuous half century, had finally achieved some political stability under Porfirio Díaz (1876-1911). Yet much of the energy of the regime was needed to prop it up. Rebellions continued, especially in the northern tier as regional political chieftains challenged the government. Throughout the country, bandits and brigands fought each other and local authorities. The army and the national police force known as the *rurales* were kept busy trying to maintain order. Even if it had wanted to, Mexico had little opportunity to expand to the north. It worried more about losing territory to the United States than acquiring it. To the south it also worried about the Chiapas-Guatemala border and the pretensions of Justo Rufino Barrios, the president of Guatemala, to build a united Central America. Barrios's plan failed, freeing Mexico from the threat of another war.

Canada had its own obstacles. It had both a western and northern frontier, and both still represented challenges in the late nineteenth century. And, like Mexico, Canada lacked an army and navy capable of international expansion. For it, "imperialism" meant the continued close alignment with Britain and the integration of Canada into a broader pan-British association.

Reform and Revolution

The late nineteenth and early twentieth centuries were extraordinary times in much of North America. Changes came fast, almost as if the seasons of the year had been squeezed into a few moments. Most glaring were the vexing social and economic problems that blighted the landscape — the squalor of the new tenements, the increasing violence, and the poor wandering the byways in search of work. Each problem called forth its preacher, demanding a rejection of sin and a return to Christian values; its politician, proposing reforms at every level of government; and its social prophet, who saw the chance for new utopias in the gloom of the onset of urbanization and industrialization.

In the United States a national movement of protest and reform took shape. Informally known as the Populist Party, the People's Party of the USA was born in

1891 and ran a candidate for president in the election of 1892. The Populists called for widespread reform of the economic and political system. Though they lost the election, the demands for reform continued with the emergence of the Progressive movement. More of an urban than a rural movement, the rise of Progressivism confirmed the shift of political power in the United States from the countryside to the city. Focused on corruption in the cities and the evils of capitalism, the Progressives demanded reform legislation from the local to the national level.

Canada had its own reformers. Cooperative movements sought to pool capital and labor and share the proceeds more justly. Farmers had their own organizations, such as the Canadian Grange, to fight the common enemies of tariffs and transportation costs, which they believed protected and furthered the interests of the manufacturing classes. Farmers, frustrated at the difficulties of selling their goods abroad and the high prices of the manufactured goods they bought at home, organized into the National Progressive Party in 1920. It had goals similar to the Populist Party in the United States, with which it had close ties. By the 1920s reformers were afoot in every corner of the country, whether they were farmers pushing their agenda through the Progressive Party or workers organized into labor unions and demanding higher wages and better working conditions.

Mexico followed a radically different course, responding to its social, economic, and political makeup. Still primarily an agrarian and rural society, Mexico continued to suffer from the sharp divisions that separated Indians from their European and mestizo masters. Mexican Indians had little opportunity to escape from their oppressive social and economic conditions and few means of protesting the system and implementing programs of gradual change. The best organized opposition came late in the form of liberal journalists and labor agitators who published a "Liberal Plan" in 1906 calling for sweeping reforms of the regime. Significantly, the plan was published in St. Louis, Kansas Missouri, not in Mexico, where many of the proponents of reform had been jailed or exiled.

Agitation continued. The political stirrings and social unrest in Mexico reflected deep tensions and frustrations. The excessive concentration of land and power in the hands of a few, the widespread social and economic inequalities, the increasing influence of the United States, and the oppressive politics of Díaz led to revolutionary change. After a slow beginning in 1910, the revolution exploded in a fury that engulfed the nation. Big in scope, violence, and bloodshed, the twentieth-century's first social revolution only began to subside in 1917, when warring factions agreed to a constitution embodying many of the principles of the modern Mexican nation. While the United States and Canada experimented with progressive reforms, Mexico followed the path of revolutionary change. Much of the twentieth century was an effort to live up to the ideals of the Constitution of 1917.

The years of reform and revolution were also years of war. World War I broke out in 1914 and first affected Canada, more closely attuned to European affairs than

Mexico and the United States. As a member of the British Empire, Canada quickly pledged its support for Britain, and eventually 625,000 Canadians served in the war. At the Battle of Vimy Ridge (April 1917) the Canadian Corps distinguished itself as an elite fighting force and contributed to the growing pride of the country. As the war dragged on, Canada had to pass conscription legislation to enlist enough men for service. Quebec, as it had in the past, resisted, further aggravating the deep tensions in Canadian society. The war, though, did mark a major transition in Canada, hastening the change from an agrarian to an industrial nation and giving it a heightened sense of its own international importance.

The United States held back until April 1917 when it joined the war. Its small army of 200,000 men jumped to over 4 million and was crucial in turning back the German offensive in the spring and summer of 1918. The armistice of 11 November 1918 finally ended the hostilities. For President Woodrow Wilson, the end of the war was an opportunity to insist on his League of Nations, an assembly of nations committed to peace throughout the world. The U.S. Senate failed to ratify the League, but the idea lived on and was reborn in the United Nations after World War II. Despite refusal to join the League, the United States emerged as a global economic and political power after the war.

World War I meant much less to Mexico as it struggled with its own problems. Angered over U.S. intervention, Mexico maintained a policy of neutrality during the war. It might have been tempted by the famous Zimmerman proposal, in which Germany promised Mexico the return of its northwest (the southwest of the United States) in return for support during the war, but it realized that Germany could offer little help in recovering lost territory. Despite flirting with the German proposal, Mexico and the United States shared a sense of continental isolation in terms of active participation in the early phases of World War I. Soon Mexico would be mired in social revolution, however, and the United States had to intervene on occasion to prevent the violence and bloodshed from spilling over the international border.

The 1920s, the Great Depression, and World War II
Change accelerated in the "Roaring Twenties." Unprecedented increases in production and consumption of clothing, household appliances, and automobiles heralded a new prosperity. The fascination with jazz and obsession with sports reflected both the cultural and technological changes sweeping the continent. But there were limits, defined mainly by poverty and isolation. In the hollows of Appalachia, the dirt-poor farms of the Great Plains, the scattered communities in the far north of Canada, and the Indian villages of Mexico, the new manias of the 1920s made few inroads.

The stock market crash of 1929 in the United States signaled the end of the boisterous and overconfident 1920s. The market crash was only the most visible of the complex domestic and international economic problems that caused the Great Depression. One root cause was that the supply of goods began to exceed demand as inequality in income distribution prevented increased consumption. Inventories began to grow, which soon forced prices down. Companies laid off more workers, increasing unemployment and further constricting demand. All had widespread international implications. Countries such as Canada and Mexico that relied heavily on the export of primary products to the United States faced weaker markets and more competition. Conditions in all three countries spiraled downward, leading to new reform policies.

In the United States the federal government entered into new social and economic arenas, creating a host of programs and policies aimed at increasing employment, managing production, subsidizing agriculture, improving rural life, regulating banks and the stock market, and providing for social security. Known as the New Deal and orchestrated by President Franklin Delano Roosevelt, it was an energetic, controversial period in U.S. history that culminated the reformist effort that had started in the late nineteenth century.

In Canada the crisis also caused widespread unemployment and a slowdown in agriculture and industry. Ontario and Quebec with their mixed economies suffered less than the Maritimes and the western provinces. Overall, by early 1933 national income had dropped by some 50 per cent, with the wheat, fishing, and timber industries suffering the most. Under Conservative Prime Minister Richard B. Bennett, the government passed several measures, but these failed to address the structural problems of an economic crisis that was becoming increasingly continental in scope. In 1935 Bennett initiated a Canadian version of the New Deal, offering a comprehensive package of unemployment and health insurance, minimum wages, and working conditions. More far-reaching reforms, which laid the foundation for Canada's postwar welfare state, followed under William Lyon Mackenzie King, whose lengthy service as prime minister from 1935-48 came on the heels of being prime minister during most of the 1920s. As in the United States, the federal government began to assume more and more responsbility for social and economic policies previously reserved for the provinces. Tensions between federal and provincial power would continue to haunt Canadian politics through the twentieth century.

In Mexico falling demand similarly crippled agriculture (especially the export crops of cotton and sisal), mining, and petroleum, aggravating the country's already vulnerable economy. Under Lázaro Cárdenas, Mexico's most famous and respected president of the twentieth century, Mexico began to implement the goals of the 1917 Revolution in a much more aggressive and comprehensive manner. Cárdenas went much further than either the United States or Canada in using the power of the central government to try and resolve social and economic problems during the 1930s. His efforts to redistribute land in the form of *ejidos*, or traditional communal landholdings, as well as to organize the urban working class, had a particularly lasting impact on the nation. Cárdenas's decision to nationalize the oil industry in 1938 despite heated opposition from the United States was the ultimate expression of state power.

World War II helped to end the Great Depression as all three countries increased production to assist the war effort. Similar to its actions in World War I, Canada entered the conflict early (now as an independent nation), declaring war on Nazi Germany on 10 September 1939, only seven days after Britain had done so. The United States struggled to maintain its neutrality, but the Japanese attack on Pearl Harbor on 7 December 1941 led to a declaration of war the next day. Both countries carried a heavy war burden on the front and at home. Industrial and agricultural production increased as the economies went on a war footing. Unemployment declined and workers tightened their belts as they joined to make the war economy more efficient and productive. At every level, new initiatives were advanced in the cause of the war. The most significant scientific and military advance was the development and then dropping of the atomic bomb on Hiroshima (6 August 1945) and Nagasaki (9 August 1945). The war ended in September 1945.

The Mexican war effort was more intense than in World War I. Mexico declared war in May 1942, after Germany sunk two Mexican ships. It increased production and held prices down on resources such as copper, lead, and cadmium destined for the war effort. It also sent an increasing number of workers to the United States, who labored primarily in agriculture as U.S. workers went into industry or the war front. Mexico also helped more directly by sending an air force squadron to the Philippines. As Mexico produced raw materials for the war it found it increasingly difficult to import goods from abroad, thus contributing to more of an emphasis on domestic industrial production. In a way similar to the United States and Canada, it received a significant economic boost from the war.

Postwar Trends
New social and economic trends transformed all three countries after World War II. Economically, pent-up consumer demand spurred economic growth, especially in the industrial sectors as factories turned out large quantities of automobiles and household goods. The consumerism of the 1920s that had been interrupted by the Great Depression helped to drive the new growth. The television was the darling of these new goods in the 1950s, much like the radio was in the 1920s and the computer would become in the 1980s.

On several fronts, Mexico's postwar change was more dramatic than in the north. Population growth provides one insight into the dynamics of change. Mexico's population has increased almost fivefold since 1940, while that of the United States doubled, and Canada's almost tripled. In 2007, the population of the United States stood at 301,139,947; Canada has 33,390,141 people; and Mexico has 108,700,981 (Central Intelligence Agency, *The World Factbook* 2007). Mexico City, in particular, prospered and suffered at the same time as it earned the dubious status of being one of the largest cities in the world in the 1980s and 1990s. Urbanization was pronounced throughout the country, as rural peoples migrated to the cities, leaving the life of the country behind. Instead of finding employment in the new industries of the city, most encountered frustration as industrialization lagged behind urbanization.

Mexico's social problems, part demographic, part economic, and part political, overshadowed those in the north, but all three countries had to struggle with serious social problems. Canada went the furthest in the development of a "welfare state" by creating comprehensive government health and social assistance programs. The United States made its own leap forward in creating a welfare state with the "Great Society" of President Lyndon Johnson in the 1960s, but it never went as far as Canada. Mexico has been the least successful in creating programs for the poor. Population increases always outran the resources of the government to address social problems. Programs in all three countries have been the subject of widespread criticism and reformist efforts.

The 1960s was a particularly turbulent decade. In Canada it was the time of the "révolution tranquille," the Quiet Revolution, when Quebec entered a period of unprecedented change led by the slogan of "masters in our own house," a phrase reminiscent of the Mexican call of "Mexico for Mexicans." Culture, politics, religion, economics — all changed as Quebec sought to transform itself into a modern society. One part of the quiet revolution was not so quiet as separatist attempts led to violence. Many of the issues that led to the referenda of 1980 and 1995 when Quebec voted on autonomy had their origins in the 1960s.

Violence in Mexico shocked the nation and the world in 1968 when the Mexican army killed and wounded hundreds of students in what became known as the "Massacre of Tlateloco." Violence also affected rural life as programs to help the poor and landless slowed, leading to unrest and peasant attempts to take the land. Despite these problems, Mexico continued its strong economic growth during the 1960s, but population increases diluted the benefits of this growth for most Mexicans.

In the United States several powerful forces converged to challenge the very nature of society in the 1960s. Society was deeply divided by opposition to the Vietnam War; increasing racial conflicts and threats from the Black Power movement; the political emergence of Native Americans, Asians, and Latinos; heightened criticism of the corporate culture of the country; and fear over the very future of the planet with the population explosion and the degradation of the environment. Student activism was at the base of much of the protest and demand for change. University campuses were scenes of intense debate and all too often of violence. The end of the Vietnam War eased some of the tension, but the issues of the 1960s continued to frame society through the 1990s. The list of contentious issues is long and not easily summarized — race, ethnic, and gender relations; access to adequate housing and education; environmental concerns; immigration; the drug trade; and foreign policy.

As North America begins the new millenium the weight of the recent and distant past is everywhere present. Certainly three themes have fashioned the contours of early twenty-first-century North America: continental security, health issues, and immigration. The Al-Qaeda terrorist network that highjacked four planes in the eastern United States on 11 September 2001 promoted a focused yet limited unity among the three nation-states of North America. It was the first time in the post-industrial age that the continent had been attacked so brazenly and with so much loss of life. The attacks against the World Trade Center in New York and the Pentagon in Washington, DC exposed weaknesses in the ability of the United States to protect the continent not from large standing armies from distant lands but from much smaller, more mobile terrorist cells that took deadly aim against US and Western policy in the Middle East. Although Canada, Mexico, and the United States could identify varying degrees of international engagement and diplomacy over the years, the terrorist attacks shattered the geographical dimensions of continental isolation that had buffeted North America for so long.

The events of 9/11 also revealed a complacency that had taken root in post-Cold War North America. With the collapse of the Soviet Union in 1991 and with China a rapidly emerging capitalist force despite its political totalitarianism, policy-makers in the United States, Canada, and even Mexico had set their sights on free trade agreements, overseas investment, and renewed economic growth in Latin America and the Pacific Rim without integrating the Middle East in any meaningful way. Moreover, particularly in the short run, 9/11 has ruptured the previous gloss of North American unity that appeared on the continent after the passage of NAFTA, as the United States under George W. Bush has tended to interpret continental unity in much more rigid terms than his predecessors. The nature of Canadian or Mexican support of U.S. foreign policy objectives has become the marker by which the United States measures continental convergence. Mexican and Canadian leaders have emphasized more consensual approaches that seek to advance their respective national interests while at the same time linking those interests to a broader diplomatic framework sensitive to continental integration.

On 26 March 2003, the premier of Ontario declared SARS, or Severe Acute Respiratory Syndrome, to be a provincial emergency when two hospitals in Toronto were shut down after having been exposed to the illness. The health crisis sparked another show of continental unity, as Canadian, Mexican, and U.S. medical personnel scoured the many airports throughout North America in search of passengers who exhibited symptons of SARS, which include high fever, headache, sore throat, shortness of breath, and a dry cough. Although there have been no new reported cases of SARS in Ontario since May 2003, the virus was linked to 247 probable cases in Ontario, four in British Columbia, and 44 deaths in 2003. In the United States, there have been eight confirmed cases, 19 probable cases, and no deaths. SARS does not seem to have entered Mexico, although there were several suspected cases in 2003 that were discounted later as something else. As the first severe infectious disease to have fashioned national, regional, and global health policy in the twenty-first century, SARS had an economic impact on Canadian tourism, as the cities of Toronto and Vancouver, in particular, witnessed a precipitous drop both in visitors and receipts.

Just when Canadian health officials had contained the SARS virus, a single cow in northern Alberta was diagnosed in May 2003 as having bovine spongiform encephalopathy (BSE), more commonly known as mad cow disease. International reaction was swift and economically devastating: more than 30 nations refused to receive Canadian beef, including Japan, Australia, and the United States. The latter's ban on Canadian beef was particularly difficult for Canadian ranchers to accept because the United States had accounted for 90 per cent of all Canadian beef exports. Soon the wholesale slaughter of cattle took place throughout western Canada as health officials put the region under quarantine.

Finally, another health scare has frayed continental health security. A strain of avian flu virus from Southeast Asia was found in the poultry farms of the Fraser Valley in British Columbia. While avian bird flu seems to pose little risk to humans, it has proved deadly to chickens. Close to 20 million chickens were slaughtered between February and May 2004, and a substantial number of poultry farms received comprehensive decontanimation treatment. While the exact figures still require an additional tally, the economic loss incurred by farmers and ranchers was immense. The Canadian beef economy, for one, lost billions of dollars, as agricultural and ranching income declined more than 40 per cent in 2003 alone.

Immigration promises to remain the one hot-button issue that defines the ebb and flow of cooperation between Mexico and the United States, even more so than the price of petroleum. In 2006, millions of documented and undocumented Mexicans and supporters of immigration reform took to the streets to protest proposed changes to U.S. immigration law. The cities of Los Angeles, Chicago, Dallas, and Phoenix became instant protest centers as the Spanish-language media, including Spanish-language blogs on the Internet, encouraged Mexicans living in the United States to articulate and coordinate their concerns. Even urban areas with fewer numbers of Mexican migrant workers, such as Madison, Wisconsin, or Des Moines, Iowa, experienced large crowds of protesters waving Mexican and U.S. flags and carrying placards to express the political message that the current anti-immigrant sentiment in the U.S. Congress would be met with resistance. While the Mexican government under President Vicente Fox tried to champion the rights of undocumented Mexican workers in the United States, post-9/11 security concerns have redefined the ways in which the U.S. government approaches immigration policy. Just like their predecessors, recently elected executives Stephen Harper (Canada) and Felipe Calderón (Mexico) will grapple with the more unilateralist foreign policy of George W. Bush, although the 2006 Security and Prosperity Partnership of North America offers some hope that continental cooperation will endure.

On the other hand, as we have summarized here, the contours of the North American experience are complex and multilayered across time and space, and recent efforts to deepen continental integration are often painted with the brush of inevitability. Convergence and divergence collide often enough in the guise of political economy and cultural values that sustained integration is neither certain nor inevitable. It is easy to find citizens of all stripes who view economic integration and facile political cooperation as a threat to national sovereignty, particularly if one unit, group, or ideology dominates the process, such as the export of U.S. mass culture, Mexican laborers, or Canadian internationalism. The different periods of the past are closely connected, however, and each provides insights into previous and later periods. Knowledge of the main currents of the North Ameican past will not allow us to predict future periods, but it will enable us to understand the processes that are shaping that future.

CHAPTER 3
REGIONS AND RESOURCES

Geography is a basic tool for understanding the history and culture of any people. Human activity takes place in space; that activity influences and is influenced by space. In North America, with its many climatic and vegetation zones that stretch from the arctic north to the tropical south, space assumes special importance in explaining the varieties of human experience. The boundaries that delineate each nation-state within North America are artificial creations that emerged in the nineteenth century; these borders, drawn as they were by men of their time, illustrate in concrete fashion the political and diplomatic features of the North American past. Sometimes the landscape served as an agent of convergence, particularly in terms of developing resources and facilitating trade. Other times the perception of bounty and an empty untamed wilderness, coupled with the political desire to exercise dominion over others, contributed to divergence, including invasions and the disregard for the indigenous peoples that had inhabited the continent for millennia. The political framework of North America, past and present, is the result of human interaction with and adaptation to the many geographic faces of the continent. The interaction has resulted in the emergence of historical regions, which in turn have influenced the course of North American history.

Size

Little agreement exists on the geographic extent of North America, an area defined in different ways according to the purpose and inclination of authors. Frequently, it has included Canada and the United States but excluded Mexico. This is particularly objectionable because it ignores the geographic and historical connections between the countries. Used in a broader continental sense, North America could embrace all of the territory from the Arctic Ocean to the Isthmus of Panama, including the Caribbean. Much of southern North America, though, is often simply called Central America. For the purposes of this study, North America includes Mexico, the United States, and Canada. Definitions might change, but these will always be the primary countries of North America. They also are three of the largest countries in the world.

The largest is Canada (9,970,610 square kilometers), the second largest country in the world after Russia. The United States (9,372,614 square kilometers) is second in the continent and fourth in the world (China is third). The size of Canada and the United States overshadows that of larger countries of the world. Canada is over three times as large as India, the seventh largest country in the world; the United States is over four times as large as Saudi Arabia, the twelfth largest country in the world. Mexico is a distant third in North America, with a total area of 1,958,201 square kilometers. While it is small in comparison to its northern neighbors, it is large in a global context, ranking as the thirteenth largest country in the world. Mexico dwarfs its Central American neighbors to the south and Caribbean ones to the east. It could easily embrace all of these countries within its borders and have room left over. Indeed, Mexico is much larger than any European country and could fit Britain, France, Spain, Italy, and Germany within its borders.

If independent, some of the states and provinces within Canada, the United States, and Mexico would rank among the largest countries in the world. The Northwest Territories of Canada (3,380,000 square kilometers) is larger than India; Quebec, less than half the size of the Northwest Territories (1,541,000 square kilometers), would be the eighteenth largest country in the world if independent. Alaska (1,530,700 square kilometers), the largest state in the United States, is almost the same size as Quebec. Chihuahua, the largest state in Mexico (244,938 square kilometers) is much smaller, but it is still almost three times the size of Portugal and nine times the size of Belgium.

The large size of the countries suggests commonalities in their histories and development: the struggle for the effective occupation and settlement of the land, the extraction of resources, the building of transportation systems, the desire to attract immigrants, and the political struggles between central governments and states and provinces. Space, some of it hospitable and comfortable, much of it hostile and forbidding, influenced how these historical processes unfolded over time.

Continental Features

The global positioning of the land mass continues to influence life. A dominant feature is that much of North America, in contrast to South America, lies within the temperate zone. Even in the subtropics in Mexico, much of the land mass sits at a high elevation, giving it a cooler, drier climate. Climates and soils in temperate regions are suitable for grain agriculture and have been the traditional centers of human development. As the climate turns cooler and agriculture becomes more difficult, populations become thinner. Thus, another important feature of the continent is that much of Canada is still uninhabited.

Canada is home to a fundamental geological structure known as the Canadian Shield (or the Precambrian or Laurentian Shield), a massive area of ancient rock extending over much of central and eastern Canada that can be likened to a granite

Map 3. Physical Features of North America.
From JohoMaps-website. Copyright © 2004. Reproduced by permission of JohoMaps.

skull-cap sitting atop much of the continent. Old and wrinkled from millennia of glaciation, its surface is twisted and scarred. Much of the topsoil has been washed away, but many minerals remain, giving the region its wealth. It is a land of lakes and streams, hillocks and rock outcroppings, muskeg and bog and deep forest. When compared to the broad river valleys of the south, it is a forbidding and difficult land. In many areas hard for agriculture, the land has traditionally supported only a small population that has extracted a livelihood from minerals and forests.

The major relief features of the continent are the mountains that run northwest-southeast in the west and northeast-southwest in the east. The oldest and most eroded are the Appalachians in the east, a complex system found from Alabama to the Maritime provinces. Eroded and lower in elevation (Mt. Mitchell in North Carolina at 2,037 meters is the highest) than western mountains, the Appalachians still represented a formidable barrier to European expansion. Their timber, water, and coal resources would eventually lead to settlement in the eighteenth and early nineteenth centuries.

In contrast to the worn and rounded Appalachians are the high elevations and abrupt relief of the western ranges. In the far northwest of Alaska the cordillera begins with the Brooks Range that extends south to the Canadian and U.S. Rockies. South of the Brooks Range is the Alaska Range, the site of Mt. McKinley, widely known as Denali, the highest mountain in North America (6,178 meters). Close by in the Yukon Territory is Mt. Logan (6,050 meters), Canada's highest mountain and the second highest in North America. The Alaska Range loops south into a number of imposing coastal ranges, including the Cascades in Washington and the Sierra Nevada in California. Mt. Whitney, the highest peak in the continental United States at 4,420 meters, dominates the Sierra Nevada.

The cordillera extends into Mexico where the two dominant ranges are the Sierra Madre Occidental and the Sierra Madre Oriental, parallel extensions of the Rocky Mountains. In Baja California there are other ranges, most notably the broken and rough San Pedro Mártir that reaches up to almost 3,000 meters. Volcanic activity has been associated with the western cordillera. The most famous of the volcanic peaks is Popocatépetl (5,426 meters) and Iztaccíhuatl (5,230 meters), which can still be seen from Mexico City on a clear day. The highest mountain in Mexico is Pico de Orizaba (5,636 meters), sometimes referred to by its indigenous name, Citlaltéptl or "Star Mountain," which overlooks the city of Orizaba in the state of Veracruz.

Between the coastal ranges and the Rockies is the Great Basin, a land of high plateaus, basins, and ridges that supports sagebrush, bunch grass, and cactus. To the east, one finds the Great Plains. They stretch from Canada into the south-central United States. For most of the history of the continent, the plains were formidable lands, sparsely populated and home to wandering peoples. Only with the technological innovations of the late nineteenth century did the tall grasses and scrub brush become attractive for permanent settlement. The mechanization of farming and the advent of the railroad helped convert the plains into one of the major producers of grains and animal products in the world. Now, 100 years later, diminishing water supplies threaten their future agricultural life.

To the east, with increasing moisture from the Gulf of Mexico, the plains gradually turn into a land of piney woods, marshes, swamps, and bayous. This coastal plain runs south to the Yucatán Peninsula and north to Chesapeake Bay. To the south and west of the plains, the lack of moisture creates two great deserts, the Chihuahuan, which embraces much of south central Texas and the Mexican state of Chihuahua, and the Sonoran, which covers parts of southern California, Arizona, and the Mexican state of Sonora. Here is a land not only of hard rock, sand, and heat, but of beautiful and resilient vegetation. The giant saguaro, the lithe ocotillo, the baroque cholla, and many other types of cactus adorn the landscape. As these deserts move south, they gain in elevation and moisture. They also taper toward the south until they are squeezed by the converging mountains of central Mexico.

Water

North America is almost an island, only thinly connected to southern land masses by the isthmuses of Tehuantepec and Panama. Water resources have been essential to its development since the first migrants crossed the Bering Strait ages ago. Later settlers crossed the Atlantic Ocean and established their first communities along the coast. These communities — Charleston, Savannah, Baltimore, Philadelphia, New York, Boston, Halifax, Quebec City, and Montreal — continued as commercial and population centers into the twentieth century. Along the Pacific Coast, the main cities — San Diego, Los Angeles, San Francisco, Seattle, and Vancouver — were founded later, but they still maintain their hegemony over western life.

Mexico was different. The first European settlement was Veracruz on the Gulf of Mexico, but it prospered only intermittently and never competed with interior cities for power and influence. Acapulco on the Pacific Coast was more marginal and only came to life when the Manila galleons brought trade goods from the Philippines. The interior cities have always lorded over the coast in Mexico, symbolically demonstrating how insignificant water resources, such as fishing, power, and transportation, have been in Mexican history. The contrast with the north is striking, especially since Mexico has a much longer coastline in relationship to land mass than either the United States or Canada. Spaniards, attracted by the dense populations and wealth of the highlands, went inland, and there they stayed.

Lakes and rivers cut across the central and northern part of North America. The arc of giant lakes swinging from northwest to southeast along the edge of the Canadian Shield connects the middle of the continent. The northernmost is Great Bear Lake, which straddles the Arctic Circle. To the south are Great Slave Lake, Lake Athabasca, Lake Winnipeg, and then the Great Lakes — Superior, Michigan, Huron, Erie, and Ontario. The Quebec historian Lionel Groulx called the Great Lakes, "a vast interior Mediterranean…almost half the size of France. Like a giant octopus projecting its tentacles in all directions this sea has provided the link of river communications in the center of America" (Groulx 1956, 68). North and south, east and west, the lakes are tied to the rivers that integrate the North American continent.

The St. Lawrence and the Mississippi Rivers have been the principal waterways in the continent. The St. Lawrence River basin is hemmed in between the Laurentians on the north and the Appalachians on the east. It has always been the center of Canada, home to the largest concentration of people, industry, and wealth. It has also been Canada's link to the Great Lakes and the middle of the continent. Beginning with the early missionaries and explorers, the St. Lawrence was the first large step on journeys that carried European culture to the farthest reaches of the continent. The link with the Mississippi River tied the northern boreal forests with the subtropics of the Gulf of Mexico. Along the Mississippi, French settlers founded community after community, ending in New Orleans. Mark Twain has immortalized this river in *Life on the Mississippi*, first published in 1874. He begins the book by simply saying that "The Mississippi is well worth reading about. It is not a commonplace river, but on the contrary is in all ways remarkable" (Twain 1923, 1). Less known and less traveled but no less remarkable is the Mackenzie, the second longest river of the continent, draining much of the center of Canada and flowing north to empty into the Beaufort Sea.

Dozens of smaller rivers have helped to shape the destiny of the continent. The St. John in New Brunswick, the Hudson in New York, the Delaware and Susquehanna in Pennsylvania, and the Ohio, Missouri, Platte, Arkansas, Red, and Assiniboine that cross states and provinces in the United States and Canada gave rise to trade, transportation systems, and towns. Rivers helped to span the continent. From the vantage point of Morgantown, West Virginia, for example, the Monongahela River flows through northern West Virginia on the western edge of the Allegheny Mountains. It is possible to put a boat in there and travel to Montana without touching land. Heading in the other direction, ships actually sailed from Pittsburgh, Pennsylvania, to London, England, in the nineteenth century. The very popular *The Navigator; Containing Directions for Navigating the Monongahela, Allegheny, Ohio and Mississippi Rivers…*, first published in 1801 and then quickly going through 12 editions, put it succinctly: "No country perhaps in the world is better watered with limpid streams and navigable rivers than the United States of America…" (Cramer 1966, 13). With the advent of railroads, the relative value of rivers declined, but many remain major arteries of transportation for bulk resources.

In contrast to Canada and the United States, Mexico has few large navigable rivers. The Rio Grande, or Río Bravo as it is known in Mexico, serves more as a political boundary between Mexico and the United States than as a transportation artery. At the opposite end of the country is the Coatzacoalcos River that opens into the

Gulf of Mexico. This river was often considered part of a plan to build an isthmian canal in the south of Mexico, but efforts proved fruitless. In the center of the country the two largest rivers, the Lerma and the Balsas, offer little navigational opportunities. The same is true of the Río del Fuerte, the Río Yaqui, and the Río Sonora, rivers that flow out of the Sierra Madre Occidental into the Gulf of California. Since the 1960s, though, these rivers have been invaluable to the agricultural development of northwestern Mexico, making it one of the most productive regions of North America.

Water for drink, transportation, power, and irrigation continues to define life in North America. Its uneven distribution has long been a divisive political issue for regions and nations. Canada, home to most of the fresh water resources of the continent, has, according to some estimates, about 20 per cent of the global supply of fresh water, a resource of incalculable value. Many have dreamed and schemed of moving water from Canada to the dry regions of North America; now there are practical plans in place to export bulk water on a global scale. In 1999 the Canadian government moved to place a moratorium on such exports until the provinces and the national government could agree on an export policy.

As water resources are depleted in many parts of the world, they will doubtless become even more significant in shaping regional identity and national politics than in the past. There is in North America a clear example of how the historical water practices and traditions of one country have influenced those of another. Early Mexican water law, that is, the water law in force prior to the U.S. invasion of Mexico in 1846, survives today in the U.S. Southwest and Great Plains because the Treaty of Guadalupe Hidalgo, which ended hostilities between the United States and Mexico in 1848, obliged the U.S. government to respect the property of those Mexicans who were suddenly residing north of the newly established border. Since water was considered property under Spanish colonial and later early Mexican law, the U.S. courts act as surrogates for Hispanic water law. Of course, Anglo common law traditions continue to shape the U.S. judicial system, which inevitably creates a juridical tension in the adjudication of water disputes in New Mexico and Arizona, for example, since the Hispanic civil law system — derived as it was from Roman Law — contained neither the riparian nor appropriative components of Anglo common law. Judges and lawyers in the United States who are involved in such disputes look to historians to unravel the complexities of the Mexican civil law of property. Moreover, contemporary judicial interpretations of the property protections afforded to Mexicans in the Treaty of Guadalupe Hidalgo have the capacity to either sustain or disrupt the links between today's successors-in-interest (primarily Hispanic and Indian farmers, irrigators, and ranchers) and those natural resources essential to their cultural identity and physical livelihood: water for domestic use, grazing of stock animals, and wood-cutting to cook food and heat homes during the winter months.

Defining Regions

The concept of "region" helps to explain the geographic complexity of North America. Unfortunately, there is little agreement on the main regions of North America or of the regions within the countries. "Region" itself is a difficult term to define, full of nuances that make it hard to apply to a given space.

Despite the difficulties, basic characteristics usually define a region. The most obvious and basic are the physical ones. Some of these are surface features, readily observable to the eye: mountains and deserts, rivers and lakes, rocky ground and grasslands. Climate and weather are as important. Hot and cold temperatures, humidity and aridity, sunshine and cloud cover influence the history of regions; so do soil quality, mineral resources, and more threatening geological conditions such as earthquakes and volcanoes.

As a direct result of soil, mineral, and water resources, the economic characteristics of regions traditionally have sprung from the physical. The Maritime provinces in Canada, facing toward the Atlantic and the marine riches of the Grand Banks, lived primarily from the sea. Newfoundland in particular has an economic history intertwined with the Atlantic fishery. As the 1990s have shown, when this fishery is in decline, the province faces economic disaster. The bituminous coal deposits in Appalachia, the cotton fields in the southern United States, the wheat fields in the middle of the continent, the silver and gold mines running the entire length of the cordillera from Mexico into Canada are just a few examples of physical characteristics influencing economic ones. With current technological transformations, physical characteristics are starting to lose some of their power. The drive to create "software centers" in regions remote from traditionally important natural resources is one example.

The cultural characteristics of regions also need emphasis. Southern California is different from New England; Chiapas is different from Sonora; British Columbia is different from Quebec. These differences depend on language, race, ethnicity, immigration, occupation, and a host of other factors such as amenity, or the choices that individuals and groups make to improve their lives. These lead to psychological differences, as groups within a region begin to think of themselves as sharing qualities that are different from groups in other regions.

All of the above can receive specific political expression that have conditioned the past and have the power to influence the future. The sectional crisis that led to the Civil War was the most momentous for the United States. For Mexico, the loss of Texas was partly a result of political regionalism. The sovereignty question in Quebec reflected the political influence of regionalism in the late twentieth century. Regional political issues do not usually have such continental consequences. The political liberalism of northern California conflicts with the conservatism of southern California but will not likely lead to the dissolution of the state. The politics of Dade County, Florida, with its large Cuban exile orientation, is different from the politics of the Florida panhandle, but the state continues to survive.

Regions continue to shift and change, often due to economic transitions and population movements. Examples that have been significant for the history of North America include the frequent migration of Indian peoples before and after 1492; the outward thrust from the first European settlements; the many gold, silver, and land booms and rushes; the migration of African Americans from south to north in the United States; the movement of Québécois into New England and the steady stream of Mexicans to the United States; the flow of rural peoples to urban areas in all three countries; and the flight from the industrial east to the south and southwest in the United States. These and many other changes have altered regional alignments in North America.

It is difficult to take the above generalizations about regions and apply them to specific geographic entities. Time, human activity, and physical characteristics make the discussion of regions a challenging, often controversial, task. Nevertheless, it is a useful one, since it provides a context for understanding broad patterns of historical change. Moreover, geographic regions often overlap national boundaries in ways that complicate the national histories of the three political states that occupy the North American continent. The Prairies do not stop at the international border with the United States, nor does the Rio Grande (Río Bravo in Mexico) only irrigate fields in Texas.

Regions of Canada

Canada's size and harsh climate prevented easy settlement. Early arrivals struggled to establish outposts and then to find routes across the central land mass or through northern ice-choked seas. Though varied, the climate is dominated by polar air masses that create extreme winter conditions in much of the country, shortening the growing season and thwarting human habitation. The Canadian Shield exercised its influence as well, deflecting the flow of human settlement south along the great rivers and lakes, and remained an obstacle to Canadian development until the advent of new technologies in the twentieth century. The result is that much of Canadian history has been played out in the southern latitudes, close to the border of the United States.

From a broad perspective, there were four chronological and regional phases of colonization: first, the Atlantic and eastern region, dating from the first years of colonization in the early seventeenth century to 1776; second, the age of central Canada, lasting until the twentieth century; third, the settlement of the Prairie provinces and the Far West in the late nineteenth and early twentieth centuries; fourth, the exploration and settlement of the North, a process spanning most of Canadian history and continuing today. Efforts to settle these regions and fuse them into a nation are keys to Canadian history.

Atlantic Provinces

The Atlantic or eastern region includes the Maritime provinces, Newfoundland and Labrador. All share an Atlantic orientation. The Maritimes — New Brunswick, Nova Scotia, and Prince Edward Island — are separated from the rest of Canada by the Appalachians. Much of the Maritimes (including parts of Maine) was known as Acadia until 1763. French-speaking and Catholic in religious orientation, the Acadians were caught between the imperial ambitions of France and Britain. Their efforts to maintain their neutrality ended with their expulsion by the British from Acadia in 1755.

Geographically, the Maritimes are as much an extension of New England as of the St. Lawrence basin. The state of Maine, reaching to just south of the St. Lawrence, almost severs the Maritimes from the rest of Canada. One of the chief features of the region is the rounded ridges and shallow valleys of the Appalachians from which came coal, lead, zinc, asbestos, and foods such as potatoes, peas, and fruits. The Maritimes eventually prospered due to their location and their natural resources. Great forests of dark and brooding conifers, pines, firs, spruces, and cedars spread across much of the land. The most famous tree was the white birch, from which Indians made their canoes. Later the timber was used to build sailing ships that linked the region to Europe. As a result, Halifax, the capital of Nova Scotia, became a leading seaport and commercial center.

The geographic centrality of the Maritimes declined in the late nineteenth century with the rise of industry in Ontario and Quebec. Even the construction of a railroad to the west did not integrate the Maritimes with the rest of Canada. As the center of Canada shifted westward, the Maritimes slipped into economic decline until the end of the twentieth century when new industries such as off-shore oil, tourism, and trade sparked revitalization.

Newfoundland and Labrador is the other Atlantic province. The island of Newfoundland was the first region of the New World known to Europe, thus its name of "new found land." Eric the Red or one of his descendants discovered the island around 1,000 AD, and settlements soon followed. In the fifteenth century Breton and Basque fishermen frequented the cod banks off the island. In the sixteenth century, literally hundreds of ships sailed from France, Spain, Portugal, and Britain to fish there. Settlement of Newfoundland was delayed by a colonial policy that sacrificed everything to fishing. Colonial governors tried to prohibit permanent settlement and agriculture in order to insure sufficient labor for the cod boats. St. John's, the capital city, was known by early visitors for its distinctive fishy smell.

Labrador, on the northeastern mainland, has traditionally been one of the least understood and explored regions of Canada. Though its population swelled in the summer months to maybe 30,000 as fishermen took advantage of the short but profitable season, the permanent population was seldom more than 10,000 people, most of whom were Inuit, Cree, and Montagnais. Moravian missionaries founded the first permanent European settlements in 1752, which still remain small and isolated. Despite its small population and marginal economy, Labrador represents a difficult political problem. Quebec, which shares over a 3,500-kilometer border with it, continues to contest a decision made in 1927 that declared it a part of Newfoundland. In 2001, the Canadian Constitution was amended to rename the province as the Province of Newfoundland and Labrador.

St. Lawrence River

The St. Lawrence River, which extends for almost 1,200 kilometers from Lake Ontario to the Gulf of St. Lawrence, unites a small but vital region of North America. It has a geographic and economic significance that spans the European history of the continent. From the earliest days of settlement, it was the center of Canada, the region with the largest population and the most dynamic economy. The first Europeans built their homes along the river and used it for food and transportation to penetrate the interior of the continent. The great city of Montreal, until recently the largest in Canada, thrived because of its location on the St. Lawrence.

The opening of the St. Lawrence Seaway in 1959 (linking the Great Lakes with the Atlantic Ocean) revitalized the region. With the seaway, large ocean-going cargo vessels had access to the interior of the continent, making Toronto, Chicago, and smaller towns international ports. Traffic through the Great Lakes and the St. Lawrence Seaway is still some of the heaviest in North America. The seaway helped Toronto to eclipse Montreal as a commercial and financial center, as it became Canada's largest city.

Quebec

While the river gives geographic unity to the region, it does not eliminate cultural divisions. Quebec and Ontario (earlier known as Lower and Upper Canada), the one mainly French-speaking and the other mainly English-speaking, share the river. Quebec, which is Canada's largest and culturally most distinct province, contains three geographic regions. The center is the St. Lawrence River region. North of the river is the largest part of the province, embracing the Canadian Shield and curving northward around Hudson Bay. The Laurentian Highlands, a part of the southern edge of the Shield, are a series of broken ridges that rise to their highest peaks in the Parc des Laurentides north of Quebec City. South of the St. Lawrence are the Appalachians that Quebec shares with the four U.S. states of New York, Vermont, New Hampshire, and Maine.

Quebec has abundant timber, mineral, and water resources. The traditional influence that outsiders (especially U.S. investors) have had over these resources supported arguments that Quebec was a colonial economy and fortified nationalist sentiment. Since the 1960s the province has assumed more control over its resources, best illustrated by the massive hydroelectric projects in the James Bay region. Though much of its industry still derives from its natural resources of pulp, wood, and metal products, Quebec today has a highly diversified economy.

Culture and language distinguish Quebec more than its economy. The French language has long unified the Québécois, underlining their differences with the rest of Canada and North America. The province has the largest concentration of French speakers in all of North America, which has given rise to demands for increased political autonomy and the guarantee that Quebec will be able to maintain its cultural distinctiveness. Political friction over language and politics continues.

Ontario

Ontario occupies the southern section of the St. Lawrence River valley and spreads north and west into the Canadian Shield. Its population distribution reflects typical Canadian patterns: most is in the south, close to the Great Lakes and the border with the United States. Toward the north and away from the rivers and lakes, Ontario is a harsh and unforgiving land, spotted with bogs, marsh, and granite outcroppings. The northern section represents about 90 per cent of the province's land mass but contains only about 10 per cent of the population. Despite the difficulties of the northern terrain, it shares with Quebec rich mineral and forest products. In addition, on its southern and western edge good soils support a flourishing agricultural economy.

Industry, more than agriculture, has defined the Ontario economy. A fortunate combination of location, natural resources, and transportation networks led to the early development of the province as the leading producer of manufactured goods in Canada. This was confirmed when Ford, Chrysler, and General Motors decided to locate in Ontario. The automobile industry, with its many economic linkages, became the leading industry in the province.

Prairies

The Prairies open to the west of Ontario and rise in three distinct steppes from less than 152 meters in eastern Manitoba to over 1,000 meters in Alberta. Broad belts of black, brown, and chestnut soils run east-west across the Prairies, providing the basis for agriculture, ranching, and dairy farming.

The provinces of Manitoba, Saskatchewan, and Alberta were settled in a land rush beginning in the 1880s. The completion of the Canadian Pacific Railway opened up the land, bringing in settlers and, as importantly, transporting the goods of the Prairies back to the industrial heartland, much the same as what had happened in the Great Plains of the United States after the Civil War. Agriculture, especially grain production, drove the settlement of the Prairies and increased the population from about 75,000 in 1871 to 1.3 million in 1911. Winnipeg was the epicenter of the wheat economy of the Prairies and of the world in the early twentieth century.

The discovery of significant reserves of oil in Alberta in 1947 shifted the economic axis of the Prairies—and the country—westward. Oil attracted new wealth, hastened economic diversification, and unavoidably accented the differences between the oil rich west and the energy dependent east. Ontario and Quebec consumed over 50 per cent of Canadian petroleum, while Alberta produced over 80 per cent of it. With the increase of oil prices in 1973, the federal government acted to minimize the impact on the energy dependent east. This precipitated an ongoing struggle over who controlled Canada's energy resources—the federal government, the provinces, or private industry. The federal government responded by creating Petro-Canada in 1973, a government-owned oil company aimed at increasing production. It followed in 1980 with the National Energy Program, designed to increase both production and Canadian ownership of energy resources. In 2004, Petro-Canada was privatized as part of a larger effort to loosen government strictures on such a profitable sector of the Canadian economy.

Far West

British Columbia, a land of islands, coastal ranges, and the Canadian Rockies, is Canada's westernmost province. Distance and the Rockies have separated it from the rest of Canada and given it a distinctive orientation toward the Pacific Ocean and Asia rather than toward Central Canada and Europe. Vancouver, the largest city, is a coastal metropolis that depends on seaborne trade and transportation for its growth. Much like in the major towns of the west coast of the United States, many settlers came from the sea, and the sea remains essential to the region's survival. The traditional fishing industry, especially salmon and halibut, still provides employment and income, so do interior resources of timber and minerals. Gold, silver, copper, tungsten, iron, and some coal and oil have also contributed to the prosperity of the province.

While the traditional industries hold on, the modern metropolis of Vancouver prospers more from communications, transportation, education, and its links with Seattle to the south and Japan and China to the west. This orientation increases its political distance from Central Canada and fosters identities and aspirations that give the region its identity.

North

For chronological accuracy the North should be discussed as Canada's first region, not its last. Migrants from Asia, and possibly from Greenland, occupied the North far earlier than the first Europeans. For Europeans the frontier of Canada is still the North, a vast expanse of land that cuts across every province and includes the Northwest Territories and the Yukon Territory. As of 1 April 1999 it also includes Nunavut, a new territory carved like a giant glacier from the Northwest Territories. The three territories, which include about 40 per cent of Canada but less than

1 per cent of the population, are divided from southern provinces by the 60th parallel.

The North is actually many different sub-regions of ice, tundra, permafrost, forests, and prairies. For simplicity, it is possible to divide it into the Near North of boreal forests and the Far North of permafrost and tundra. In the Near North, indigenous peoples, though speaking different languages, call themselves the Dene, "the people," and live from forest and fresh-water resources. They also work with recent arrivals in the mining camps and towns. Gold was and is a basic resource. Yellowknife, the largest city and the capital of the Northwest Territories, was founded as a trading post in the late eighteenth century but only entered its modern period of growth on the heels of the discovery of gold. Much of the region is made up of the Mackenzie Lowlands, the vast area drained by the Mackenzie River and including the Great Slave and Great Bear Lakes. It is an area of limited development but of storied potential.

The Far North spreads beyond the tree line and has less vegetation and fewer people. It is the home of the Inuit, who traditionally depended primarily on the sea for their livelihood. The region has been the least important economically in all of North America, but with the development of aviation, it became strategically valuable, leading to new military installations. In addition, recent oil and gas discoveries have led to new investments and settlements. In the late twentieth century, change came rapidly to the Inuit of the Far North, and the creation of Nunavut, a political entity that they govern (they represent 85 per cent of the population), gives them the opportunity to determine their own destiny.

The North is a special place in the history and culture of Canada. Canadians have even coined the term "nordicity" to describe the phenomena associated with it. It is a region of great complexity but also one that often falls prey to simple stereotypes, much like the West does in the history of the United States. Despite the inaccuracy of some of these stereotypes, the North, more than any other region in the country, fires the imagination and speaks to the determination, strength, and self-reliance of Canadians. Perceptions of the North, sharpened by art, literature, and folklore, are strongly imprinted on the historical consciousness of Canada and will continue to influence Canadian culture.

Regions of the United States

Regional diversity in the United States has challenged successive waves of colonists. As the colonies and then the country grew, they incorporated temperate, subtropical, desert, and arctic lands, each with their own resources, and often with their own histories of earlier occupation.

The history of the United States, much like the history of Canada and Mexico, is the growth and interaction of its regions. There were, however, distinguishing features about the interplay between geography and history that make the U.S. experience different from that of its neighbors. First to emphasize is the broad coastal plain that greeted the earliest colonists. Despite the hardships experienced, the mid-Atlantic seaboard offered fewer challenges for settlement than the rugged northern coasts or the southern tropical ones. Hemmed in by the Appalachians, the colonies grew slowly, maturing and building, until finally they broke through the confines of the coastal plain and squeezed through mountain gaps, spilling out on the central lowlands. This broad fertile plain promised and then yielded agricultural bounties that fed the early nation and continue to do so today. Another distinguishing characteristic was the humid temperate climate that encouraged early settlements. Broadly comparable to the European climatic patterns of the early settlers, the coastal climate was usually more accommodating than debilitating, especially compared to that which confronted settlers in the north and south. By the time that the United States started to expand in earnest in the nineteenth century, new technologies helped to overcome the harsher climates of the interior of the continent.

South

There were two early centers of colonization that gave rise to the most pronounced regions until the Civil War—the South and North. Chronologically, the first was the South, an offshoot of the Jamestown settlement founded in Virginia. Here in the tidewater along Chesapeake Bay the seeds of plantation society quickly took root; plantations inched north until climate and soil limited further expansion and then thrust deep into the South, creating a distinct way of life wherever they went. Chesapeake Bay was a transition zone between the North, encompassing what later became known as the mid-Atlantic and New England regions, and the South.

Different types of agricultural production existed in the South, but the plantation with its enslaved African workers and unequal distribution of land defined it. Tobacco was the first crop, followed by rice, indigo, and cotton. By the middle of the nineteenth century, "King Cotton" more than any other crop gave the region its social and economic individuality. With cotton as the draw, Southern society marched across the Gulf States and into Texas. There was manufacturing, but it failed to supplant agriculture until after the middle of the twentieth century. No longer fettered by a failed agricultural and social system, the South in the final decades of the twentieth century sported revitalized cities (Atlanta's claim as capital of the South was strengthened when it hosted the Olympics in 1996), new industries, increasingly prestigious universities, and the election of a president in 1976 (Jimmy Carter) and 1992 (Bill Clinton).

North

The second line of colonization began with the founding of Plymouth by the Puritans in 1620. This settlement initiated a period of development that led to remarkable results by the end of the nineteenth century. If the region is defined by industrialization, which became its dominant feature, it encompassed the middle-Atlantic states of Maryland, Pennsylvania, New Jersey, and New York (though these are often treated as a distinct region) and extended northward through New England. Early on the economy was mixed, with a balance between farming, fishing, and artisan production. The availability of natural resources (coal and iron) and water transportation increased the opportunities for industrial production. By the end of the eighteenth century, the region was producing everything from ships to textiles. Expansion in the nineteenth century led to the industrial rise of cities such as Pittsburgh, Detroit, and eventually Chicago. Industrial America had come of age. This was a land of factories, cities, and railroads that had a larger concentration of wealth and population than any other region of North America.

Historically, some regions in the United States have also been described as sections, a practice that the federal government initiated in the late eighteenth century for administrative purposes. Sections and sectionalism are most often emphasized when analyzing the economies of the North and South. At times interpreted as distinct entities whose economic resources dictated specific political objectives, the different sectional interests aggravated the tensions that led to the Civil War. The northern industrial economy clashed with the southern agricultural one, and both competed with the interests of the slowly developing region of the Old West.

Midwest

Once settlers pushed past the Appalachians, they encountered what was known as the West in the early nineteenth century, a thinly populated land that is today referred to as the Midwest. The region sprawls across the central lowlands of the continent and offered newcomers rich soils, adequate rainfall, good river transportation, and some minerals. The states of Ohio, Indiana, and Illinois made up the central core of the new region, bordered by Minnesota, Wisconsin, and Minnesota in the north and Kentucky and Tennessee in the south.

Maize and wheat came to define the center of the Midwest; dairy products shaped the northern states, while mixed farming characterized the southern ones. The large grain elevators and silos seen everywhere in the farming belts are monuments to the agricultural riches of the region, just like the small, often worn and broken corn cribs around Mexican subsistence plots testify to the agricultural poverty of much of Mexico. Already by the late nineteenth century pockets of manufacturing complemented agriculture, spurring the growth of cities. Chicago benefited the most from the transportation and processing systems that moved products from farm to market.

Great Plains

West of the Mississippi River the lowlands begin to gain elevation and then rise sharply around the 98th parallel to an elevation of about 1,500 meters on the Missouri Plateau. Here the Great Plains take over, a region marked by a harsh climate and unpredictable rainfall that stretches from the Canadian Prairies into north central Mexico. Drought, wind, and extreme temperatures continue to hamper agriculture in the plains. The recent drought of 1996 recalled memories of the Dust Bowl of the 1930s, immortalized in John Steinbeck's *The Grapes of Wrath* (1939) and reinforced once again that nature was still the final arbiter of life on the plains. Mining and cattle booms and busts, not agriculture, prompted the early settlement of the northern tier of the plains—what became the states of Wyoming and North and South Dakota. After the Civil War, cowboys drove herds of longhorn cattle north from Texas along trails known as the Chisholm and Western, helping to tie distant regions together. The westernmost trail, known as the Goodnight-Loving Trail, ran from Pecos, Texas, to Cheyenne, Wyoming, and firmly entrenched ranching as an economic activity.

Settlers continued to push into the plains, searching for land and opportunity. The movement climaxed in the Oklahoma Land Rush of 1889 as thousands of settlers scrambled for 1,920,000 acres in the Oklahoma District. The following year the U.S. Census Bureau officially announced that the frontier was closed. Using an arbitrary definition of the frontier as a land with not less than two and not more than six persons per square mile, the pronouncement had little impact on settlement patterns. It did, though, influence interpretations of the history and culture of the country. Frederick Jackson Turner, a young history professor at the University of Wisconsin-Madison, wrote "The Significance of the Frontier in American History" in 1893, arguing that it was the area of free land on the western edge of settlement that defined the history and culture of the country.

West

As the country expanded westward, it incorporated more land. More precisely, there was some "leap-frogging" that took place which resulted in the incorporation of much of the Southwest and Far West into the United States before the semi-arid plains entered the Union. The Texas rebellion and the war with Mexico helped create the continental empire. What had long been Spanish and then Mexican acquired an Anglo veneer that became more entrenched with each passing decade.

Now the West is many different regions, cultures, and economic systems. The northwest of Oregon and Washington is more akin to British Columbia than to southern California. The southern Sonoran and Chihuahuan deserts have climates and settlement patterns distinct from the northern intermontane basin and the Rocky Mountains. All are part of the West, and all have changed rapidly in the last 50 years. The greatest changes have been at the coastal extremes. In southern California there is almost a continuous line of development between Los Angeles and San Diego. The orange groves and sleepy coastal villages all but disappeared as southern California leapt forward after World War II. At the northern end there has also been rapid growth. The corridor between Portland and Seattle has prospered from the demand for new technologies, transportation, and tourist opportunities. Alaska and the Great Basin region of Nevada, Utah, and Idaho have been slower in growth, but they have benefited from the outflow from southern California. In the early 1990s, the population movement from west to east was so pronounced that it was dubbed a reverse Oregon Trail.

Out of this geographic, economic, and cultural diversity is it possible to find a core, a region equivalent to the St. Lawrence River in Canada? The closest historical equivalent to a regional center is the coastal strip that runs from Washington, DC northward through Baltimore, Philadelphia, New York, and on to Boston. This narrow coastal belt controlled the country for much of its history. In the nineteenth century a spur shot westward through Pittsburgh and then on to Detroit and Chicago; another led to Cincinnati and then to St. Louis. By the middle of the twentieth century, new polar points had developed, most noteworthy the new megalopolises of Los Angeles, San Diego, Dallas, Forth Worth, Houston, Denver, Atlanta, and Miami. From this perspective, the history of the United States has been the increasing regional dispersal of power, wealth, and population.

Regions of Mexico

Geography has influenced Mexico as much as it has the United States and Canada. Three prominent geographic features divide the country: the Isthmus of Tehuantepec separates the far south from the center; the Yucatán Peninsula arches northeast from the coastal plain and has its own distinctive geography and culture; and the Baja California Peninsula running south from California has long been isolated from the rest of the country. In addition, mountains, basins, tropical forests, and deserts break Mexico into hundreds of localities, each boasting their own traditions and history. These *patrias chicas*, or little homelands, make Mexico a complex country, rich in geographic and cultural differences.

Adding to the complexity is the influence of climate on Mexican history. The Tropic of Cancer runs through the middle of the country and exaggerates climatic differences that depend on altitude. In the middle of the country, three broad climatic zones exist, often within just a few kilometers of each other. The *tierra caliente* is found in the hot lands along the coast where plantation and African influences were the strongest. Next, starting at about 1,000 meters is the *tierra templada*, a transitional cooler zone, traditionally home to the largest populations. Higher still is the *tierra fría*, a region over 3,000 meters where the population thins and agriculture becomes more difficult.

Geographers and historians have a difficult time compartmentalizing these differences into regions. What follows is one of the simplest regional schemes possible, dividing the country into the Center, South, West, and North.

Center

The history of the Mexican nation has been in many ways the struggle to overcome the geographic and cultural divisions that fragment the country. The Center, especially the nucleus of the Valley of Mexico and the central highlands, has been the key cultural and political force in this struggle. The highlands are a mosaic of geographic and climatic extremes, a land of fire and ice, of towering peaks that reign over a wild and uneven landscape, of violent volcanic and seismic activity, and of humid valleys and eternal springs. This is a land of extremes, where within a few miles travelers can go from dense tropical forests to the perpetual snows of the high peaks.

Mexico City is the dominant city of the central highlands. Until the nineteenth century it was the largest city in North America; it regained that distinction in the late twentieth century. Mexico City dominates the rest of Mexico, extending its influence into every corner of the republic. Long before the arrival of Spaniards, Tenochtitlán was the capital of a political confederation that embraced millions of subjects. The Spanish conquest ushered in a new era in the city's history, giving it a Spanish facade, but beneath that much remained the same. Languages, foods, clothing, and religious beliefs from the past continued into the Spanish period. Indian markets in rural areas still demonstrate examples of cultural characteristics that survived the new intrusions. After the flurry of activity in the sixteenth century, the city experienced another phase of growth during the late nineteenth century and then again in the late twentieth century.

South

Gradations rather than clear demarcations separate the South from the Center. South of the central highlands, the mountains continue, fracturing into different chains and ridges. The Sierra Madre del Sur runs close to the Pacific Coast and converges with the central Sierra Madre de Oaxaca at the Isthmus of Tehuantepec. Here are the states of Oaxaca and Chiapas, traditionally isolated regions with dense Indian populations. Both are very poor states, neglected and on the periphery of recent economic growth. While geographically they might show similarity to the mountains and basins of the center, culturally, economically, and politically, they have been disconnected from many of the currents influencing national development.

To the southeast of the central highlands, the land softens until it becomes part of a broad coastal plain running along the Gulf of Mexico. At the southeastern extreme is the Yucatán Peninsula, a limestone plateau that is similar in surface features to the peninsula of Florida. Tabasco, Campeche, Yucatán, and the state of Quintana Roo dominate this region. Home of the Maya, the peninsula was the center of intense cultural activity that led to the construction of the majestic sites of Palenque, Uxmal, Chichén Itzá, and countless others. The process of the rediscovery and reconstruction of these sites continues today. For increasing numbers of tourists going to

Mexico, the new beach resorts of Cancún and Cozumel are as important as the Mayan ruins. As in the Gulf States of the United States, tourism has come to play a critical role in the regional development of the South.

Just as important are the vast petroleum reserves of Mexico, most of which are located in the Gulf of Campeche. The power of petroleum, if defined by crude oil reserves, has shifted from the United States to Mexico. In the 1970s, for example, Mexico was third in the continent in crude oil reserves, with 6,000,000 barrels. Ten years later it was number one, with 31,250,000 barrels, and by the 1990s it had double the reserves of the United States and ten times those of Canada, though it was producing far less than 50 per cent of U.S. production (*Energy Statistics Sourcebook* 1996). Mexican petroleum reserves have not yet created a wealthy society, but they do guarantee, despite short-term fluctuations in oil prices and inefficiencies in production, that Mexico will influence the political and economic future of the continent.

West

Geographically, the West is the smallest of the four regions, encompassing only the states of Jalisco, Nayarit, Colima, and parts of Zacatecas. The central characteristic of the West is the dominance of Guadalajara, the second largest city in Mexico and today a thriving industrial and commercial metropolis. It began as an administrative and agricultural town in the sixteenth century as settlers arrived to take advantage of the good soils. Without a large Indian population to provide labor and tribute, Spaniards took to the land themselves and became proprietors of *ranchos* (small and medium sized farms). The most famous product of the land in Jalisco was and is tequila, a beverage distilled from the juice of the agave. Today the West shares many characteristics with the Center and the North, but the *tapatíos* (residents of Jalisco) boast of their economic accomplishments and cultural distinctiveness.

North

The center of northern Mexico is the *meseta central*, a high plateau broken by *bolsones* (deep pockets) and spurs from the Sierra Madre Oriental and Sierra Madre Occidental that run north and south. As one moves northward from the center, the terrain becomes more even, rainfall more irregular and scarce, population density smaller, and the Indian influence less pronounced.

The North is the largest region of Mexico and can itself be subdivided into a Northwest, Center, Northeast, and Border region (discussed below in the next section). The Northwest has its own special features, with climate ranging from Mediterranean to arid to subtropical. Lower California, for long a neglected territory, is now the states of Baja California del Sur and Baja California del Norte. The peninsula is separated from the mainland by the Gulf of California, also known as the Sea of Cortés. On the eastern shore are the states of Sonora and Sinaloa. Earlier a region of sparse population, isolated mines, and ranches, these states now boast very productive agribusinesses.

In the Center North are the large states of Chihuahua and Durango, again known for their mineral resources. Rimmed by the sierras on the east and west, they are lands of high plateaus, sharp ridges, and broken valleys. The Northeastern states are Coahuila, Nuevo León, and Tamaulipas. Monterrey, the capital of Nuevo León, dominates the region as an industrial, transportation, and commercial center. It is the seventh largest city in Mexico, full of an entrepreneurial dynamism that has helped to transform the Northeast in the last 50 years.

Borders

The political, economic, and cultural characteristics of the regions presented above are dynamic and subject to change. North America has been and will continue to be a continent of regional shifts and alignments. Two examples of the changes are the "border" region between Mexico and the United States and the emerging region known as Cascadia in northwestern Canada and the United States. In both cases, international boundaries distort and sometimes complement the geography of North America. At first glance, the Rio Grande (or Río Bravo) appears as a natural border made of water, but it was a boundary born of expansion and war. As this chapter has shown, natural borders and political boundaries are not carved by the same hand.

The Mexican Border Region

The border is a new region with an old history. It is new in the sense of a recently arrived and rapidly growing population, a manufacturing economy, and profound social and environmental problems. It is old in the sense that it traditionally represented the northern extreme of the Spanish empire and then the Mexican nation. On the far periphery of the great cities and political power of the Center, it emerged with a different culture and economy. Less rigid, more mobile, and more antagonistic to the centralizing tendencies of the federal government, the border has usually been viewed with suspicion and caution by the Center.

Post-World War II growth of the border is the most dynamic example of the new bi-national regions and regionalism influencing North America. Mexico's population growth and expansion northward occurred as the U.S. southwest was experiencing a boom. These two trends produced far-reaching changes along the Rio Grande and in southern New Mexico, Arizona, and California. Given the geographic and economic differences present in this area, it is best to recognize that there are several "borders," each with its own regional identity: the Gulf Coast, stretching from Brownsville-Matamoros to Laredo-Nuevo, Laredo; the Central Plateau dominated by El Paso and Ciudad Juárez; and the California border, running from Calexico-Mexicali to San Diego-Tijuana; and the Arizona corridor.

There is little agreement about the commonalities that tie the borders together. Older terms such as frontier provide little help. In Mexico the "North" is still at times referred to as "*la frontera*," but it is not the frontier of the past when the "North" was an empty land, a place of refuge or of economic opportunity. In the United States the frontier meant more specifically the edge of settlement or a divide between European and Indian occupation. More than a boundary or the outer edge of settlement, the border has been a place where different people, technologies, and cultures overlap and intersect. The intensity of this interaction can be far-reaching and extend beyond the international boundary line and plunge deep into both countries. As an example, Monterrey, Nuevo León, and San Antonio, Texas, lie deep within their own countries, but both share characteristics of the border.

There are many questions and problems associated with the border in the late twentieth and early twenty-first centuries. In the United States attention focuses on the increasing pressure on human, economic, and environmental resources. In short, public services of all types are overwhelmed by larger populations. Undocumented immigrants are blamed for everything from overcrowding in schools to a decline in medical services. Moreover, post-9/11 security issues have further complicated the politics of immigration, galvanizing those adamantly opposed to the free movement of peoples while creating a new consciousness among those who support guest-worker programs and legal residency for migrants. In Mexico, there are frequent complaints about the illegal and discriminatory treatment of Mexican citizens in the United States.

Both countries also worry about the political future of the border. Many in the United States point to the "Mexicanization" of the Southwest, while Mexico feels threatened by the "Americanization" of its North. Mexicans even stereotype their northern residents, calling them *agringados* or *pochos*, derogatory terms suggesting that they are less Mexican than those in the Center and the South. History heightens Mexican anxieties, and while there is little fear of another U.S. military invasion of Mexico, there are concerns about the long-term effects of U.S. consumer culture and materialism on Mexico's youth.

Rather than focusing on the border as a mingling of two cultures, perhaps the emphasis should be on the formation of a *new* culture, which, according to some interpretations, is evolving from the fast blending of languages, customs, and cultures. Mexicans living along the border often do differ from those in the Center and the South: they are bilingual, have higher incomes, and are integrated economically and culturally into the United States. They also often have close family and personal ties on both sides of the border. Does this mean that they are less Mexican? The same question can be asked of U.S. citizens living along the border. The answers are not clear, but there is little doubt that the border does have its own distinctive dimensions. How this will be expressed politically remains to be seen, particularly in light of 9/11 and the protests in the United States and Mexico over immigration reform.

Between the United States and Canada there are also several borders. None, though, expresses the cultural distinctiveness of the Mexican border or portends changes that might alter the political future of North America. Similarities in language, culture, and economic levels overshadow the differences. Even along the Quebec-U.S. border, where two distinct languages and cultures co-exist, there has not arisen a new culture based on a fusion of these differences.

Cascadia

One northern border region has attracted increasing attention in recent years. Cascadia, a name derived from the Cascade Mountains that run from British Columbia to northern California, has replaced the earlier names of Ecotopia and Pacifica to describe the central northwestern part of the continent. According to Toronto's *Globe and Mail*, "Cascadia is a reflection of a new attitude, optimism and internationalism that is manifesting itself in Alberta, British Columbia and the U.S. Pacific Northwest" (25 January 1992). From the population centers of Vancouver, Seattle, and Portland in the west to Calgary and Edmonton in the east, Cascadia is geographically larger than the European Community and according to estimates in the early 1990s had the world's tenth largest economy. In North America, it is the closest region to Japan and China, giving it a decided advantage in the emerging Pacific market.

Cascadia's vibrancy and growth distinguish it from other northern border regions. Its economy is bi-national, based on the aircraft industry, shipping, information technologies, and tourism. It has become a powerful new region, noteworthy for its economic activities and regional integration. The traditional activities of forestry and fishing continue, but they no longer dominate the economy.

The economic integration contributes to the movement of people north and south. Border crossings between Washington and British Columbia topped 30 million in 1990. Cascadia also draws a large number of immigrants from Asia who serve to strengthen the economic orientation eastwards and influence everything in Cascadia from languages in schools to food in restaurants. Still another commonality is the widespread concern for the environment and dependence on outdoor recreational activities. Once planned regional transportation systems are in place and bi-national regional policy boards gain more clout, Cascadia may emerge as an even more distinct economic and cultural reality in the northwest of North America.

Places

This quick survey of regions only suggests the historical and cultural richness of the landscape. The countries are so vast and so diverse that it is difficult to select one or two sites, monuments, or cities that serve as cultural eyes, peering into the past and offering perspectives on the present.

Our own list of icons of place is brief. For Mexico it is the *Plaza de las Tres*

Culturas, or the Plaza of the Three Cultures, situated in the center of Mexico City. The plaza has many dimensions. Its sunken excavations of an Aztec temple (Tlatelolco) pay homage to the Indian past, although at the expense of African influences in Mexico. Its beautiful church of Santiago Tlatelolco reflects both the dominance of Spain and the fusion of Spanish and Indian that created the *mestizo*. Overlooking the plaza is the modern skyscraper of concrete and glass that houses the Secretary of Foreign Relations, symbolizing the modern Mexican nation. Finally, a plaque in the plaza marks the place where hundreds of students were gunned down in 1968 as they protested government policies on the eve of the Olympics. Perhaps there is no other place in all of North America that fuses so much history in so little space.

In Canada, the Plains of Abraham help to tie much of the country's history and culture together. Just outside of the wall of old Quebec City, the ramparts overlook the St. Lawrence River. Here on 13 September 1759 the British under General James Wolfe defeated the French led by the Marquis de Montcalm. The battle was an essential part of the Seven Years' War that ended French control over much of North America and contributed to the formation of Quebec's identity as well as British dominion over much of the northern tier of North America.

It is difficult to find one defining site in the history of the United States. We suggest three. The Statue of Liberty, sitting on a small island in New York harbor and dedicated in 1886, symbolizes the immigrant history of the country and the prevailing ideology of freedom and social mobility. With the words "Give me your tired, your poor, your huddled masses yearning to breathe free…," the statue welcomed millions of immigrants to the United States. As their experiences demonstrated, immigrants often faced oppression and discrimination, but this did not undermine the deeply imbedded belief that opportunity and social mobility awaited those willing to make the journey to the United States, a belief still held in many parts of the world. The current debate over immigration reform in the U.S. Congress, not to mention the groundswell of support for Mexican workers that has taken the form of peaceful protests and demonstrations throughout major U.S. cities and towns, suggest that the centrifugal and centripetal forces that shape contemporary immigration have their origins in perceptions, both real and imagined, of what constitutes a place and how this place might improve one's lot in life.

To the south are the great battlefields of the Civil War, monuments to the pride, passion, and prejudice of Americans. There is the famous and popular Gettysburg, where Robert E. Lee sought to bring the scourge of war to the North. It also provided the poignant backdrop of Abraham Lincoln's "Gettysburg Address." Not too far away is the moving battlefield of Antietam where the clash of forces on 17 September 1862 left 23,000 dead and wounded, the bloodiest day in the nation's history.

Hollywood, that eclectic mix of fantasy, creativity, and fads, presents a different perspective on the United States. Hollywood symbolizes the rapid growth of the

West, the rise of the entertainment industry, the excesses of a good time, and the tawdry aftermath of a society out of control. Alongside the sports cars and trendy restaurants are the homeless, those adversely affected by the rapid economic growth of the 1990s, as well as runaways. Hollywood embraces them all.

The places belong to landscapes and regions that shift and change. Mexico, with the continued dominance of Mexico City, has shown more stability in regional alignments than the United States and Canada, but even in Mexico the rise of the northern tier is gradually reducing the power and influence of the Center. In all three countries historical shifts have altered population distribution, economic wealth, and political life. They have not recently altered political borders, but there is little guarantee that these borders are immutable. The geography of North America overlaps the national boundaries created in the nineteenth century. Mother Nature and diplomats, it seems, step to the beat of different drummers.

CHAPTER 4
POLITICS AND POWER

Geography and the location and distribution of natural resources facilitated, as we have seen, similar and dissimilar trajectories of economic growth and social change in North America, with most historians emphasizing differences rather than commonalities. As the dawn set on European colonialism in the late eighteenth and early nineteenth centuries, the political history of North America also seemed to fracture as each country confronted a particular set of problems. The commonalities in colonial administrations dissolved into three political histories, each with so many threads running in so many different directions that it is difficult to weave them into a coherent whole. The emergence of federalism and political parties, however, provides a continental context for understanding the main lines of political change in each country and for appreciating the influence of political culture on national development. Moreover, the exercise of power, conditioned as it often is by domestic politics and national concerns, has had a direct bearing on the ways in which each nation-state views continental integration and tri-national cooperation. Politics and power, therefore, illustrate quite nicely the forces of convergence and divergence.

Federalism

All three countries have a federal system of government. Federalism divides power vertically between the central government and the states or provinces. In addition to federalism Mexico and the United States have a horizontal separation of power among executive, legislative, and judicial branches of government. Canada differs in the joining of executive and legislative functions, best represented in the office of the prime minister. Seldom absolute, these powers often interface and overlap, causing problems of jurisdiction among the different branches of government. While all three countries are federal, the extent of power of the central government varies in each country, with Mexico and Canada representing the two extremes of centralization and decentralization and the United States falling in the middle.

In general, a parliamentary system fuses power among the branches of government in an effort to facilitate cooperation and encourage the effectiveness of government policy and majority rule. The legislative branch selects the prime minister, who represents the majority party in parliament. Moreover, there are no term limits in the parliamentary system, as the prime minister remains in office for as long as he or she continues to enjoy majority support. The specter of divided government, therefore, casts few doubts on the legislative programs of the majority party. In fact, once an election is over, the party with the most votes controls both the legislative and executive branches. The parties with fewer votes become the so-called loyal opposition, and sometimes the leaderships of minority parties seek alliances as a way to dislodge the majority party from power. Finally, in a parliamentary system, the head of government (prime minister) serves an indefinite term of office, linked explicitly to how long his or her party remains in the majority. If the party loses majority support, the prime minister resigns from office. Two practices have developed in the system: first, the prime minister can call early elections to capitalize on his or her party's popularity or to determine the extent to which the party platform has the support of the people; second, a "vote of no confidence" can be taken among the members of parliament to ascertain support for the prime minister in the legislature. Prime ministers resign from office when they lose a vote of no confidence.

A republican system of government divides and distributes power to prevent its concentration in the hands of one branch, although in the United States and Mexico there is the tradition, as we will see, of a strong executive branch. Divided government can be part of the political landscape in the republican system, as one party controls the legislative branch and another the executive branch. Unlike in the parliamentary system, a politician cannot simultaneously hold office in two branches of government, and there is a complex set of checks and balances among the branches of government. Moreover, the minority party can exercise a myriad of procedures to shape legislation, dilute bills passed by the majority party, and even prevent the executive branch from appointing key personnel.

Perhaps the most pointed difference between the two systems of government is found in the positions of head of state and head of government. In the republican system, the chief executive (president) holds both positions. A president is expected to foster and embody national unity despite the political differences that exist. As the leader of a political party, however, the president also creates or endorses legislative programs and foreign policy that reflect a certain political ideology or set of ideas. Political turmoil often ensues when a president is perceived to have acted as a partisan rather than as a national leader. In the parliamentary system, the head of state and head of government are distinct persons. In the case of Canada, the monarch is the head of state (the monarch of Canada is also the monarch of the UK), while the prime minister serves as head of government.

Federalism in the United States
The U.S. Constitution designed a simple and delicately balanced federal system, the oldest in all of the Americas. It divides powers between the federal government (cur-

rency, postage, defense, war, taxation, and foreign and interstate commerce) and the states (education, health, police, and local government). It further specifies divisions between the executive, legislative, and judicial branches of government, each representing a check and balance against the other. In addition, its first ten amendments include a carefully articulated "Bill of Rights" that protects the rights of citizens against the government. "Freedom of Speech" is the most often cited of these fundamental freedoms. The Constitution, like a fine Shaker chair, durable, beautiful, and functional, continues to serve the political needs of the country.

The balance between state and federal (central) rights and the strength of the different sectors of government have been major political issues in the history of the United States. From the first days of the republic, intellectual and political battles charted the course of government. Thomas Jefferson and Alexander Hamilton were at the forefront of the debates. Jefferson viewed citizens as rational beings who could be trusted to act in their and the nation's best interests; thus, he fought for a limited central government with power and wealth widely diffused. Hamilton disagreed, believing in a strong, active government that would promote a diversified economy. He preferred power to be held in the hands of the elite rather than in the hands of the people, who could not be trusted to conduct the affairs of government.

One of the first battles fought over these principles was the proposal for the Bank of the United States (1791). Jefferson strongly opposed it, viewing the bank as a violation of the Constitution; Hamilton supported it as necessary for the economic development of the country. *The Alien and Sedition Acts* (1798), which gave the president the power to fine, imprison, or exile citizens or aliens deemed threatening to the United States, caused more concern. In the *Kentucky and Virginia Resolutions* (1798-99), Jefferson and James Madison argued against the constitutionality of the acts, since they violated the freedom of individuals and undermined the power of the states.

These and other dilemmas never threatened the stability of the republic. The issue of slavery did. It flared in 1817 when Missouri wanted to enter the Union as a slave state, which threatened the balance between "slave" and "free" states in the Senate. The Missouri Compromise (1820) allowed Missouri in as a slave state and Maine as a free state. In addition, it banned slavery in the northern parts of the Louisiana Territory. The balance was preserved, but the future of the country was not secure. Abolitionists kept the cause alive, arguing for an end to slavery. After the Mexican-American War, the Compromise of 1850 once again helped to delay a final solution to the slavery question. The legislation allowed for the entry of California as a free state and the organization of the New Mexico and Utah territories according to popular sovereignty (the will of the people would decide whether the states would be slave or free). It also called for the federal government to help return fugitive slaves and abolished the slave trade in the District of Columbia. This still did not settle the issue. The *Kansas-Nebraska Act* (1854) opened Kansas to settlement under the principle of popular sovereignty. This was interpreted as a rejection of the Missouri Compromise and led to heated debate and widespread violence in the new territories.

These two great compromises, so deeply imbedded in the political memory of the nation, postponed but did not eliminate the sectional threat of slavery. Again it emerged in 1861, when the Civil War engulfed the country as the South formed the Confederate States of America and attempted to secede. The war was long and costly, but the United States did survive intact, unlike Mexico, which had lost Texas to foreign invasion and sectional disputes. As a result of the war and the period of Reconstruction that followed, the power of the federal government expanded at the expense of the states.

Since the Civil War the United States has not experienced any direct internal threats to its sovereignty. It has, though, faced a range of problems, most stemming from social and economic conflicts rather than from purely regional or sectional divisions, which have influenced the balance between federal and state power. Racial conflict, violent strikes, and the harsh treatment of immigrants plagued the United States, much more so than they did Canada. Monopoly capitalism and the rise of the great trusts intensified economic and social inequalities and led to increased calls for regulation, initially on the state level, eventually on the federal.

In response the Progressive movement and the New Deal helped to shift the balance toward the federal government. Complex and subject to many interpretations by historians, both movements aimed at using the power of government to improve the life of citizens. The Progressives, never a unified group, struck out at the poverty and despair of the fast growing cities, the corruption of the political bosses, and the extremes of monopoly capitalism. Their legislation was a prelude to the emergence of a new and more powerful federal government during the 1930s. In response to the crises of the Great Depression, President Franklin Delano Roosevelt used the government to intervene in social and economic matters traditionally reserved to the states. Agriculture, banking, currency, employment, energy, industrial production, stock transactions, trade, social welfare, and more came under federal control.

The current balance of power between states and the federal government derives from the Great Depression and post-World War II period as the power of the federal government and the presidency grew. The tradition continued through the Great Society years of the 1960s as the federal government expanded even further into education, social welfare, transportation, energy, health and safety, and economic development. The changes did not take place uncontested. Under President Ronald Reagan Republicans challenged the increasing power of the federal government and promised to roll back programs and budgets, with limited success. In the second administration of President Bill Clinton, Democrats as well as Republicans argued for a smaller, more efficient federal government.

Federalism in Canada

Canada has not followed the same trajectory from a weaker to a stronger central government. Despite many efforts by the federal government, the provinces have recently reasserted themselves and flex far more muscle than the states in the United States. Their strength, though, was little evident in the first years of Confederation.

In 1867, the *British North America Act* created the Dominion of Canada, bringing together Ontario, Quebec, New Brunswick, and Nova Scotia. Manitoba and the Northwest Territories, formerly parts of Rupert's Land and the North-Western Territory acquired from Britain and the Hudson's Bay Company, joined in 1870, British Columbia in 1871, Prince Edward Island in 1873, the Yukon Territory in 1898, Saskatchewan and Alberta in 1905, and Newfoundland in 1949.

Canada's first prime minister, John A. Macdonald, believed that the federal government should direct national affairs. The *British North America Act* gave support to his efforts, since it granted all power to the federal government not explicitly delegated to the provinces. This differed from the U.S. Constitution, which delegated all power to the states not expressly given to the federal government. Specifically, the act gave the federal government power over defense, trade, taxation, currency, Indian affairs, navigation, and more control over interprovincial trade than in the United States. The provinces retained control over education, health, prisons, taxation related to the provinces, and property and civil rights. While the provinces held these broad powers, the federal government had the authority to disallow their legislation within a year after passage.

Despite Confederation and the move toward political autonomy, Canada maintained a strong monarchical connection, which was represented in some of its political institutions and traditions. The governor general, for example, who represents the monarch in Canada, is the head of state, as opposed to the prime minister, who is the head of government. With powers mainly ceremonial and ritualistic, such as summoning and dissolving parliament, the governor general has also had "prerogative power," which could be used during times of crisis. Another link with the monarchy is the Queen's Privy Council of Canada, a large group of current and former officials and citizens, which advises the Crown.

Much seemed to favor centralism, but by the end of Macdonald's administration Canadian courts had already made many rulings in favor of the provinces that confirmed the "Compact Theory of Confederation." The theory stated that the provinces, as sovereign entities, had created the central government, and thus it could not be modified without their unanimous consent. In the late nineteenth century the specific political issues affecting the balance of power included methods to absorb new territory (and to protect against U.S. expansion), the monopoly control of the railroads, and the resistance by some indigenous and Métis groups in Manitoba and Saskatchewan.

One of the most disruptive issues was the Manitoba schools question of the 1890s. The *Manitoba Act* of 1870 protected and supported both English- and French-language schools in Manitoba. By 1890 the English-speaking population far surpassed that of the French, leading to calls for a province-wide English educational system. The provincial legislature decided to exercise its rights to control education granted by the *British North America Act* and declare English as the sole language of instruction. Other provinces in Canada followed suit. French-speaking residents throughout Canada viewed this as a direct violation of the rights of French speakers to education in their own language. The federal government intervened to persuade the Manitoba government to accept a compromise: wherever there were 10 or more French-speaking students, instruction could be in French.

The strength of centralism ebbed and flowed with the tide of political events. Under the National Policy of Macdonald the central government had the power to encourage railroad construction, attract immigrants, and stimulate industrialization. Yet the future of central control was anything but assured. Acts that increased control, especially during the crises of World War I, the Great Depression, and World War II, could provoke a hostile reaction. Conscription laws, for example, which gave the central government the authority to force citizens into military service, provoked a harsh reaction in Quebec, further aggravating the tensions between Quebec and the central government.

To give backing to central control, the Royal Commission on Dominion-Provincial Relations (1940) recommended that the federal government assume more power over unemployment compensation, retirement, and taxation. One outcome of the recommendations was the implementation of "equalization payments," initiated in 1957. The intent was to help the poorer provinces through federal transfer payments to them from wealthier provinces. By this time the Liberals, not the Conservatives, had become the outspoken advocates of more central control.

Constitutional Issues

Canadian federalism shifted toward the provinces again in the 1960s and 1970s. Quebec was the most aggressive, demanding more respect for its cultural and political aspirations, but other provinces joined in demanding more control over spending and taxation. Any lasting resolution of conflicting provincial-federal objectives seemed elusive in the face of frustrated constitutional reforms. To resolve the issue, Prime Minister Pierre Trudeau pushed for a constitutional revision that led to the *Canada Act (1982)*, which stated that the British Parliament would no longer act as the final arbiter of constitutional change in Canada. The *Canada Act* became a part of the *Constitution Act (1982)*, which took all constitutional legislation beginning with the *British North America Act* and renamed them the *Constitution Acts*.

Two serious constitutional issues continue to beleaguer Canada. The less problematic is the Charter of Rights and Freedoms that specifies freedoms for individuals and groups in Canada. Canada already had a "Bill of Rights" (1960), but this was deemed insufficient because it emerged federally without strong support from the provinces. The new charter prevents the parliament or the government from actions or laws that limit specified freedoms. As an example, in 1917 naturalized citizens of German origin were deprived of their right to vote under the *War Measures Act*. With the new Charter in place, such action could not take place.

Much more perplexing have been the amendment provisions of the constitution. Quebec, ever vigilant in protecting its interests, refused to ratify the *Constitution Act (1982)*. After much deliberation an agreement known as the "Meech Lake Accord" was reached in 1987. This guaranteed that French and English were the official languages of Canada and that Quebec's "distinct society" would enjoy constitutional protection. It also gave each province the right to veto any amendments to the constitution. Quebec quickly approved the accord, but vetoes by Manitoba and Newfoundland prevented its passage.

The failure of Meech Lake led to more negotiations and the Charlottetown Accord in 1992. It called for Quebec's distinct society, but also for Aboriginal rights, minority rights, senate reform, and greater provincial control. In a national vote in October 1992 the proposals were defeated. In the end, the future of Canadian federalism remained uncertain.

The Quebec Question

As the federal government moved to consolidate its power, Quebec offered the stiffest opposition. Fundamental to Quebec's attitude is the strength of its political and cultural traditions. The history of the province is often interpreted as a struggle to maintain and affirm its identity as one of the founding nations of Canada. It had early success in guaranteeing basic freedoms of language and religion in the *Quebec Act* of 1774, at times referred to as the "Magna Carta" of the province, but these guarantees did not erase its insecurity. The old province itself ceased to exist with the passage of the *Constitution Act* of 1791, which divided Canada into Lower Canada (Quebec) and Upper Canada (Ontario). This insecurity grew as the *Act of Union* (passed 1840, proclaimed 1841) united Upper and Lower Canada into one government. As the center of gravity in Canada shifted to Ontario, Quebec gradually became marginalized economically and politically. It stood slightly to the side as massive social and economic changes hastened the urbanization and industrialization of Canada, which prompted some historians and social commentators to emphasize the family, church, and village as bastions of Quebec culture. Gradually, the Québécois came to recognize that a strong provincial Quebec government offered the best means for asserting their economic independence and guaranteeing their cultural distinctiveness.

Recently, discussion of Quebec nationalism has moved beyond the traditional and exclusive definitions of the past. Lise Bissonette, the influential editor of *Le*

Devoir (a Quebec newspaper), explains: "We have consciously decided that we are not going to be a nation based only on language, culture, a shared sense of history (that of Nouvelle France)…everyone who lives in Quebec and wants to live there is a part of this 'country'" (Bothwell 1998, 236). According to her, the narrow ethnic and cultural identification of nationality is giving way to a broader regional one that accommodates diversity.

The political struggle over Quebec nationalism intensified in the 1960s with the *révolution tranquille,* or peaceful revolution. Under the leadership of Jean Lesage and the Quebec Liberal Party, the provincial government moved quickly on several fronts. It assumed more control over its economy, education, and social programs. As its power expanded, that of the Anglo-Canadian community in Quebec and the Catholic Church declined. With new power-sharing arrangements with the federal government, Quebec started its own retirement plan. It also invested heavily in massive hydroelectric projects through Hydro-Québec, an electric utility owned by the province. In this and other economic activities it emphasized the role of Québécois administrators and managers and the use of the French language. In education it started the Université du Québec (1968), which eventually established several branches in the province. Every activity was in keeping with the determination to transform provincial life.

When French President Charles de Gaulle visited Quebec in 1967 he said it reminded him of Paris after it was liberated from Nazi occupation. The insult to "Anglo Canadians" continued when de Gaulle addressed the large crowd that had gathered outside Montreal's City Hall. He shouted "Vive le Québec libre" ("Long live a free Quebec") from the balcony, and the crowd roared its approval. The French president had borrowed from the rallying cry of the Quebec separatists, thus bestowing an international legitimacy to the movement, much to the chagrin of Prime Minister Lester Pearson, who shortened de Gaulle's visit to Canada. The phrase, however, summarized the new Quebec — a more powerful, economically aggressive, and culturally assured society within Canada but also within North America. With the articulation of its growing strength came calls for more political autonomy within the Canadian Confederation. Most politicians phrased the calls within the context of party platforms and political rhetoric; a few went beyond and advocated violence to achieve political independence. The bombings and kidnappings that did take place brought a harsh reaction, uniting the province and the rest of Canada against the radical separatists. Quebec, like the United States and Mexico in the late 1960s, realized how vulnerable its civic institutions were to violent attacks.

The end of violence did not eliminate the commitment to a new relationship within the Canadian Confederation. The Parti Québécois, inspired by René Lévesque, united many of the groups committed to change. This was a separatist party, committed to sovereignty but in association with Canada. Seldom clearly defined, sovereignty-association envisioned redefining linkages and interdependence between equal peoples and states. Voters brought the Parti Québécois to power in 1976, and it soon started leading the province toward a vote on sovereignty. When the vote came in 1980 it dealt a crippling blow to the separatists — 60 per cent voted against sovereignty.

While separatist sentiment subsided, the language issue kept the question of the political future of Quebec alive. In 1977, the Parti Québécois passed *Bill 101* that strengthened earlier language legislation. It declared French the official language of Quebec and required all signs and billboards to be in French. In addition it insisted on French as the language of education, except for the children of English-speaking parents who had lived in the province before 1977. This and subsequent legislation inspired heated political fighting and judicial debate. It remains an unresolved issue.

The failure of the Meech Lake and Charlottetown Accords rekindled anxiety over the future of Quebec and led once again to serious consideration of separation. When Jacques Parizeau brought the Parti Québécois back to power, he pledged another referendum on separation. The separatists lost again in 1995, this time in an exceptionally tight vote — 49.6 per cent voting for the referendum. When Lucien Bouchard took control of the party after the defeat, he pledged that another vote would be held as soon as "winning conditions" emerged. Canadian Prime Minister Jean Chrétien, for his part, decided to switch tactics, leaving behind the conciliatory stance taken before the referendum in favor of a more aggressive position. He brought in a constitutional expert, Stéphane Dion, a law professor from Quebec, to bolster the federalist position. Dion attacked the separatists' assertion, made for years, that "Canada is divisible but Quebec is not." In the process, he and his supporters raised an important constitutional question: could Quebec secede from Canada with only a simple majority (50 per cent plus one)? Even the Civil Code that governs Quebec stated that a simple majority was not sufficient to dissolve an entity with juridical personality, such as a political or civil organization. Quebec civil law, it seemed, required a two-thirds majority vote to terminate a legal relationship. The Chrétien government then asked the Supreme Court of Canada to make a ruling on whether or not any province could unilaterally dissolve its relationship with the Confederation. In August 1998, the Supreme Court issued its ruling, stating that provinces cannot unilaterally secede from the Confederation, even if the province held a plebiscite that was favorable to dissolution. The subtlety and nuance of the ruling, however, still left open the possibility of formal separation if a "clear question" was presented to voters and a "clear majority" voted in favor of secession. Canada would be obliged to negotiate the terms of secession. And the highest court left it to the government to decide how to interpret the subtlety of its decision.

On the other hand, Chrétien's desire to stem the tide of the separatist movement created the conditions for a political scandal that involved the use of public funds to promote federalism in Quebec. Some of the money, apparently, was detoured secretly to the Liberal Party and its supporters. Chrétien's successor, Paul Martin, was forced to cut deals with other political parties in order to prolong his own party's stay in power. Despite the recent scandals—dubbed the sponsorship scandals in the Canadian press—that have plagued Canadian politics, virtually every poll taken in Quebec since 1995 suggests that support for formal separation is mitigated by a desire to avoid yet another referendum.

Some Canadians wondered whether the election of Conservative Party leader Stephen Harper as prime minister in early 2006 would substantially recast the federalist question. In November 2006, after nine months in office, Harper asked the House of Commons to recognize Quebec as a nation. More concretely, the prime minister introduced a motion declaring that "the Québécois form a nation within a united Canada." Harper called it an "act of reconciliation," a way of recognizing that many Québécois see themselves as a distinct people with their own culture, language, and traditions. Was the new prime minister opening the door to formal secession and independence? He was quite firm in this regard: "Do the Québécois form a nation within Canada? The answer is yes. Do the Québécois form an independent nation? The answer is no, and the answer will always be no." Most political analysts point to the provincial elections that must be held by the end of 2008, when the Liberal premier, Jean Charest, is set to run again. His party is trailing the Parti Québécois in the polls, and Harper would much rather avoid another referendum should the Parti Québécois win the election. Others suggest that Harper crafted a pre-emptive strike in the House of Commons in an effort to improve the long-term political fortunes of his Conservative Party in the province. At this early juncture in Harper's tenure as prime minister, it is unclear whether his decision to recognize Quebec as a nation within a nation hinders or promotes formal independence. As long as Quebec demands recognition of its separate status to the point of threatening secession, the future of Canadian federalism remains uncertain.

Federalism in Mexico

Mexico, currently de facto the most unitary of the three countries, has a centralist tradition that dates to the viceregal system, when the viceroy represented the king of Spain in the political life of the colony. Centralism, at least according to the theory of government, continued during the colonial period, when all power emanated from the center. In practice, divisions and subdivisions of power splintered political life at the local level. Local power contenders, regardless of the wishes of king and viceroy, dictated political decisions in towns and provinces. From monarch in the colonial period to *caudillo* (regional or national strongman who combined military power and a charismatic personality) in the nineteenth century, centralism has struggled against regional forces. Centralism prevailed, demonstrated by the extensive power of the Mexican president, but only after a long struggle and despite a formally federal structure.

Mexico's nineteenth-century history was a violent struggle of contending factions, expressed in ongoing personal, group, and regional animosities that far surpassed anything experienced in Canada and the United States. From the first years of independence Mexico faced fundamental decisions on the type of government, on who was going to rule, and how they were going to rule. Answering these questions was more difficult than in the United States and Canada. Regional realities posed one of the most serious problems for Mexico. It emerged as an independent nation when it still controlled about half of the continent, a vast space of different resources, populations, and political interests. Creating a new political system to govern a country of such size and regional diversity was challenging and ultimately impossible. In contrast, the United States created its new government when it was still a small nation confined to the Atlantic seaboard. Canada was much larger, but the prairie and western provinces had such small populations that they could not challenge the dominance of the St. Lawrence River region. As they grew they were quickly integrated into the new nation with the completion of the Canadian Pacific Railway in 1885.

The first years of Mexico's independence portended many of the difficulties of the nineteenth century. Agustín Iturbide declared Mexico independent in the *Plan of Iguala* in 1821. The plan was not revolutionary at all. It called for a constitutional monarchy, the protection of the Roman Catholic Church, and the coexistence of Spaniards and Mexicans, all as much a reaction to the liberal reforms of Spain in 1820 as to internal Mexican conditions. Iturbide then proclaimed himself emperor.

Local conditions turned against Iturbide soon enough, driving him from office in 1823. This led to efforts to develop a new political system, confirmed in the Constitution of 1824, which rejected the monarchy and created a federal republic. The new president was the liberal Guadalupe Victoria; his vice-president was Nicolás Bravo, a conservative centralist. Before their terms ended, Bravo had revolted against Victoria.

By this time, there were already elements of the system in place that would last for much of the century. Instability was in evidence early. There were not institutional or political loyalties and commitments strong enough to prevent rebellions and overcome factionalism. Liberals and conservatives — the former usually a plank of liberals, the latter of conservatives — clashed over the military and Church, as well as over federalism and centralism. Powerful regional forces demanded an extreme federalism that struck at the core of the nation. In the north center of the country the state of Zacatecas aspired for more autonomy in 1835; in the far north Texas successfully rebelled in 1836, creating its own Lone Star Republic; in the southeast state of Yucatán Mayans waged a war of separation from 1847 to 1855. One aftermath of this war, known as the Caste War of Yucatán, was the creation of an independent stronghold of Indians in the interior of Yucatán until 1911. Regional outbreaks thwarted the centralizing tendency of the government for much of the nineteenth century.

All this unfolded against a tumultuous political history that had cliques and factions bickering and fighting each other. The army, or factions of the army, ultimately arbitrated the disputes. Events simmered, boiled, cooled, and then simmered again. As liberal factions gained control in the 1850s, they passed a series of reforms pushing their platform. Three in particular chilled conservatives. The *Juárez Law* limited the jurisdiction of ecclesiastical and military courts to canon or military law. Members of the church and military could no longer seek refuge from their criminal and civil transgressions. The *Lerdo Law* prohibited ecclesiastical and civil corporations from owning or administering real property not directly used in day-to-day operations, and while the new law was aimed at the vast holdings of the Mexican church, the *ejido*, or the communal landholdings of Indian and mestizo towns, also came under attack. While historians still debate exactly how much communal land was lost to the *Lerdo Law*, many Indian villages were forced to put their traditional lands up for auction. Finally, the *Iglesias Law* also limited the power of the church by reducing the customary fees that the clergy charged for administering the rites of baptism, marriage, and burial. And still another law aimed at the church transferred its responsibility to maintain the civil registry (keeping records related to births, marriages, and deaths) to the state. These and other restrictions were codified in the liberal Constitution of 1857.

This liberal-conservative conflict precipitated the War of the Reform (1858-61), a three-year struggle for control over the political future of Mexico. Conservatives, rallying to the cry of *"religión and fueros"* (religion and privileges) struck at the liberal reforms. Under Juárez, the liberals emerged victorious in 1861, but there was little time to celebrate victories or plan for the future. Juárez and Mexico were again at war, this time against the French, who occupied the country from 1863 to 1867 as a part of Napoleon III's global efforts to build a new French empire.

The first 50 years of Mexican independence were a struggle for survival. Beset by foreign invasions, regional conflicts, the loss of half of its territory, and economic weaknesses, Mexico had little time to build the participatory democratic institutions beginning to take shape in Canada and the United States. Stability came only in the late 1870s with the emergence of Porfirio Díaz, who ruled 34 of the 38 years between 1872 and 1910. Known as the *Pax Porfiriana*, his administration ushered in an era of relative peace and great economic growth. The modernization he initiated, especially the building of roads and railroads, helped to integrate the nation and overcome some of the regional tendencies. Skillfully using the army, an expanding bureaucracy, and international capital, Díaz overcame some of the obstacles that had limited Mexico's growth. Regionalism was not dead though and broke out with fury in the Mexican Revolution of 1910. The Constitution of 1917 helped to allay the tendencies toward regional violence by creating a nominally federal system, but pacification came slowly under a group of leaders that hailed from the northwest of Mexico and who were known as the Sonora Dynasty.

By the end of the 1930s, the regionalism that so long had disrupted Mexican life was under control. So were the church and the military. The central government had overcome its foes, and the power of the Mexican chief executive far exceeded that of his counterparts in the United States and Canada. Known as *presidencialismo*, the Mexican system confers on the president vast powers of appointment and influence over the legislative process. Until 2000, much of his power derived from his role as head of the main political party, the *Partido Revolucionario Institucional* (Institutional Revolutionary Party), or PRI. As president, he selected his successor as president of the party and the country. The PRI candidate had always won the presidency until Vicente Fox turned the political tide in Mexico with his victory in the election of 2000.

Mexico's centralist system stands in contrast to the federalism of the United States and Canada for several reasons. In addition to a strong executive branch, the federalist framework in Mexico includes a bicameral legislature (Chamber of Deputies and Senate) and the Supreme Court. For most of the twentieth century, the executive branch, through its party patronage networks, doled out money and favors to state and local officials in an effort to structurally transform the PRI into a national party. Often emphasized in discussions of Mexican political history is the tradition of the colonial period, when Spain struggled to impose its political weight on its colony, severely limiting efforts at independent political action. Yet the success of Spanish absolutism is overemphasized, as problems of distance, inefficiency, corruption, and the sheer magnitude of the problems of administration weakened Spanish rule. More telling is the political history of the late nineteenth century, when there was an effective concentration of power under Díaz. This was shattered during the revolutionary period but slowly reassembled beginning in the 1920s. Three considerations aided this process: the rapid growth of Mexico City, the political, economic, and cultural center of the country; the emergence of a revolutionary development ideology whose implementation fell on the shoulders of the president; and the concentration of revenue in the hands of the national government, including the almost total dependency of state and municipal governments on external sources of funding.

Even the election of Vicente Fox in 2000, the first candidate from an opposition party to win the Mexican presidency, did not radically alter these considerations. The result has been centralized rule within a constitutional federalism, although Fox was more hesitant to intervene in state politics than his PRI predecessors. The 2006 protests in Oaxaca are a good example of Fox's approach to federalism. When teachers and students demanded improvements in the state educational system, the governor of Oaxaca balked. Soon the main plaza in downtown Oaxaca was overrun with protestors who demanded the governor's resignation. Tourism, which normally fills municipal coffers with revenue, plummeted as Mexicans and foreigners alike avoided the city. After denying repeated requests for executive intervention, Fox finally responded to the chaos in the waning months of his administration by dispatching 4,000 federal police agents to Oaxaca. His successor, Felipe Calderón, displayed less timidity with federalism upon taking office in December 2006. He sent the military and federal police agents to his home state of Michoacán to battle the drug lords whose street battles have produced gruesome beheadings and hundreds of deaths.

Political Parties in the United States

The formation of political parties accompanied the emergence of independent nations in North America. New constitutional arrangements guaranteed, at least according to law, political freedoms unknown during the colonial period. Individuals organized into groups to further their political beliefs, and some of these groups became political parties. In the United States political parties with well-defined ideologies formed in the 1780s and 1790s around the leaders of the independence movement and the constitutional debates. The ideas of Thomas Jefferson, charged with a distrust of the power of the central government and wealthy financial and industrial groups, led to the formation of the Republican Party (also known as Democratic-Republicans and then just Democrats). The ideas of Alexander Hamilton, infused with a commitment to a strong central government to promote industry and commerce, provided the planks for the Federalist Party.

The early differences between Republicans and Federalists constituted one of the great divides in the political history of the United States. The Federalist Party did not survive, but its principles did as they became essential to the ideology of the National Republicans, which split from the Republican Party in the 1820s. The party took shape with the election of John Quincy Adams in 1824 (he appointed the first minister to Mexico, Joel R. Poinsett, in 1825) and advocated the use of the federal government for national improvements. Andrew Jackson's party became known as the Democratic Republicans and then simply as the Democratic Party. The old Republican Party of Jefferson also was now known as the Democratic Party. Another party emerged in 1834. Known as the Whig Party, it was a broad coalition of National Republicans, northern industrialists, and southern planters. In a twist common to political life, a group broke with the Whig Party and formed the Republican Party in 1854. It formed in reaction to the *Kansas-Nebraska Act* and had as its unifying principle the opposition to slavery. The election of Abraham Lincoln as president in 1860 catapulted the party to national power. The two great parties (Republicans and Democrats) that would dominate the future of political life were now set, though their policies and constituencies would continue to change.

After the Civil War, the Republicans dominated political life, occupying the presidency 14 out of 18 times between 1861 and 1933. This was a period of tremendous economic expansion, bolstered by favorable tariffs, subsidies for railroads, stable currencies, and cheap labor and resources. At the same time, farmers and urban workers experienced increasing difficulties as commodity prices fell and wages stagnated. Frustrated by efforts that failed to reform the party system, grass-roots political movements often splintered into new parties.

The New Deal was pivotal in turning the Democratic Party into a popular, broad-based party identified with the needs of working people. Republican domination during the 1920s was an easy explanation for the poverty and suffering of the Great Depression. Voters now placed their hopes in the new assistance programs of Roosevelt and the Democrats. At the same time, African Americans started their political migration to the Democratic Party, a process accelerated in the 1950s and 1960s. As the Democratic Party emerged from the 1930s it was more closely identified with working people, African Americans, the new immigrant groups, and the South. The Republicans were more closely associated with industrial interests, Midwestern agriculturalists, and middle- and upper-class income groups.

By this time, the principles of the parties had changed. The Democrats, the heirs of Jefferson, had reversed his disdain for government intervention into a belief in the power of the federal government to solve social and economic problems. The Republicans, the heirs of Hamilton, had turned his commitment to an activist government into a criticism of government intervention in economic and social affairs. In the most general terms, Democrats were more willing to support higher taxes, especially on upper income groups; more spending on social welfare programs and education; and, beginning in the 1970s, reductions in defense spending.

By the end of the twentieth century it was no longer as easy to distinguish a Democrat from a Republican as it had been in the 1930s. Much of Bill Clinton's political, social, and economic programs, for example, were an amalgam of centrist Democratic and moderate Republican ideas. He pitched his campaign to so-called "middle America" and, taking political advantage of a cyclical recession in the United States, beat President George H.W. Bush in the presidential election of 1992. Despite a shaky start, Clinton stayed on the middle path, thus setting up a smooth re-election in 1996. George W. Bush's election in 2000, on the heels of a sustained economic boom that seemed to work, oddly enough, against Al Gore, the Democratic candidate and Clinton's vice-president, also showed how a Republican candidate for president could read from the opposition's playbook. Bush campaigned as a "compassionate conservative," one who was eager to deploy the power of the federal government to effect changes in American society. Nevertheless, one characteristic of party politics did not change. Despite the success of Ross Perot in the 1992 presidential campaign, polling almost 20 per cent of the vote, and his more limited success in 1996, third parties continue to face insurmountable difficulties in the United States, especially when candidates from the two major parties borrow and integrate policy ideas from one another's political platforms. In short, the U.S. electoral system discourages third parties, and when a third party does emerge, it often siphons votes from one of the two dominant parties rather than establishing a genuine political alternative.

Political Parties in Canada

Canada also has a history of two dominant parties that trace their origins to the nineteenth century. The Liberal-Conservative Party, the first major national party, formed as a variant of the Conservative Party in Britain. As in Britain, the party — and the conservative beliefs associated with it — carried the label of Tory or Toryism. With Confederation and under the leadership of Prime Minister Macdonald, the party dominated politics. In the 1870s it dropped the "liberal" and became known as the Conservative Party, emphasizing the role of the new government in promoting Confederation and economic growth. Through the National Policy the government promoted the building of railroads, attracted immigrants, and generally sided with the business interests of Ontario and Quebec. It also supported Britain and feared the emerging continental power of the United States.

The Conservatives dominated politics (except for the interlude of Alexander Mackenzie from 1873-78) until 1896, when the Liberals triumphed. Conservative successes in the twentieth century have seldom lived up to Macdonald's legacy. Progressive Conservative Party leader Brian Mulroney, however, came to power in 1984 promising voters that fiscal responsibility and national unity were part and parcel of a new conservative approach to politics. A pro-business politician, he made the political decision to link the Canadian economy with the U.S. economy and entered into negotiations for a free trade agreement. By the time he left office in 1993, his administration had accumulated the largest peacetime debt in Canadian history. Moreover, his efforts to forge national unity through a series of constitutional accords (Meech Lake and Charlottetown) seemed to have had the reverse effect, setting the stage for the Quebec referendum in 1995, a mere two years after he left office. The election of Stephen Harper in 2006, on the other hand, demonstrates that the Conservative Party can rebound even after it failed to dislodge Liberal Paul Martin in 1994. Public impatience with the Liberal Party and its corruption scandals may have played a much larger role in the Conservative Party's victory than any broad Canadian embrace of Harper's party platform.

The Liberal Party traces its origins to nineteenth-century efforts for responsible government. Liberals wanted public officials responsible to elected bodies and opposed the concentration of power in the hands of small cliques. As the century progressed, they argued against tariffs and preferred an anti-imperialist policy. Power finally came with the election of Wilfrid Laurier (1896-1911). Laurier pushed through a reciprocity treaty with the United States, a long-sought goal, but he was defeated before having the chance to implement the treaty. The next great Liberal leader was William Lyon Mackenzie King, who, with only two interruptions, dominated politics from 1921-48. After King, Liberals found strength and longevity in Pierre Elliott Trudeau (1968-79, 1980-84), who combined a commitment to a strong federation with recognition of the aspirations of Quebec. Trudeau ushered in the modern constitutional era with the *Canada Act* and *Constitution Acts* of 1982. After

Brian Mulroney's victory in 1984, the Liberals had to wait until 1993 to once again become the party in power. Jean Chrétien ended Canada's economic doldrums by cutting the budget deficit and reducing the national debt. As the global economy soared during the 1990s, Canada under Chrétien made the necessary fiscal adjustments in order to secure the benefits of globalization.

Chrétien also proposed several bold social initiatives, such as same-sex marriages and the decriminalization of marijuana, that reflected mainstream Canadian politics, but the quest for the political center had become part and parcel of politics across North America. Chrétien's downfall from power, however, came not from any conservative backlash against his social policies but rather from his own party. Paul Martin, Chrétien's finance minister, fomented an internal revolt against him. Chrétien's decision to relieve Martin of his cabinet post ignited a tumultuous debate within the Liberal Party, forcing Chrétien to step aside in late 2003. The sponsorship scandal broke shortly thereafter, and Martin had to contend with several public inquiries into Liberal Party mismanagement of funds. In many ways, Martin's re-election victory in 2004 was a turning point for the Liberal Party. Although still in control of the government, the sponsorship scandal had eroded the Liberal hold on political power. It was the first minority government in Canada since 1979; the Liberals won 37 per cent of the vote to the Conservatives' 30 per cent. In May 2005, Martin even courted a conservative member of Parliament, Belinda Stronach, to cross party lines in order avoid a "no confidence" vote in the House of Commons. As the Speaker of the House cast the deciding vote in favor of the status quo, that is, to keep Martin's government in power, it was obvious to most political analysts that the Liberal Party's days were numbered.

The results of the 2006 election gave the Conservative Party a plurality of seats (40.3 per cent, or 124 out of 308 seats) and thus the election. Paul Martin's Liberal Party won 30 per cent of the popular vote, which translated into 103 seats. As a result, Stephen Harper, leader of the Conservative Party, formed a minority government and became the twenty-second prime minister of Canada. The election was called because the House of Commons passed a motion of no confidence in Martin's government. Persistent scandal had pointed to a conservative victory, albeit a narrow one. Martin's defeat ended 13 years of Liberal rule.

Third parties have fared better in Canada than in the United States and have led some observers to describe Canada as a multiparty rather than a two-party system. Occasionally these parties have had a major influence on national political life, but they have been most pronounced on a regional level. Two parties stand out: the Cooperative Commonwealth Federation (CCF) and Social Credit. Both achieved success in reaction to the inability of the Conservative governments to stem the tide of the Great Depression. Founded in 1932, the CCF issued its platform in what is known as the Regina Manifesto. It called for the nationalization of key industries and a massive redistribution of wealth through government-sponsored welfare programs.

The CCF remained a force in Canadian politics until 1961, when it became the New Democratic Party, a democratic socialist party that still has an influence in Canadian politics. The Social Credit Party was also a western-based party that had national aspirations. Started in Alberta in 1935, the party advocated the need to reward workers with a larger percentage of the finished value of their work, a type of "social credit" that would allow them to consume more and thus combat the effects of the Great Depression. Though the party never succeeded at the federal level, it had a long string of successes in Alberta from 1935 to 1971 and survived as one of the major parties in British Columbia until the 1990s.

The influence of third parties continued at the end of the twentieth century. The Bloc Québécois, at one time led by Lucién Bouchard, defended and promoted the rights of Quebec at the federal level. In contrast the Reform Party, born from a western populist movement, argued for equal treatment of all provinces and conservative economic policies. The current prime minister of Canada, Stephen Harper, cut his political teeth as a founding member of the Reform Party, which changed its name to the Canadian Alliance before amalgamating with the old Progressive Conservative Party to become the current Conservative Party of Canada. Third parties have had much more success in Canada than in the United States and Mexico; this tradition will likely continue in the future.

Political Parties in Mexico

Formal political parties came much later to Mexico, although liberal and conservative groups organized in the nineteenth century to further their interests. Liberals espoused constitutionalism, federalism, laissez-faire economics, and the elimination of special privileges enjoyed by corporate groups (church, military, Indian villages). Conservatives favored centralized authority, the privileges of the church, and the preservation of the traditional social order. Neither group organized lasting political coalitions, but their conflicts did lead to instability and violence in the nineteenth century.

Only after the Revolution of 1910 did parties with staying power emerge. The undisputed leader of these was the *Partido Revolucionario Institucional* (Institutional Revolutionary Party, PRI), originally formed in 1929 as the *Partido Nacional Revolucionario* (National Revolutionary Party). It represented a significant achievement in Mexican politics since it provided an institutional mechanism for the peaceful transition of power. The competing revolutionary groups, who still had significant and sometimes violent quarrels in the 1920s, agreed to allow the party to arbitrate their differences. The violent quest for power that had so long characterized Mexican politics dissipated as the party bureaucratized the transfer of power. In 1938 it became the *Partido Revolucionario Mexicano* (Mexican Revolutionary Party), formalizing the participation of four distinct groups in party politics: peasantry, labor, military, and the popular (all others) sectors. In 1946, the name was changed again, this time to the *Partido Revolucionario Institucional* (PRI), which remains the name of the party.

The PRI now has three major collective constituents: the agrarian sector, represented by the *Confederación Nacional de Campesinos* (National Confederation of Farm Workers); the labor sector, represented by the *Confederación de Trabajadores Mexicanos* (the Mexican Confederation Workers); and the popular sector, represented by the *Confederación Nacional de Organizaciones Populares* (National Confederation of Popular Organizations). The popular sector is the most broad-based of all the representative groups, drawing in bureaucrats, teachers, merchants, industrialists, and others. Its growing strength has gradually diminished the power of rural and urban workers in the parties. Yet all three sectors participate in nominating party candidates for political offices. Working together, they defend the interests of party membership in the system and are formally represented in the Mexican legislature.

The PRI has been a remarkable organization. Hierarchical, authoritarian, paternalistic, jealous of guarding its power, corrupt, and very successful, the party has dominated federal, state, and municipal elections since its formation in 1929, although its influence has been challenged at the state level since the late 1980s and at the federal level since 2000. Even as its pronounced social goals of land reform and programs for the poor changed to an emphasis on economic development and political stability, the PRI stressed its revolutionary ideology. More than any other group or institution it was able to portray itself as the defender of the revolution.

Competitors appeared early, but none had lasting effect until the formation in 1939 of the *Partido de Acción Nacional* (PAN), the National Action Party, a conservative alternative to the PRI. Founded in Guadalajara as a reaction to the reform policies of Lázaro Cárdenas, the PAN espoused a classically liberal political philosophy: laissez-faire economics and limited government influence in the private sector. With its emphasis on business, the party had difficulty in attracting a popular following. It achieved an important breakthrough in 1989 when it won the governorship of Baja California, the first time a party other than the PRI had won a governor's seat in modern Mexican history, and it had some further success in the 1990s. The election of Vicente Fox in 2000, however, changed the political dynamic for the PAN. With one of its own occupying Los Pinos (the residence of the Mexican president), the party has tried to broaden its political message with limited success. The perception that Fox failed to deliver on many of his campaign promises presented a challenge to the PAN. Since most elements within the PRI political structure had embraced the neo-liberal model of economic development, *panistas* continued to look for ways to distinguish themselves from the former ruling party while trying to avoid a public disagreement with the very person who won them access to national power. The PAN still represents an alternative to the PRI and PRD (discussed below), especially in the northern cities with large middle-class business interests and other urban areas with a growing middle-class and small business ownership, not to mention the more traditional Catholic vote.

A more populist alternative is the *Partido Revolucionario Democrático*, or Democratic Revolutionary Party (PRD), founded after the 1988 presidential election, when Cuauhtémoc Cárdenas, the son of Lázaro Cárdenas and the leader of the party, lost the much disputed presidential election. The PRD brought together opposition groups from the center and left who argued for a democratic, progressive alternative to the corrupt, anti-democratic politics of the PRI.

Neither the PRD nor the PAN was strong enough to challenge the PRI successfully in the presidential election of 1994, but the absolute power of the PRI had been broken. Criticism of the PRI exposed many of its inadequacies, leading to demands for change. Scandals, especially those surrounding the Salinas de Gortari administration (1988-94), continued to haunt the party and gave even more urgency to the call for national electoral reform. Mexicans expressed their political outrage over scandals, which had emerged during the presidency of Ernesto Zedillo (1994-2000), in the mid-term elections of 1997. Cuauhtémoc Cárdenas of the PRD was elected mayor of Mexico City, the first time that a mayor of one of the world's largest cities had been elected by the people instead of appointed by the president. More importantly, however, the PRI lost its congressional majority for the first time in 70 years. The election results reflected a growing weariness among Mexican voters with the PRI political machine and its corrupt practices. While the leftist PRD performed well in the federal district, the more conservative PAN won a majority of the congressional seats reserved for the opposition. The PAN also won two gubernatorial races (Querétaro and Nuevo León). Finally, the mid-term elections of 1997 gave opposition parties control over one-half of the municipal governments in Mexico, a clear indication of public contempt for the idea, championed by *priistas* since the late 1920s, of a national party that could govern all facets of political and economic life through a system of patronage and *quid pro quo*. Moreover, the high political drama of the 2006 presidential election, which saw the PAN and PRD battle for the presidency, leaving the PRI marginalized, indicates quite strongly that the PRI no longer monopolizes the electoral process as it once had in the past.

For some groups the opening of Mexican politics was not fast enough. The *Ejército Zapatista de Liberación Nacional* (Zapatista Army of National Liberation) exploded in southern Mexico (Chiapas) in 1994, demanding a more responsible and accountable government. The *Ejército Popular Revolucionario* (Popular Revolutionary Army) emerged in 1996, demanding not simply a more responsible government but an overthrow of the government and the creation of a new society. Cries for revolutionary change in Mexico had long been dormant, subsumed under the rhetoric of an official party divorced from reality. In the late 1990s, some observers feared that the politics of change once again threatened political stability in Mexico.

The presidential election of 2000 demonstrated that this negative sentiment was misplaced, at least for the near future. With the election of Vicente Fox Quesada, the PAN candidate, the Mexican electorate soundly rejected the old political system of the PRI in the most fundamental way: by depriving the PRI candidate of the executive branch and with it the constitutional power to shape politics and budgets from the municipal to federal levels. The future political course of Mexico remains uncharted, but the 2000 election proved that Mexico had a stronger and more mature commitment to democracy than many critics believed. Even the mid-term elections of 2003, which saw the PRI gain seats at the expense of President Fox's PAN party, showed that Mexicans were willing to vent, once again, their frustration at the inability of the party in power to facilitate the necessary political and economic reforms. The 2006 presidential election shaped up as a contest between the PAN candidate, former energy minister Felipe Calderón Hinojosa, and the PRD candidate, Andrés Manuel López Obrador, the former mayor of Mexico City. That the PRI candidate, Roberto Madrazo, languished consistently in third place in most polls suggests that Mexicans were hesitant to return the executive branch to the PRI, but it also pointed to the growing popularity of other political parties, such as the *Alternativa Social Demócrata Campesina*, or the Social Democratic and Peasant Alternative, headed by Patricia Mercado, a candidate who has given voice to political feminism in Mexico. In the end, however, Mexico remained as divided politically as the United States has been since 2000. A cursory glance at the 2006 Mexican electoral map shows a nation split in half: most states north of Mexico City voted for Calderón and the PAN party, while those south of the federal capital voted for López Obrador and the PRD party. The blue state-red state divide (Democrat-Republican) that has come to characterize U.S. politics has become a blue state-yellow state divide (PAN-PRD) for Mexico. There was certainly a geographical dimension to the 2006 presidential election: Mexicans who lived closer to the U.S. border voted for the pro-free trade Calderón, while those in the poorer southern states cast their ballots for the populist candidate, López Obrador.

Political Culture

The exercise of political power usually reflects attitudes and values about socially accepted forms of behavior. Often referred to as political culture, these shared beliefs influence political life as much as formal political institutions. Generalizing about political cultures is risky, but identifying some shared values that are a part of the political process helps to explain the political history of North America.

Alexis de Tocqueville, probably the most famous commentator on political life in North America, provides a good starting point. He visited the United States for nine months in 1831 and 1832 and later wrote a highly praised account entitled *Democracy in America* (1835, 1840). Tocqueville found much to criticize in the new republic, but overall he recorded very favorable impressions. One of the most distinguishing features of the United States was "the general equality of condition among the people ... The more I advanced in the study of American society, the more I perceived that this equality of condition is the fundamental fact from which all others seem to be derived" (Tocqueville 1956, 11). In other words, little distinguished one person from another in the political and social realm. The inequalities in wealth that did exist did not create deep divisions of rank comparable to the aristocratic societies of Europe. The United States lacked an aristocracy, even in the plantation societies of the South. Without titles of nobility, special legal exemptions, or a charter of corporate privileges, large landowners failed to convert their power into hereditary positions. The inheritance laws of the United States, which allowed for the break-up of landed estates to satisfy heirs and creditors, also worked against them. There was no primogeniture (inheritance by oldest male heir) or mortmain (legal entailing of the estate so that it could not be divided).

In contrast, Mexico was built on a hierarchical conception of society that inherited deep divisions from the colonial past. The Indian world and the Spanish world were two distinct realms, the former subordinate to the latter. While they mixed at every level, the Indian, by law and by practice, did not have the same rights and privileges of Spaniards. Mestizos, mulattoes, and Africans also faced discrimination. The status of these groups changed legally with the independence of Mexico, but reality remained much the same. In addition, special groups within Mexico—the church, the military, the guild, the Indian village—had privileges and responsibilities that separated them from the mainstream. Efforts to flatten the many divisions separating races and institutions provoked turmoil but did little to grant equality. Mexico remained a pyramidal society where equality remained an elusive goal.

Canada was much closer to the United States than to Mexico in its commitment to social equality. Yet there was a difference. Instead of emphasizing the equality of individuals, the *British North America Act* designated the rights of French and English speakers, of Catholics and Protestants. There was an underlying hue to Canadian political life that emphasized group over individual rights. Even more significant was the greater emphasis given to order, stability, and the respect for authority than to equality and freedom. Canadian conservatism derived from the British Tory tradition that respected the monarchy and old values as a way of preserving social order.

Tocqueville argued that in the United States equality was more closely related to the cultural commitments than to individualism, democracy, and later to populism. The colonial New England township offered a fertile breeding ground for these beliefs. Townspeople, even though acknowledging the monarchy, literally determined their affairs by levying their own taxes and electing their own officials. It is also worth remembering that in 1619 the London Company, which had founded Jamestown, agreed to share its power with representatives elected to the House of Burgesses. These representatives had the power to advise the company on laws and to review policy.

In effect, different forms of self-government took root in the English seaboard colonies.

Here was the seedbed of democracy, the support for the rights of the electorate, and an underlying distrust of authority. While this distrust of authority also runs deep in Mexican history, it had no early institutions similar to the House of Burgesses, the New England townships, or later to Jacksonian democracy to express itself. Instead, the 1535 appointment of a viceroy, the highest representative of the king, thwarted the political ambitions of early settlers. Soon a complex world of officials, laws, and bureaucracies interacted to exercise power, but elections did not become a part of the political process. The lack of a democratic tradition frustrated nineteenth-century attempts at building new political institutions.

New France after 1663 displayed some of the characteristics of New Spain. Until that time, commercial companies, working with leading members of the church and society, exercised power. Whatever tendencies toward representative government existed under this arrangement faded with the arrival in 1663 of an intendant, who ruled with broad administrative, judicial, and military power. Politically, New France came of age under Louis XIV, a ruler committed to absolutism and the centralization of authority. In this climate, representative government had little chance of survival. Only with the fall of the French in the late eighteenth century did Canada move toward democratic institutions. Committed to the authority of the monarchy and to the continuation of a stable, orderly society, the democracy that developed in Canada differed from that in the United States.

Tocqueville's other explanation for political equality was the lack of a large class of the very rich or a large stratum of the desperately poor. In the middle lived "an innumerable multitude of men almost alike, who, without being exactly either rich or poor, are possessed of sufficient property to desire the maintenance of order, yet not enough to excite envy" (Tocqueville 1956, 265). This middle sector, continually replenished from the ranks of the rich and poor, gave ballast and stability to the political system. The key was wealth, and in the United States "wealth circulates with inconceivable rapidity, and experience shows that it is rare to find two succeeding generations in the full enjoyment of it" (Tocqueville 1956, 52). In Canada wealth did not circulate as rapidly, but access to land insured a minimum equality that was reflected in the stability of the social and political system.

Mexico's experience continued to differ. Extreme inequalities in wealth marked the colonial period and the nineteenth century. The landless poor, deprived of ownership or access to community lands, grew in size until they became a threat to the Díaz regime in 1910. The revolutionary governments of the twentieth century emphasized redistribution programs but failed to create a middle group comparable to what Tocqueville described for the United States in the 1830s.

In the case of Mexico, the Spanish conquest and early colonization explain many of the differences. Spain imposed a political culture on Mexico that respected hierarchy and authority, institutionalized in the Castilian monarchy and the Catholic

Church. This culture mingled with and slowly replaced the indigenous institutions that had their own traditions of deference for authority. The local institutions that did emerge, in contrast to the English seaboard colonies, offered little opportunity for political participation. When independence came, it was a conservative reaction to a new liberal government in Spain, not a complete break with the political culture of the past. Mexico's struggle for democracy faced obstacles from the beginning.

The United States and Anglo Canada had the same English origins, yet their political cultures veered in the nineteenth century. One of the leading students of the differences between the two countries, Seymour Martin Lipset, explains the divergence by emphasizing the independence movement in the United States. It was a great founding event for the nation, replete with battles and heroes that struggled to uphold the values of freedom, individualism, democracy, and limited state power. The non-believers and counter-revolutionaries went north to Canada, preferring tradition and monarchy to revolution. Even when Confederation came to Canada in 1867, it did not represent a dramatic break with the past. Instead, it was only the first step in a gradual evolution leading to complete independence from Britain. The revolutionary commitment to equality never found expression in Canada as it did in the United States.

Tocqueville's analysis provides many insights into political life, but in the end it leaves much unsaid about the deep inequalities in the United States, especially in the lives of slaves, Indians, women, and immigrants. It was not a utopian society by any means. These groups have had to struggle to fulfill the belief expressed in the Declaration of Independence that "all men [and women] are created equal." Efforts to achieve political equality have been one of the driving forces of politics in North America in the nineteenth and twentieth centuries.

The Franchise

The elementary basis for this equality is the right of each citizen to vote and the belief that each vote has equal weight in the political process. The task of each country has been to widen the franchise to include those who have been excluded.

The United States has been at both the front and rear of this long road toward political enfranchisement. It lagged behind in freeing slaves and creating a political climate permitting freedmen to vote. Mexico was first, emancipating slaves in 1829. Canada followed in 1834, but by this time slavery had long been unimportant in Canada. In neither country did the issue of slavery produce the convulsions that it did in the United States. The Thirteenth (1865), Fourteenth (1868), and Fifteenth Amendments (1870) abolished slavery, granted citizenship, and forbade the states from depriving citizens of the right to vote because of "race, color, or previous condition of servitude." The amendments provided the basis for the franchise, but a century of struggle was necessary to insure the vote for the African-American community. The Civil Rights movement of the 1950s and 1960s was critical in the struggle. Finally, legislation in the 1960s eliminated the remaining property and literacy restrictions that prevented some African Americans from voting in southern states.

Women and Indians achieved the right to vote later. The women's suffrage movement gathered strength in the late nineteenth century and culminated with the ratification of the Nineteenth Amendment (1920). Indians only gradually received the rights of citizenship and franchise. Finally, the *American Indian Citizenship Act* (1924) conferred citizenship with the right to vote to all "Indians" born in the United States.

Influenced by both the suffrage movements in Britain and the United States, suffrage in Canada gained momentum in the late nineteenth century and then registered widespread success in the early twentieth century. Manitoba was the first province to grant full female suffrage in 1916; the federal government followed in 1918. Women, though, could not vote in Quebec provincial elections until 1940. Mexico was even more laggard. Women only achieved the right to vote in local elections in 1946 and in national elections in 1954. In Canada, Asians and Indians had a harder time getting the vote. Males and females of South Asian and Chinese lineage had to wait until 1947; Japanese Canadians until 1948. Indians had to wait even longer. The right to vote in federal elections was not extended to all Indians until 1960, but Quebec stalled again, and did not grant Non-Status Indians the right to vote until 1969. Though Canada lagged behind the United States in granting the franchise to its minorities, it did not suffer from the widespread racial political inequalities that were so entrenched in the history of the United States and Mexico.

This brief outline of the history of the franchise shows that the ideal of political equality so eloquently expressed by Tocqueville had been a long time coming. Most of the triumphs came slowly, sculpted out of the heroism and ideals of the men and women of the continent. Their efforts to achieve the franchise provide one of the many threads to the political history of North America. While all individuals of required age and civil status now have the franchise in North America, many forces limit or undermine it. Illiteracy, apathy, wealth, and corruption circumvent the legal rights of individuals. Even when the legal rights are exercised, the extent of democracy is in question. Effective representation for all individuals and groups will be a challenge for North America in the next century.

Mexico and Canada face ongoing political problems and challenges that stem from their national histories. In Mexico, the electoral and political reforms initiated in the late 1980s and 1990s run counter to the traditional concentration of power in the presidency, the PRI, and Mexico City. In Canada, the political stalemate over constitutional issues, particularly the Quebec question within the context of the federal-provincial division of powers, makes it more difficult to anticipate the future. In the United States, multiple social problems, ranging from new patterns of immigration to inadequate access to health care, assume increasing importance with each passing year but do not yet signal fundamental shifts in political life. The conservative political cast to U.S. politics, firmly in place since Richard Nixon embarked on his so-called "southern strategy" in the 1970s, will continue to shape domestic affairs for some time to come. While the outcomes in each country are unclear, the way in which political drama unfolds in Canada, Mexico, and the United States will reconstitute the dynamics of continentalism. Foreign policy and diplomacy are other areas where we can assess these dynamics, particularly how nineteenth-century ideas of the "nation" served as a catalyst for expansion, contraction, and negotiation.

CHAPTER 5
CONTINENTAL DIPLOMACY

The political divisions of North America experienced rapid change beginning in the sixteenth century. These new divisions either built upon or eliminated the old settlement and land-use patterns of indigenous peoples. Spain, France, England, and then the United States, Mexico, and Canada clashed to determine the current borders of the continent. They did so in the face of local and regional resistance by indigenous peoples and in the context of international politics. It is a story not only of wars and diplomacy but also of competition for resources, population size, transportation routes, and much more.

Older narratives of the North American past suggest that the story chronicles the emergence of the United States as a world power in the nineteenth century and the way in which Mexico and Canada reacted to the growing strength of their neighbor while trying to shape their own national paths despite U.S. military and economic power. A broader view of the history reveals that patterns of European colonialism, national aspiration, expansion and contraction, and uneven economic growth serve as a common denominator. Historians contest how much of the story has a continental sensibility to it, however, and how much of the narrative unduly privileges the popular version articulated in the United States at the expense of Mexican and Canadian interpretations of North America.

Colonial Configurations
In broad outline the diplomatic history of the continent is easy to understand. Spain dominated North America in the sixteenth century. Its cultural and political center was the Valley of Mexico, but hundreds of smaller communities emerged with their own identity and ability to survive without connections to Mexico City. Spain in North America was comparable to a giant atom, with Mexico City the nucleus and the hundreds of satellite towns the electrons. As a result, there was an Hispanic imprint on much of the south and west of the continent.

In the seventeenth century, France established itself in the narrow confines of the St. Lawrence River system and then spread west and south. The St. Lawrence always remained the trunk of the French experience in North America, with the roots running long and thin along the Great Lakes and then down the Mississippi River Valley. By the end of the century, France had become a significant competitor with Spain, but wherever the roots linking it to the great river systems of the continent broke, the power of France weakened.

England was much more confined in the seventeenth century; it remained a coastal power, hugging the Atlantic seaboard with only slow movement west to the piedmont and the Appalachians. In early colonization, it was similar to Portugal in Brazil, which remained a coastal society until the eighteenth century. In the eighteenth century, it broke through its coastal confinement to compete with Spain and France for control of the trans-Appalachian west.

Early Diplomacy

The beginning point for the wrangling over North America is the famous Treaty of Tordesillas, issued in 1494 by Pope Alexander VI. It granted to Spain all new lands west of an imaginary line of demarcation running 370 leagues (about 1,400 kilometers) west of the Cape Verde Islands off the coast of Africa. All lands east of the line belonged to the Portuguese. The treaty portended Spanish control over the new lands in the sixteenth century, even though other European powers paid it little heed. They searched for the fabled Northwest Passage that would connect Europe with Asia; they fished for cod and set up drying stations; they tried to found early colonies; and they attempted to capture Spanish silver galleons as they returned to Spain. These voyages gradually resulted in the establishment of permanent colonies, all taking place without formal arrangements of who controlled what. The uncertainties created tensions that led to conflict and war. The wars often reflected traditional European rivalries, but they nevertheless had lasting consequences for the political configuration of North America.

Spanish holdings in central Mexico stood without challenge. Not so their feeble claims on the periphery. French expeditions set out for Florida and the Carolinas, seeking a foothold in North America. Spain took note soon enough and ended the French hopes with a series of skirmishes and the founding of St. Augustine, Florida, in 1565. Spanish missionaries then went north, establishing missions along the Gulf of Mexico. These tentative efforts came up against the claims of English settlers who attempted to colonize the Carolinas in the seventeenth century. Finally, in 1670 the Treaty of Madrid accepted the principle of "effective occupation" to determine what belonged to whom.

Meanwhile, to the north, Anglo-Dutch rivalries erupted in military confrontations. The English successfully dislodged the Dutch from the New York region and took New Amsterdam in 1664, renaming it New York. Within a decade, the Dutch had lost their trading prominence in North America. Just a little earlier (1654) they had lost control of northeastern Brazil and were relegated to the small islands of

Aruba, Bonaire, and Curaçao in the Caribbean. Dutch influence in all of the Americas had been severely reduced.

Conflicts with the French proved more difficult. Fish and furs more than other resources precipitated the struggle for the northern tier of the continent. Fish, then and now, were valuable commodities that sharpened Anglo-French conflicts beginning in the early sixteenth century. The French established pre-eminence early, but after the 1570s the English founded land bases in Newfoundland for drying fish. The French did the same in Cape Breton and the Gaspé Peninsula, thus launching a struggle that would span centuries.

The struggle for furs was also long lasting. French trappers and traders had to compete with a major new force after the founding of the Hudson's Bay Company in 1670. From its tentative beginnings, it grew into a powerful economic force; its network of trading posts extended from the Atlantic to the Pacific and from the Great Lakes to the Arctic Ocean. It was very successful in obtaining and exporting furs and even today is one of the leading fur companies in the world. (It also is a major modern corporation with extensive wholesale, retail, real estate, and energy interests.)

French explorers and traders countered the establishment of the Hudson's Bay Company with their own expansion into the Mississippi River valley, which culminated in the founding of New Orleans in 1718. Just two years later in the north, they built Louisbourg, a massive fortress on Cape Breton Island designed to insure French control over the Saint Lawrence. New Orleans and Louisbourg, today cultural artifacts to the French presence in the southern and northern tiers of the continent, failed to preserve the political and economic control of France in North America.

War

European policy objectives often spilled blood in North America. The War of the Spanish Succession (known as Queen Anne's War in North America) was the most influential in the early eighteenth century. Before Charles II of Spain died in 1700, he named as his heir Philip of Anjou, a grandson of Louis XIV of France. England tried to prevent his accession to power, and the war spread to North America. Skirmishes and battles broke out from Acadia to the Caribbean as the English, French, and Spanish tried to gain territorial advantage. When peace came in the Treaty of Utrecht (1713), England benefited at the expense of France. The treaty upheld its claims to the Hudson Bay territory and granted it Newfoundland and Acadia.

These intrigues involved indigenous peoples from the beginning. Far from simple pawns in colonial disputes, Indians actively pursued their own strategies designed to improve their position in the continent. The Iroquois War of the 1640s was only a prelude to over a century of intermittent conflict between (and among) Indians and Europeans. In many engagements, Indians played critical roles in the battles that shaped the political boundaries of the continent.

The most famous of these conflicts was the Seven Years' War, which officially began in 1756 when Britain declared war on France. Known as the French and Indian War in North America, the conflict had its background there in French and British expansion in the Ohio River Valley in the late 1740s and early 1750s. Fort Duquesne, located in present-day Pittsburgh, was a strategic point for controlling the western edges of Pennsylvania, Maryland, and Virginia. George Washington went out from Virginia as a young surveyor in 1753 to demand that the French retreat. When they refused, Washington marched west in 1754, this time leading an army of provincial troops, which was defeated by the French. Troubles also broke out in Nova Scotia, Lake Champlain, and Lake Ontario. As the war became more intense in 1758, it spread to the Caribbean, where the British hoped to wrest the sugar islands from the French. In two key northern battles, the French lost Quebec City in 1759 and Montreal in 1760, severely weakening their chances for survival on the continent.

Under the Treaty of Paris (1763), Britain became undisputed master of North America east of the Mississippi. France ceded her Canadian claims, except for the tiny islands of St.-Pierre and Miquelon in the Atlantic. France also gave up all lands east of the Mississippi River, except for the city of New Orleans. Spain, fearful of Britain's dominance, had sided with France and by the Treaty of Fontainebleau (1762) received French territory west of the Mississippi River. Spain, though, was weakened on the mainland, since it gave Britain control over east and west Florida in exchange for Cuba (which the British had occupied during the war).

The upshot of the war was the political reconfiguration of the continent. With France practically eliminated and Spain weakened, Britain enjoyed a brief dominance as master of lands that extended from the Arctic to the Caribbean. The dominance was short-lived. Rebellious colonials rather than foreign powers undermined its hegemony. Discord became more evident in the 1760s as increasing revenue measures threatened the autonomy and growth of the colonies. British measures in Quebec also had their affect. The *Quebec Act* (1774) created a permanent centralized government dependent on the Crown. It also extended the claims of Quebec to the confluence of the Mississippi and Ohio Rivers, which irritated colonists in Massachusetts, Connecticut, and Virginia who also had claimed the area. Discord turned to conflict and warfare in 1775. Colonial forces marched north to Montreal and then approached Quebec City in the hopes of weakening the British before they could mount a northern offensive. Both France and Spain supported the movement for independence, but it was France more than any other European power that aided the colonies in their struggle.

The effects of the independence of the United States for North America were profound. The Treaty of Versailles (1783) awarded the United States lands west to the Mississippi River, as well as fishing rights off the Grand Banks and in the mouth of the St. Lawrence River. Britain gave away much of the center of the continent that it had just acquired from France. As the United States consolidated into an organized and federal entity, it was poised to shape the political destiny of North America.

Events moved quickly. Within a generation, the United States was moving south, west, and north, laying claim to new territories. The age of Manifest Destiny had begun before the label was applied. Of more immediate impact was the symbolic influence of the new country. Other colonies now saw a model for breaking away from their colonial masters. Canada was the exception. It became even more committed to Britain as a result of the U.S. upheaval. Loyalist supporters of Britain fled north during and after the war, strengthening the pro-British inclinations of Canadians.

A New Era

With independence, the United States acquired global interests, but North America still offered more problems and promises than any other region. Immediately after the war, negotiations began over lands adjacent to the new nation. The Treaty of San Lorenzo (Pinckney's Treaty) of 1795 with Spain established the 31st parallel as the southern boundary of the United States and the Mississippi River as the western. It also guaranteed to the United States the use of the Mississippi River and the right to commercial access to New Orleans.

Pinckney's Treaty was a prelude to the most significant acquisition of the young republic. In 1803 under President Thomas Jefferson, the United States purchased the Louisiana Territory from France (which had received it from Spain in 1800) for about $15,000,000. The purchase doubled the size of the United States, extending it from the Mississippi River to the Rocky Mountains and assuring that it would become the dominant power in the continent. Eventually 13 states were carved out of the new territory. Even before the purchase, Jefferson had spoken of his grander vision of North America (1801): "It is impossible not to look forward to distant times, when our rapid multiplication will expand itself beyond those limits, and cover the whole northern, if not the southern continent, with a people speaking the same language, governed in similar forms, and by similar laws" (LaFeber 1989, 51). On the heels of the purchase came the annexation of West Florida (1810). Finally, the entire Florida question was settled with the Adams-Onís Treaty (1819). Under the treaty, Spain relinquished control over East Florida and recognized U.S. control over West Florida; in addition it ceded its interest in the Pacific coast region of Oregon. In return, the United States recognized Spanish claims to Texas. All took place quickly, as if the United States had just made the opening moves in a continental chess game, easily capturing Spanish and French pieces and designing the strategy that would see Texas and Mexico fall in the endgame.

In contrast, the War of 1812, the first major conflict after independence, did not lead to territorial acquisitions. It did set the stage, though, for a stronger interest in Canada and increased fear in Canada over that interest. Canadians interpret the war as one of the defining moments in their history, a definitive rejection of the new republicanism to the south and an affirmation of British traditions and institutions.

The war prompted the Rush-Bagot Agreement of 1817, which prompted the demilitarization of the Great Lakes. A year later, the United States and Britain signed the Convention of 1818, establishing the 49th parallel west of Lake of the Woods as the Canadian-U.S. boundary. The problem of the Oregon Territory remained unsettled until the 1840s.

Until Mexico's independence in 1821 and recognition by the United States in 1822, continental policy was aimed at Spain and Britain. After independence Mexico, not Spain, was the focus of U.S. policy. Mexico emerged from its independence movement economically weakened and politically divided. It was little match for the fire storms that soon swept across its northern frontier, severely curtailing its continental influence.

Manifest Destiny and Beyond

Developments in the 1820s and 1830s helped to position the United States to expand. Population increased, agricultural production soared, manufacturing jumped, and roads and canals began to crisscross the nation. Indian populations were silenced or expelled, reducing any serious internal threats to the nation. Diplomatically, the United States issued the Monroe Doctrine, anticipating later efforts at expansion. The doctrine declared the existence of two spheres — a European and an American. Europe should not extend its influence or attempt new colonization in the American sphere, and the United States would not intervene in the European sphere. More important was the growing nationalism of the still young country. Manifest Destiny would not become a common term until the 1840s, but already U.S. expansion had a sense of inevitability, a belief that destiny would lead the country to the west coast and maybe beyond. All opened the way for the two major salvos of expansion fired before the Civil War.

Texas was the first target. From the entry of U.S. settlers into Texas in 1821, there was a threat to Mexican sovereignty. The combination of political turmoil in Mexico and increasing Texan demands led to conflict and recriminations, which sparked the Mexican General Santa Anna's siege of the Alamo in 1836. The Mexicans won the Battle of the Alamo but were soon on the defensive and lost Texas before the year was out. The United States recognized the Lone Star Republic in 1837 and then welcomed Texas as the twenty-eighth state in 1845.

Mexico also had problems to the south. Within a year of independence in 1821, the Mexican empire extended south to include all of Central America except for Panama. A revolt tried to throw off the Mexican yoke but was easily suppressed. Desire for independence festered in what was the old Audiencia of Guatemala and finally erupted again in 1823, leading to the creation of the Central American Confederation in that year. Only Chiapas, now the southernmost state of Mexico, decided to stay with Mexico. The confederation splintered into the independent countries of Guatemala, Honduras, Nicaragua, El Salvador, and Costa Rica in 1837.

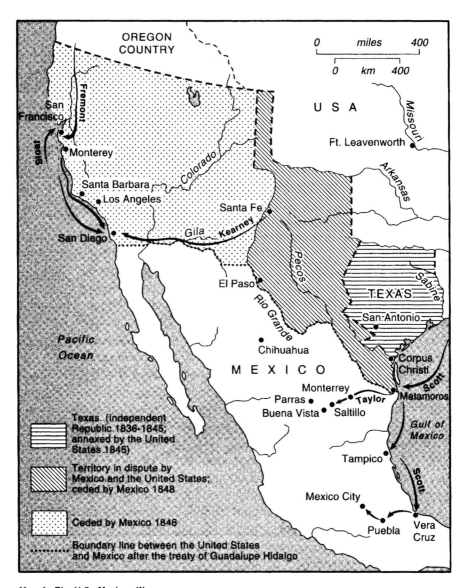

Map 4. The U.S.-Mexican War.
From *Americana: The Americas in the World, around 1850* by James Dunkerley. Copyright © 2000 Verso Press. Reproduced by permission of Verso Press.

Panama remained a part of Columbia until 1903. What might have emerged as an ongoing threat to Mexico's southern border disappeared with the demise of the Central American Confederation.

For Mexico, the northern boundary was always more vulnerable than the southern. After the loss of Texas, internal conflict and economic difficulties absorbed the country, preventing it from shoring up its northern, poorly defined, and contested boundaries. Texas stood alone for nine years, and Mexico could not bring it back. Mexico claimed the Nueces River as the border of an independent Texas, but Texas and then the United States claimed the Rio Grande (which doubled the size of Texas). Disputes over this area led to the Mexican-American War (1846-48) and another defeat for Mexico. In the Treaty of Guadalupe Hidalgo (1848), Mexico lost one half of its territory, a national humiliation that deeply penetrated the Mexican psyche. On the other side, the United States added Arizona, Nevada, California, and sections of New Mexico, Colorado, and Wyoming. An additional insult was the sale of the Mesilla Valley in southern Arizona and New Mexico for $10 million (the Gadsden Purchase). The treaty rewarded the United States with another 30,000 square miles.

The war was disastrous for Mexico. Rather than leading to national unity and economic growth, the country slid into yet another decade of struggle. Contending foes in Mexico now had a common enemy, united in their hatred and fear of the United States. This "Yankee phobia" remained a characteristic of Mexican history into the late twentieth century. For the United States, the war brought the splendid results of still more territory, making it truly a continental country. An added bonus was the rich deposits of gold discovered in California in 1848. The policy of Manifest Destiny had paid rich dividends. Culturally and politically the United States boasted confidence and optimism. The country took shape during a time of expansion and growth, of apparently infinite resources available for the taking. The drawback was the problem of slavery in the new territories, which eventually led to the Civil War.

Territorial questions to the north of the United States were settled without war. In 1842, the Webster-Ashburton Treaty settled the long-standing dispute between Maine and New Brunswick, adjusted the boundary between Vermont and New York and Canada, and granted the United States land west of Lake Superior, which soon yielded iron ore riches. Shortly thereafter the Oregon Treaty was signed (1846), formally extending the 49th parallel to the Pacific. The old northern limit of the Louisiana Territory now became the northern boundary for the northwest of the United States. With smooth diplomacy and very little saber rattling, the United States had acquired an area that had been in dispute since the 1820s.

Both Britain and the United States were satisfied, but the treaty did spur a more rapid settlement of the Canadian west. The Hudson's Bay Company, which previously had trading and trapping rights in the Oregon Territory, was now confined to the north of the treaty line. It established a settlement on Vancouver Island that became the nucleus for the development of British Colombia. The discovery of gold, the rise of agricultural communities, and increasing trade to the south led to the growth of the Canadian west. Canada, like Mexico, had a growing fear of the emergence of the United States as a continental power.

Civil War in the United States

The Civil War in the United States had many consequences in Canada and Mexico. British sentiment generally supported the Confederacy, and an early incident almost triggered war between the Union and Britain. In 1861, the Confederacy sent two representatives to Britain on a British mail steamer, the *HMS Trent*. The ship was intercepted by the Union and the two representatives imprisoned. In response, Britain sent over 10,000 troops to Canada to strengthen defenses and prepare for war. Other incidents followed, including a Confederate attack launched from Montreal on St. Albans, Vermont, in 1864. The attackers hoped to provoke the Union into pursuing the rebels into Canada, thereby involving the British in the war. It almost worked, as the Union demanded reparations from the attack. Witness to the expansion wrought by Manifest Destiny, Britain feared for the survival of Canada if the Union won the war.

Tensions continued after the war. Concrete justification for Canadian fears appeared with the Fenian raids. The Fenians, an armed and ideologically committed group dedicated to the independence of Ireland, struck at Britain through Canada in 1866; they struck again in 1870. The raids did little except to exacerbate the general uneasiness in Canada about its exposed southern flank. More momentous was the U.S. purchase of Alaska from Russia in 1867, a further sign of the rapidly growing strength of the United States. The architect of the purchase was William Henry Seward, Secretary of State from 1861 to 1869, who at times made grandiloquent references to continental expansion. In one speech, he claimed that the United States should include "Canada and all British America to Behring's [sic] Straits, and Spanish America to the Isthmus of Panama, and perhaps to Cape Horn" (Paolino 1973, 9).

Canadian Confederation and the passage of the *British North America Act* in 1867 were partly in response to the Civil War. With the victory of the North, Britain recognized the increased difficulty of protecting its colonies and moved quickly toward the formation of a nation. John A. Macdonald, one of the architects of the new nation, believed that excessive states' rights had led to the Civil War. He vowed not to repeat the mistake and argued for a stronger centralized government than in the United States. The Treaty of Washington (1871) helped to resolve a long list of grievances that Canada, the United States, and Britain had that stemmed from the war, but left many on both sides of the border disgruntled.

By a twist of historical timing, the Civil War also affected Mexico's sovereignty. British and Spanish troops landed in Mexico in late 1861 to collect debt payments from Mexico. French troops followed in 1862 and soon started marching on Mexico

City. En route they engaged Mexican defenses in the city of Puebla. Mexico won the battle, which is remembered yearly in the Mexican national holiday of *cinco de mayo* (5 May), but ultimately could not prevent the French from controlling the country and installing Ferdinand Maximilian, Archduke of Hapsburg, as the puppet Emperor of Mexico in 1864. The United States, engulfed in its own war, could do little about the pleas of Benito Juárez for assistance. One practical reason was that it worried about encouraging the French to enter into an alliance with the Confederacy. The French occupation was the most flagrant violation yet of the Monroe Doctrine, but it brought no response from the United States. With the victory of the North, the United States pursued a more activist policy. Secretary of State Seward pressured France to withdraw. More importantly, the United States sold arms to Juárez and allowed his troops and supplies to move back and forth across the border. In addition, Civil War veterans fought directly on the side of Mexico against the French. Juárez and Mexico claimed victory in 1867 and set about rebuilding the country once again.

The 1860s were especially significant for the political formation of the continent. The United States survived as a single entity and began to integrate the new territories that it had acquired in the south, west, and north. Canada was now a confederation and moved to settle and develop its west. Mexico, finally freed from foreign domination, consolidated its center and began the development of its much reduced north.

Expansion Modified

Expansionist sentiment in the United States continued after the Civil War, but it was tempered by geography and the realities of recovering from the war and settling the newly acquired lands. The United States had already taken what it wanted from Mexico. What remained was distant, arid, and inhospitable. Late nineteenth-century interest in Canada was stronger than in Mexico. A contemporary observer phrased it well:

> In any case there is no perceptible difference of race, language, or literature between the Anglo-Saxon populations on either side of the political frontiers, while the differences in customs or institutions are either slight in themselves, or carry little weight in the presence of such momentous issues. For Americans and British Canadians alike the amalgamation would involve social and political changes of comparatively little importance. (Reclus 1886-95, 1:453)

Even some Canadians agreed with this assessment, giving support to the idea of eventual union with the United States. The same was not true of French Canada, which had little enthusiasm for the idea.

As the century drew to a close, the foreign policy aspirations of the United States extended beyond the continent. Three events had particular significance for Canada and Mexico. First, the United States bullied Britain into accepting arbitration of a boundary dispute between Venezuela and British Guiana in 1895. The United States made its position unmistakably clear in a message to the British:

> Today the United States is practically sovereign on this continent, and its fiat is law upon the subjects to which it confines its interposition. Why?…It is because, in addition to all other grounds, its infinite resources combined with its isolated position render it master of the situation and practically invulnerable as against any or all other powers. (Bemis 120, 1943)

The tone was frightening and unmistakable. The United States would countenance little opposition to its foreign policy objectives.

Second, the United States achieved success in the Spanish American War of 1898, acquiring an empire that included control of Cuba, Puerto Rico, the Philippines, and several smaller islands. Possessions in both the Caribbean and Pacific hastened the third development—the construction of a canal across the Isthmus of Panama. In 1850 the United States had agreed with Britain that neither country would have exclusive control over an isthmian canal. Negotiations in 1900 and 1901 produced the Hay-Pauncefote Treaties that rescinded earlier agreements and gave the United States the exclusive right to build the canal. Next, the United States acquired the rights to a canal from the newly created (with the assistance of the United States) nation of Panama in 1903. The implications were ominous for Canada and Mexico.

After nearly a century of influence, Britain had retreated from the Americas, leaving Canada even more vulnerable to the United States. When it wanted to act, the United States did so decisively and with conviction. Canada felt the pressure first in the Alaska Boundary dispute of 1903. Canada hoped that it would have access to the Pacific Ocean from the Yukon Territory across the southern panhandle of Alaska. The discovery of gold made the question urgent and led to the controversy. President Theodore Roosevelt used "Big Stick" diplomacy to intimidate Britain, sending troops to Alaska and threatening to take the land by force. Instead, a commission settled the dispute in favor of the United States, teaching the Canadians once again that they did have something to fear from their southern neighbor.

Mexico was next. As the calm of the Porfirio Díaz era broke into protests and then full-scale conflict, the United States watched with increasing concern. Then it acted, directly and indirectly. First, Henry Lane Wilson, the Ambassador to Mexico, connived with opposition forces in the murder of the popularly elected Francisco Madero in 1913. Second, it sent troops ashore in Veracruz to prevent Mexico from receiving arms from a German ship in 1914. Third, it retaliated against Pancho Villa for his 1916 raid on Columbus, New Mexico, by sending General John J. Pershing into Mexico in a failed attempt to capture the elusive Villa. The failure had broader international repercussions, convincing the Germans to expand submarine warfare in the belief that they had little to fear from the United States. All three incidents slipped into obscurity in the United States as it joined World War I. However, they remain widely known and discussed events in Mexican history.

The asymmetry of power relationships stood in bold relief in the early twentieth century. No country in the Americas challenged the United States, which often viewed its closest neighbors with a casual indifference. The neighbors, given its rapid expansion, could not afford to neglect the United States. Mexico had a deep-seated and understandable fear that resulted directly from its nineteenth-century history, a time of frustration and territorial loss. The past remained as an insult to Mexico and strengthened the nationalism unleashed during the Revolution of 1910.

Canada was stung by the Alaska boundary resolution, not to mention the failure of Britain to defend its claim. Negative sentiments surfaced against the United States and Britain, but the negativity was complicated by the reality of the Canadian situation. The Canadian political system ensured that its foreign policy would continue with a strong British orientation, while its language, culture, and economy drew it toward the United States. In Canada, the point of view known as continentalism, never widely accepted, embraced a shared heritage and the wisdom of a common future. Specifically, continentalists wanted lower tariffs, foreign investment, and free trade. Goldwin Smith, an historian, journalist, and outspoken advocate of continentalism, argued in *Canada and the Canadian Question* (1891) that each Canadian province was tied to the United States and that the French-English dilemma could not be solved. In other words, the new Canadian Confederation was destined to fail. Canada and the United States would eventually join together in a marriage that had been arranged by geography and history. Quebec demurred. It was not about to be the handmaiden to a union that threatened its own cultural aspirations.

Early Twentieth-Century Issues

After the Alaska dispute, diplomacy in the north turned on the more prosaic issues of trade and the regulation of waterways. One of the triumphs of this diplomacy was the signing of the Boundary Waters Treaty (1909) and the formation of the International Joint Commission to resolve disputes. These negotiations occurred while Canadian control over its foreign policy was on the rise. In 1909, Canada established its Department of External Affairs, an initial step to an active foreign policy. It independently negotiated for the first time its own treaty, the Halibut Fisheries Treaty with the United States in 1923. Finally, in 1927, it had its own permanent representation in Washington, DC. Like much else in Canadian history, the emergence of an independent foreign policy was a gradual process, achieved through negotiation and compromise. All was formalized in the *Statute of Westminster* (1931), which gave Canada control over its political life, domestically and internationally, although Britain still maintained ultimate authority over constitutional changes.

The *Statute of Westminster* had broader implications. Former British colonies came together in the Commonwealth, respecting each other's independence and autonomy but united in their allegiance to the British Crown. As they achieved independence, they maintained ties to the British monarchy and freely participated with other former dependencies to discuss issues of mutual concern. The Commonwealth was particularly attractive to countries such as Canada, fearful of the bold expansionist tendencies of the United States. In addition, through tradition and political heritage, Canada was closely involved in British foreign policy. This was evident long before the formal formation of the Commonwealth through Canadian involvement in the South African Boer War (1899-1902) and World War I.

The Commonwealth evolved into a formal organization of independent nations (48 in the 1980s) tied to each other through a common language, former membership in the British Empire, shared political institutions, and similar economic and defense interests. The Commonwealth never became a *supra* nation, meeting only biennially to address issues of common interest.

The Commonwealth represented one direction for Canadian foreign policy. Quebec and the *Francophonie* represented another. The Francophonie, a term that became widely used only after World War II, lacks the history and formal structure of the Commonwealth. It refers to both the French-speaking countries of the world and to the increasing number of multilateral organizations among French-speaking nations. Rather than bound by an allegiance to a central figure or institution, the Francophonie is held together by the French language and themes of common interest. The *Agence de coopération culturelle et technique*, designed to promote educational and scientific development, is one example. Canada is a member, as are the provinces of Quebec and New Brunswick.

Membership in the Commonwealth, and to a lesser extent the Francophonie, exemplifies the European and global dimension of Canadian foreign policy in the twentieth century. Canada, especially after World War II, became an international actor with increasing influence, yet its main focus and preoccupation remained the United States. History and the reality of the power and wealth of the United States set the course for North American international relations.

Mexico differed from Canada in the lack of a European dimension to its foreign policy. Unlike Britain and France, Spain did not create an international organization equivalent to the Commonwealth or Francophonie to give Mexico and other former colonies an opportunity to participate on a wider political stage. It also differed in the lack of domestic support for continentalism. Mexico was too different from the United States, its past too scarred by imperialism to seriously consider closer integration with the colossus to the north. That would have to wait until almost the end of the twentieth century.

There is another significant difference. Mexico and the United States had a much more troubled relationship in the 1920s and 1930s. The heightened nationalism engendered by the Revolution posed a threat to foreign investment and led to threats and counter-threats. President Calvin Coolidge helped to ease the tension by appointing Dwight Morrow as Ambassador to Mexico in 1927. In contrast to the despised Henry Lane Wilson of earlier years, Morrow charmed Mexicans with his grace and respect. He treated Mexicans as equals and understood the sensitivity of issues affecting Mexican sovereignty. As one example, he changed the sign outside of the embassy from the "American Embassy" to the "United States Embassy" in recognition that the United States was not the only American nation.

Despite the successes of Morrow's efforts and the emergence of a broader "Good Neighbor Policy" that aimed at improving cooperation between the United States and Latin America, friction continued. "Mexico for the Mexicans" was an increasingly popular slogan after the Revolution that riveted attention on the extent of foreign investment. The origins of the growing criticism are in Article 27 of the Constitution of 1917, which reasserted the Spanish colonial legal principle, "all subsoil rights belong to the nation." Mexico now legally owned all the minerals and oil in the nation. These could be leased but not sold in perpetuity. Foreign investors complained, and the Mexican Supreme Court resolved the question in 1922 with the principle of "positive acts." This stated that companies that had made investments and improvements in the land before the Revolution could continue to exploit those lands as if they owned them, an agreement formalized in the "Extra-Official Pact" of 1923.

Under President Lázaro Cárdenas, the problems of foreign influence reached crisis levels, precipitated by labor disputes in the oil industry. Article 123 of the Constitution permitted the organization of labor, and the Cárdenas administration encouraged it for nationalistic reasons. The National Petroleum Workers Syndicate formed as the umbrella union for the 21 smaller unions of petroleum workers in 1935. With newfound strength and government encouragement, the syndicate began to demand concessions from British and U.S. oil companies. A long, troubling period of negotiations began over some 250 issues, wages being one of the most important. When the government and the companies failed to reach a compromise, partly because of the companies' demands that Cárdenas give them a written statement of his willingness to compromise, Cárdenas nationalized them on 18 March 1938. This is still celebrated as a national holiday of economic independence.

The action led to boycotts, embargoes, and threats of an invasion, but it was clear that President Franklin Delano Roosevelt had little interest in going to war to recover the petroleum. Instead, he encouraged negotiations. A satisfactory settlement became increasingly important since Mexico was selling oil to the Axis powers. Finally, on 19 November 1941, just before Pearl Harbor and the U.S. entry into World War II, Mexico and the United States signed the Mexican-American General Agreement. This agreement spelled out the repayment schedule for the nationalized oil (finally paid in 1947) and settled the land claims still carried over from the 1910 Revolution. Mexico had its oil and became an active supporter of the Allies in World War II.

Postwar Directions

No issue as dramatic as the 1938 oil expropriation has troubled Mexican or Canadian relations with the United States since World War II. Difficult problems arose, but they did not threaten the stability of North America. Indeed, the main trend in all three countries has been an increased willingness to negotiate difficult issues.

The rhetoric, though, was not necessarily softened. Daniel Cosío Villegas, one of Mexico's leading historians, wrote the following about the United States in the early 1960s:

> The century-old crushing process undergone by Mexico has now entered its final stage. It is taking place in all fields, since the pertinacious, the unassailable North American [United States] influence is felt everywhere: in customs pertaining to food and dress; in the language, in thought, in the ideals of life; in the economy, in society, in religious policy, in education and the arts; in all interior and exterior acts … That is why North American influence on Mexico is now like the God of the Christians: omnipotent and omnipresent. (Cosío Villegas 1964, 41-42)

Less noticeable at the time but clearly growing in the southwest of the United States was the increasing Mexican influence in everything from food to language. In the late 1990s, the Hispanic influence had spread throughout much of the United States, leading in some cases to a fear of the Hispanic influence similar in tone to that of Cosío Villegas 30 years before.

The 1960s were years of intense anti-U.S. sentiment in much of the Americas. The growing influence of the United States and the unilateral exercise of power ignited a strident reaction, personified by Fidel Castro. The Cuban revolutionary leader became the leading spokesman for anti-imperialist and anti-U.S. rhetoric in the Americas. Much to the dismay of the United States, Mexico, under President Adolfo López Mateos (1958-64), continued diplomatic relations with Cuba and opposed attempts to expel Cuba from the Organization of American States. However, at least one significant diplomatic act of the period was in direct contrast to the stereotypes of U.S. imperialism. In 1964 the United States returned to Mexico the Chamizal, a 600-acre patch of land near El Paso, Texas, that had been disputed for 100 years. In one sense this was the end of the story that began with the Mexican-American War. Mexico had claimed this land since a shift in the Rio Grande in 1864 moved the border to the south. President John F. Kennedy initiated the negotiations in 1962, and in 1964 President Lyndon Johnson officially returned the land to Mexico.

The return of the Chamizal was, perhaps rightly so, interpreted as little more than a gesture on the part of the United States and did not represent a significant shift in attitude. Nor did it soften the nationalistic tone of Mexican foreign policy that continued to emphasize the principles of non-intervention, self-determination, and control over foreign investment. Given the asymmetry of power in the hemisphere, Mexico could do little more than vocalize its nationalistic aspirations. When it came to actually negotiating, the United States usually held the upper hand. In addition to Cuba and Castro, there is a long list of issues that has preoccupied diplomats since the 1960s. At the top belong immigration, energy issues, trade (especially the importing of Mexican agricultural products), debt, and in the 1980s and 1990s the drug trade. These issues continue to elicit rancorous comments on both sides of the border, and while they will not provoke a diplomatic break in U.S.-Mexico relations, they will fashion tension and stress in the post-9/11 reconfiguration of continental security.

The same is true of the issues that have divided Canada and the United States since World War II. Increasing U.S. domination of the global economy, its ferocious energy consumption, its contributions to pollution and acid rain, and even its military conflicts, such as the Vietnam War of the late 1960s and early 1970s and the current war with Iraq, as well as the perceived undermining of Canadian culture, have troubled the relationship. As with Mexico, an independent policy toward Cuba has also distinguished Canadian foreign policy. When Jean Chrétien visited Cuba in April 1998, he reaffirmed Canada's long-standing policy of dialogue and trade in contrast to the embargo maintained by the United States. None of these issues, however, has seriously jeopardized Canadian-U.S. relations.

While the diplomatic history of North America has been dominated by Mexican and Canadian bilateral relationships with the United States, Canada and Mexico do have a diplomatic and commercial history that extends back to the late nineteenth and early twentieth century. Yet it was not until 1944 that the countries exchanged ambassadors. From that point, the relationship gained strength as the focus of Canada's Latin American policy slowly shifted from Argentina, Brazil, and Chile to Mexico. Their co-chairing of the North-South Conference held in Cancún, Mexico, in 1981 signaled the convergence of important principals of their hemispheric policy. Canada and Mexico agreed, in contrast to the United States, that the political crisis in Central America was more a result of failed development than of communist aggression. As the 1980s and 1990s unfolded, diplomatic attention shifted to economic, educational, and cultural exchanges between the countries.

The political boundaries and foreign policies of the United States, Mexico, and Canada have been shaped in response to the strengths and weaknesses of each country. For Mexico and Canada, the asymmetry of continental power has helped to determine national boundaries and national identities. Boundaries have undergone major changes in the past, as have national priorities. The recent success of NAFTA is the best example. It is inconceivable that during the 1960s, a period of intense nationalism in Mexico and Canada and of lingering uncertainty over the expansionist policies of the United States in the hemisphere, that NAFTA could have been signed. Economic integration and foreign investment, once seen as threats to national sovereignty, are now seen as the best avenues of growth. National policies have changed enough to support or at least accept the new policies. At the same time, Canada and Mexico have cultivated a strong and encompassing relationship that exists alongside of NAFTA. Despite the ongoing disagreements among all three countries, harmony and compromise have replaced the discord and extremism of earlier years, although the U.S. preoccupation with security issues after 9/11, as well as the preemptive war with Iraq has introduced a new wrinkle in continental diplomacy.

When Vicente Fox broke the political monopoly that the ruling party (PRI) had enjoyed in Mexican politics by defeating Francisco Labastida in the 2000 presidential election, many U.S.-Mexico watchers assessed the victory not only in narrow political terms but also in a broader diplomatic context. Certainly the relationship between the United States and Mexico had improved since the debt crisis of the early 1980s, when Mexico defaulted on its loan obligations, thus souring its relations with both Washington, DC and Wall Street. As the administration of Carlos Salinas de Gortari (1988-94) embraced the neo-liberal model of economic development, including free trade, relations improved to such new heights that the diplomatic result was a monumental trade agreement, NAFTA. Ernesto Zedillo (1994-2000) continued the economic policies and diplomatic measures of his predecessor despite the corruption scandals and economic crisis that emerged in the early days of his administration. Both the United States and Canada applauded the Mexican transition to electoral democracy and the peaceful transition that took place when Zedillo handed the presidential sash to Fox in December 2000.

The U.S. government, however, now headed by George W. Bush, sent a strong signal that U.S.-Mexico relations were key components in the U.S. post-Cold War foreign policy. Bush's experience as a governor of Texas facilitated an awareness of border problems, foreign investment, and immigration. And both Bush and Fox fashioned themselves as cowboys, *vaqueros*, with each owning ranches in their respective home states (Bush in Texas, Fox in Guanajuato), which suggested a personal affinity that could overcome potential barriers in their diplomatic relationship. The two presidents even met at Fox's ranch in February 2001 to initiate talks related to the creation of a guest-worker program as well as an adjustment of the legal status of Mexicans working in the United States. That the visit to Mexico was Bush's first foreign trip as president was more telling than any broad agreement that might be reached on immigration or guest-workers. Canada had to wait until Bush was re-elected in 2004 for his first official visit. Clearly Mexico was enjoying its elevated status during the early days of Bush's first term, which seemed to give high priority to issues important to President Fox, while affording President Bush an opportunity to tone down the Republican Party's anti-immigrant rhetoric. The two leaders decided to meet again, this time in the White House for Bush's first official welcome of a foreign head of state.

Amidst the pomp and circumstance of President Fox's first visit to the Bush

White House in early September 2001, terrorists were days away from hijacking four planes departing from various East Coast airports and using them as missiles to attack certain targets. Just days before September 11, 2001, during a joint news conference with President Fox, Bush remarked, "The United States has no more important relationship in the world than the one we have with Mexico." While Bush's words pleased those interested in promoting U.S.-Mexico relations to a higher level, they certainly created an uncertainty among some Canadian-U.S. watchers. A few days later, however, as hijacked airplanes slammed into the World Trade Center in New York and the Pentagon building in Washington, DC, the Bush administration quickly reconfigured U.S. diplomacy in ways that identified homeland security — not Mexico or Canada for that matter — as the principal determinant of policy. For his part, President Fox, eager not to lose the momentum of his own foreign policy initiatives, expressed his country's solidarity with the United States, rejecting terrorism and pledging to cooperate in terms of tightening border security, although he committed neither troops nor air support in the retaliatory strikes against the Taliban in Afghanistan. To do so would have completely overturned decades of Mexican unwillingness to militarily support U.S. foreign policy objectives.

Canada's reaction to 9/11, however, had a certain immediacy to it, as the United States shut down its airspace, grounding all outgoing flights and diverting incoming flights. Approximately 250 airplanes, carrying over 43,000 passengers, were forced to land at various airports across Canada. Canadians of all political stripes expressed their condolences and friendship to the American passengers aboard those diverted flights. Soon thereafter, Jean Chrétien's government sponsored and pushed through Parliament sweeping anti-terrorist legislation (Bill C-36) that mirrored the Bush administration's *Patriot Act*. Both laws significantly enhanced police powers, surveillance of suspected terrorists, and the gathering of personal information. While debate over each act's ability to curtail privacy and individual rights was stronger in Canada than in the United States, both C-36 and the *Patriot Act* became the laws of their respective lands. Poll after poll demonstrated that Canadians and Americans preferred security and safety over individual rights and freedoms. In 2006, however, the courts in Canada and the United States started to review anti-terrorism legislation, striking down key provisions in each nation's respective laws regarding privacy and due process. The Ontario Superior Court of Justice, for example, has argued that the government's fight against terrorism cannot be waged without regard to constitutional protections defined in the Canadian Constitution, including the freedoms of religion, expression, and association.

When the United States began its retaliatory strikes against the Taliban in Afghanistan in October 2001, Canada quickly joined the ranks of other close U.S. allies to support the U.S.-led invasion. The 3,000 Canadian troops that participated in the strikes constituted Canada's largest military operation since the Korean War. Because of budget cuts, the initial tour of duty lasted only six months. After the

Taliban were overthrown and Al-Qaeda forced to flee Afghanistan, Canadian troops assumed the familiar role of peace-keepers in the aftermath. In August 2003, Canadian troops formed part of a United Nations International Security Assistance Force (ISAF) whose goal was to stabilize the country as well as prevent the return of the Taliban and Al-Qaeda. Following a distinguished history of service to the international community, Canada provided over 2,000 military personnel in what was the largest contribution of any participating nation. Canadian involvement in U.S. foreign policy objectives had its limits, however, and when President Bush began to justify plans for a pre-emptive war with Saddam Hussein's Iraq, Canada, as well as Mexico, resisted. In fact, neither Canada nor Mexico supported Bush's decision to invade Iraq. Jean Chrétien announced publicly that Canada would not join the United States without the support of the United Nations Security Council, which was not forthcoming.

Vicente Fox, for his part, maintained continuity in Mexico's foreign policy despite the close relationship that he had forged with Bush in previous years. In the past, Mexico often opposed U.S. efforts to project its military power, and while the circumstances surrounding the preemptive strike against Iraq reflected the post-9/11 security emphasis that had permeated U.S. diplomacy, the Mexican president decided that holding true to Mexican diplomatic principles — rooted as they were in the Mexican past — was more important than political gain. As a result, Fox's public opposition to the war cost him crucial White House support for immigration reform. The Bush administration even hinted at the possibility of diplomatic and political reprisals, which were never fully defined, if Fox did not openly support the U.S position in the United Nations. U.S.-Mexico relations had reached their lowest point since the early 1980s, something that most political analysts in Mexico and the United States, operating and working as they were in a post-NAFTA spirit of continentalism, had not anticipated. A thaw began in 2005 when Bush revisited the idea of a guest-worker program in his State of the Union speech. By then Mexico had participated in a series of security exercises with the United States, including Operation Centinela that involved 18,000 Mexican troops and 12,000 federal police officers securing Mexico's northern and southern borders against a possible terrorist attack. The purpose of the exercise was to demonstrate that Mexico could indeed assist its northern neighbor with efforts to secure large areas of strategic interest to the United States and stop potential terrorists from entering the United States.

As Mexicans look beyond the 2006 presidential election, which placed Felipe Calderon in the presidency by the slimmest of margins, and Canadians adjust to Stephen Harper's Conservative government after 13 years of Liberal rule under Jean Chrétien and Paul Martin, the formalities associated with continental diplomacy continue (official state visits, binational and trinational meetings, educational exchanges, etc.), but the continentalism of the late 1980s and 1990s was butting heads with the post-9/11 tendency to measure diplomatic relations in terms of support for U.S. foreign policy objectives. Once again, the willingness and ability of the United States to flex its military muscle to secure its national interests have caused small but growing fractures in the continental cooperation that had emerged since the passage of NAFTA in 1994. While North American diplomatic unity remains elusive, a rapidly changing economy, not to mention the push and pull of demographic forces, will press Canada, Mexico, and the United States to maintain, or in some cases mend the framework of continentalism that the three nation-states had worked so hard to design. Certainly some North America watchers had cast the march toward continental integration as an inevitable conclusion to decades of spirited negotiation and diplomacy. There are so many national and regional threads woven into the historical fabric of the continent, however, with the forces of divergence often outpacing those of convergence, that it is quite difficult to find a structural unity in the diplomatic narrative of the North American past.

CHAPTER 6
INDIANS AND EUROPEANS

While the building blocks of continental diplomacy may seem abstract without its biographical components (Jefferson, Santa Anna, Macdonald, etc.), the story of the interaction between Indians and Europeans is vast and touches on many dimensions of North American history. The archaeological record reveals the human drama of Indian North America long before Christopher Columbus arrived in the hemisphere, while ethnography and oral history tell us much about the richness and diversity of indigenous culture. Europeans advanced quickly in some cases, slowly in others, but the advance was relentless, always narrowing the spaces between Indian culture and that of the new arrivals.

Within a continental framework, the national boundaries created in the nineteenth century failed to recognize Indian communities, dividing numerous Indian societies that inhabited North America in ways that reflected the attitudes of the dominant culture toward indigenous peoples. The business of nation-state building proved even more detrimental to their polities than European colonialism. By the early twentieth century, the power of Mexico, the United States, and Canada was uncontested everywhere in North America. But the story was only half told. In all three countries, Indians during the 1960s re-emerged as powerful actors who began to shape their future, insisting on and gradually receiving the legal and political recognition that guarantees their survival. Many political and economic issues remain unresolved, but the cultural survival of Indians is not one of them.

Problems of Definition

Clarification of the word Indian is useful at the outset. It is a word, with its accompanying definition, coined by non-Indians in the dominant culture and used in multiple ways—often derogatory—since 1492. In Mexico, the country with the largest Indian population in the past and in the present, *indio* (Indian) is still commonly used, along with *las razas indígenas* (indigenous races), or simply *indígenas*. In the United States, the term Indian has been used for centuries, though it came under criticism beginning in the 1960s. Numerous replacements have been suggested and are in use: American Indian, Native American, Amerind, and Amerindian are most common. Indigene, the noun most closely resembling the Mexican indígena, is not widely used. In Canada, First Nations and indigenous peoples are used, along with the increasingly common Aboriginal peoples.

The problems of definition assumed more importance with the political, legal, and cultural battles of the twentieth century. Mexico, with its great complexity and large mestizo population, led the way in trying to define an Indian. Alfonso Caso, director of the *Instituto Nacional Indigenista* (National Indian Institute) stressed four characteristics essential to a definition: racial, cultural, linguistic, and psychological. None of these is pure or absolute. Racial mixing has been continuous in North America since 1492. The idea of a "pure" racial type has little relevance except in the political rhetoric that surrounds racism. The same is true of culture. Beliefs and behavior are not insular categories whose origins can be traced back to pre-contact days. Speaking an indigenous language is a good measure, but the declining use of Indian languages weakens its usefulness. Fewer and fewer people speak Indian languages, though the number of Indians is on the rise. The final point is now recognized as exceptionally important. Psychological identification with Indian culture and an Indian community or group, along with acceptance by that group, identifies an Indian more specifically than other criteria. Alfonso Caso summarized his definition:

> An Indian is one who feels that he belongs to an Indian community, and an Indian community is one in which non-European somatic elements predominate, that speaks by preference an Indian language, that possesses in its material and spiritual culture a strong degree of indigenous elements, and finally that has a social sense of isolation from the communities that surrounds it and that is also distinguished from white and mestizo communities. (Caso 1948, 16)

The United States Bureau of the Census uses the term Indian to include "those who indicate their race as 'American Indian,' entered the name of an Indian tribe, or reported such entries as Canadian Indian, French-American Indian, or Spanish-American Indian" (Census 1990, B-29). Generally, individuals who claim origins in any of the original peoples of North America and have a cultural identification with a tribe are recognized as Indians. Since the question of origins can be difficult to ascertain, tribal identification has often been more important than race in determining status.

Canadian nomenclature has its own complexity. The general term Aboriginal Peoples is commonly used, much in the same way that Native American is used in the United States. It includes the First Nations, the traditional Indian tribes such as the Mohawk and Cree; the Inuit, the later arrivals formerly referred to as Eskimo; and the Métis, the people of mixed Indian and European ancestry. The *Constitution Act (1982)* defines all the above as Aboriginal Peoples.

Legal definitions in Canada are more precise. There are two types of Indians.

Status Indians are those who "took treaty" or entered into an agreement with the British Crown in a treaty, which often meant that they surrendered land claims in return for other benefits from the Crown. Status Indians are also registered Indians, those who for whatever reason have not taken treaty but are still legally considered Indians. Non-status Indians, the second group, are not legally considered Indians. They are people of Indian ancestry who married non-Indians or who forfeited their treaty status. For example, an Indian woman marrying a non-Indian man lost her Indian status, and their descendants were not considered Indians. The denial of Indian status provoked litigation and the eventual restoration of Indian status to many women and their children. The issue of having "status" assumed monetary significance when land, mineral rights, entitlements, and gambling revenue were at stake.

Despite the diversity of terms and their legal and cultural implications, the term Indian is recognized and used in all three countries and is commonly used in this chapter.

Early Interactions

Several conditions influenced the early interaction between Indians and Europeans. Population size had an extraordinary impact, everywhere conditioning the successes and failures of European and Indian objectives. Maybe some 25 to 30 million people — 25 million in Mexico, 2 million in the United States, and 1 million in Canada — lived in North America in the early sixteenth century. The numbers are controversial and will always be little more than sophisticated estimates. It is nevertheless clear that large populations, with their sedentary agricultural systems and hierarchal institutions, made it possible for Europeans to more rapidly establish control; small, nomadic populations proved more elusive and difficult to dominate, frequently remaining outside of colonial control until the late nineteenth century.

Viewed from the perspective of Europeans, Indians often represented a valuable resource. As interpreters and traders they acted as auxiliaries in the first stages of colonization. Soon they began working in the emerging colonial economies, either freely or bound in servitude. As Europeans began to build their colonial economies around other resources — the list is long: land, fish, fur, food, precious metals — the need for labor grew and dictated the way in which Indians and Europeans interacted.

The ability to exploit resources depended on population size, which in turn depended on biological changes. Most destructive was the intrusion of diseases that Europeans brought with them. Smallpox, typhus, influenza, measles, mumps, and other pathogens weakened and then killed millions, making it easier for Europeans to take control. Along with the diseases came new plants and animals. Some, such as the horse, offered new opportunities for mobility; others, such as cattle, sheep, and pigs, provided new sources of protein; still others, such as sugar, led to new demands for labor. All in one way or another changed Indian culture.

Mexican Conquest

Spaniards already had suspicions about the size and strength of the Aztec world when they landed in Veracruz in 1519. As they climbed up from the coastal plain to the cool central valleys, they encountered large populations living in towns and cities and participating in complex social and political systems. With surprising speed, Spaniards overthrew the political superstructure of the Aztec confederation. Within a generation they had elaborated their own complex administrative and legal apparatus to govern the colony. Many of the governing polices aimed toward the Hispanization of Indians, providing mechanisms for their incorporation into the Spanish religious, political, and economic realm.

Church and state joined together to convert Indians into Spaniards but never in a consistent or uniform manner. Too many conflicting interests distorted or waylaid the policies of Hispanization. Out of the complexity, one feature of colonization did not change. Law and military strength dictated that Indians had an inferior position in Spanish society. According to the Spanish theory of empire, they lived in segregated neighborhoods, performed forced labor, paid tribute, and faced limitations in dress and ownership of weapons and horses. Spain attempted to create dual societies, a "republic of Indians" and a "republic of Spaniards," the former subordinate to the latter but both having their internal rights and responsibilities. Again according to theory, through a gradual process of Hispanization, this dualism would eventually lead to the full integration of Indians in the Spanish world.

Strict legal separation seldom ruled the relationship between Indians and Spaniards. Instead of separation, interaction took place at every level of material, cultural, and spiritual life, dictated primarily by the size of the Indian population and the location of resources. Laws were enacted to protect Indians from rapacious Spaniards who wanted to exploit Indian labor, but these laws neither constituted nor conveyed a special status to Indians simply because they were Indians. In other words, Spanish colonial jurisprudence sought to protect Indians from the more egregious effects of the colonial enterprise, but it did not grant Indians special rights or even more rights than those enjoyed by the Spanish population. In central Mexico, Spaniards relied on Indian labor and tribute to build their colony, a process described in Chapter 8. As Spanish influence expanded, that of Indians receded. Slow and irregular, control came easiest in the central areas, as Spaniards used Indian traditions of dominance and subordination to their own ends. On the periphery, where the population was sparse and nomadic, they had a more difficult time physically subduing Indians. There the missions, founded primarily by the Franciscan and Jesuit orders, became the outposts of Spanish society. As in the southwest and Great Plains of the United States, final military dominance did not come until the late nineteenth century, and even then it often was tenuous at best.

Despite Spanish power in Mexico, Indian cultures survived. Violent resistance in the central and southern valleys and the deserts of the north momentarily slowed the spread of colonial institutions but did not stop it. More essential in the struggle for survival was the strength of the Indian pueblo, the village that held Indian life together. Through membership in the village, Indians belonged to a specific language and cultural group and shared customs and festivals. Through the village they had access to land, which was controlled in common by the village. As long as the land-based village survived, the Indian survived, even if surrounded by European culture. Paradoxically, Spaniards envisioned the village as one of the main forces of colonization, gathering Indians in them and imposing a Spanish political structure on them. Like islands in a stream, the villages were susceptible to erosion and reconfiguration, but they did survive. When the stream became a river in the nineteenth century and the islands were submerged, Indian cultures faced new threats, but again they survived.

During the first century of colonization, the prevailing attitudes of Spaniards toward Indians became evident. First and foremost they regarded Indians as "a problem" — a military, political, economic, social, and ultimately a cultural problem that strained the best minds of the day. At root were European perceptions of civilization and the failure of Indians to conform to them. European ambivalence toward Indians also characterized their behavior. Spaniards described the Aztec city of Tenochtitlán with awe and wonderment and marveled at the artistry and creativity of its builders. In another breath they criticized their barbarity and brutality, especially their religious practices. This attraction and revulsion found expression in everything from art to educational policy through the centuries. Still another attitude emphasized the need for special programs and policies for Indians. Most were paternalistic, predicated on the belief that Indians acted childlike and needed the protection and guidance of Europeans. These ideas, all evident during the first generation of European occupation, guided policy for centuries.

Quebec Trade

French colonists also encountered diverse languages, cultures, and economies. The French, like the Spanish, pursued a policy of Christianizing and assimilating Indians. Unlike the Spanish, they made little progress in these goals, given the small European population and the dispersed settlement pattern of the Indians they encountered. Furthermore, the economics of the new colony dictated against assimilation. With the colony's most valuable resource — beaver pelt — spread across thousands of square kilometers of land unknown to Europeans, Indians served as guides, trappers, and traders. New France was little more than a trading outpost, similar to the colonies that the Italian city states had established in North Africa or the Portuguese in Brazil. With very few colonists and an economy based on trade, the French had much less interest in control over the land than did Spanish and English settlers.

Successful colonization in Quebec depended on the assistance of several tribes. The Montagnais and Algonquin in the northeast and the Cree and Ojibwa in the northwest helped in the expansion of the fur trade. In the center and southwest lived the Huron, the largest and most powerful group in the region. Organized into a confederation of five tribes, the Huron dominated an area in modern Ontario that Europeans labeled Huronia. Champlain early on established a trading relationship with the Huron, who provided fur to the French and European goods to western tribes. Indians quickly developed a desire for European goods—metal tools, cookware, weapons, and alcohol. Groups such as the Huron, already accomplished traders, became intermediaries in an expanding circle of commerce that was a part of the larger Atlantic trading system. To profit from the trade, the French learned Algonquian and Iroquoian languages. The geographic extent of these languages allowed them to communicate with peoples throughout the Great Lakes region. They quickly adopted the canoe for trade and travel. Furthermore, they lived with and married Indians, creating the Métis, who in turn became very successful traders. The Dutch and then the English struggled to establish similar relationships with the Iroquois, the traditional enemies of the Huron. Competition among and between Indians and Europeans set the stage for centuries of conflict that culminated in the French and Indian Wars.

English Policies

English toehold settlements along the eastern seaboard of the continent also depended on Indians but not to the same extent as the French and Spanish. The fundamental overriding difference was the failure of English policy to provide for mechanisms for coexistence with Indian groups. Instead, policy emphasized a separation and isolation of Indians from Europeans, of pushing them away from the new colonies, and of creating barriers or of allowing Indians to live in enclaves for short periods before expelling them. Even the periodic efforts to "civilize" or assimilate Indians did not deflect the underriding currents of isolation.

As with the French, early English settlers from Newfoundland south through Nova Scotia, New Brunswick, and Maine struggled for control over fishing grounds and established trading relations with Indians when it benefited them. The largest group in the far northeast region was the Mi'kmaq (Micmac), fishing and hunting people who migrated yearly between coast and interior. They participated early in the fur trade, but as it moved westward they had difficulty competing. Gradually, many of them found work in the slowly expanding economy of the Maritime provinces, but they were soon driven to the periphery.

Farther to the south, Algonquian-speaking Indians occupied the coastal region. In Jamestown, as elsewhere, the early settlers depended on the Indians for trade and food. As tobacco agriculture expanded after 1612, colonists took more land, leading to Indian retaliation and intermittent skirmishes. In New England, the Puritans maintained cordial relations with Indians until the Pequot War of 1637, a reaction of the Pequot tribe against increasing loss of land. In 1675 war broke out again. Known as King Philip's War (Philip was a Wampanoag chief), the conflict ended serious Indian claims to land in New England.

In the interior lived the Iroquois, a more powerful group that had created a political confederation by the sixteenth century, initially composed of the Mohawk, Oneida, Onondaga, Cayuga, and Seneca. In the eighteenth century the Tuscarora joined them. The extent of political organization and power of the Iroquois confederation is still debated by historians, but there is no doubt that in the seventeenth and eighteenth centuries the Iroquois affected the destiny of the continent. Centered near Albany, New York, the Iroquois raided (in the Iroquois Wars) to the north, attacking the French and their allies, the Huron. The Iroquois continued to influence trade and settlement patterns throughout the eighteenth century.

Land remained a troubling issue for Indian-European relations. Europeans, with their well-worked out arrangements of land ownership, often misunderstood Indian land-use patterns. Indians used the land for hunting, gathering, and farming. They did so without ownership rights in the traditional European sense, thus leading to many conflicts over land. Yet even if there had been legal agreement over the extent of land rights, Indian lands still would have been vulnerable. The expansion of the European colonies from Newfoundland to New Spain depended on control over land. Wherever Europeans demanded land, Indians were vulnerable.

Fundamental differences in the interaction of Europeans and Indians shaped the history of North America. Spaniards built their colonies on the backs of Indian labor, creating a social order based on race and ethnicity. The presence of large Indian populations allowed the Spanish to do what no other colonizing power could. The French acted differently, carefully nurturing commercial relationships with tribes to continue the fur trade. Their economic interests and small population did not lead to the acquisition of large tracts of land beyond the St. Lawrence River Valley. The English followed another course. They displaced Indians, forcing them farther and farther from the seaboard colonies. Only in the eighteenth century, when Britain seriously began to contest the French, did it seriously cultivate commercial relations with the Iroquois.

After the Seven Years' War, the British government issued the Royal Proclamation of 1763. Hailed by many Indian groups through the centuries as justification of their land claims, it recognized the legal existence of Indian tribes and accepted their limited sovereignty. It prohibited English settlers from occupying lands west of the Appalachians, declaring them a vast Indian reserve. Indians had the power to enter into treaty agreements but did not achieve recognition as equal to European nations. For its part, the Crown hoped to stabilize an increasingly turbulent region, control a growing trade, and deflect new settlement to the north and to the south. The proclamation failed in its objectives, but it served as an important background document to the subsequent discussion of the extent of Indian sovereignty and land titles in the United States and Canada.

Post-Colonial Relations in North America

United States
In the United States after independence, Indian affairs presented a challenge. As the country expanded westward, it entered into treaties with Indian tribes, thus confirming their sovereignty. During George Washington's presidency (1789-97), westward movement accelerated, settlers clamored for new lands, and hostilities flared. To meet the challenge, the country adopted a policy of regulating Indian affairs, which often had trade and land cessions as major goals. There was also the stated goal of "civilizing" and assimilating Indians, forcefully articulated under Thomas Jefferson (1801-09). He saw the Indian as a "natural man," fully capable of assimilation into U.S. society. Through education, intermarriage, and economic productivity, Indians would become full citizens.

The policy failed, stymied at every step by the expansion of the new republic. As populations increased and land values climbed, settlers violated treaties and pushed Indians farther west. A great expulsion took place in the 1830s, as government policy forced over 100,000 Indians in the southeast from their homes. Cherokee, Chickasaw, Choctaw, Creek, and Seminole followed a "trail of tears" on the way to their new homes in Oklahoma. In exchange for their rich farm lands in the southeast, they received promises of land "forever" west of the Mississippi River. Much of the land was harsh and barren and reached into sections of the country referred to as the "American Desert" and the "Indian Territory." Consequently, it held little initial appeal for settlers, giving hope to government officials that the policy of isolation and exclusion would hold.

Isolation did not last long. The annexation of Texas, the settlement of Oregon, and the Mexican Cession opened up half the continent to U.S. colonization. The country now pursued a policy of "concentration," signing treaties that settled individual tribes on designated lands. By segregating the tribes, the government opened new lands for settlement and prevented Indians from forming a confederation that might threaten U.S. control.

The end of the Civil War unleashed a new rush of settlement. From the Mexican to the Canadian border, settlers bought lands, opened mines, and harvested timber. Completion of the transcontinental railroad in 1869 brought in more settlers. Some 6 million poured into the Great Plains and basins of the west between 1865 and 1890, squeezing even more the 200,000 Plains Indians and everywhere impinging on their land. The Sioux and Blackfeet in the North, the Cheyenne and Arapaho in the center, and the Apache and Comanche in the south experienced increasing pressure on their cultures of mobility. Soon war engulfed the plains from north to south.

The advantages of numbers and technology insured victory for the expanding United States. Indians in the Plains, the Great Basin, and the far northwest fell before the wave of settlers and machines. As the buffalo disappeared and hunting grounds shrank, Indians had fewer opportunities for survival. A new policy of "confinement" followed in 1867 and 1868. Plains Indians were moved to two large reservations, one in the Black Hills of the Dakota Territory and the other in the Oklahoma Territory. Again the policy failed to stymie the land grabbers, prospectors, dirt farmers, and ranchers who formed an unstoppable wave in their desire for opportunity and wealth. Conflicts broke out again, and new treaties and smaller reservations tried to accommodate the conflicting interests, only to end at the Massacre of Wounded Knee in 1890. The military occupation of the West was now complete.

War did not solve the social question of the future of Indians. The policies of containment, confinement, and reservations had not worked. There was now a return to earlier ideas about assimilation. The *Indian Appropriations Act* (1871) gave the government the power to act without the cooperation of Indians. No longer respected as independent powers, tribes were seen as a barrier to individual Indian assimilation. Policy-makers hoped that by presenting Indians with the benefits of modern industrial life they would forsake their way of life.

Private property emerged as the guiding principle of the new policy. The *Dawes General Allotment (Severalty) Act* (1887) encouraged Indians to divide tribal lands into private units of 160 acres per family. According to prevailing social beliefs, ownership of property would transform Indians into petty capitalists who would work to acquire the supposed benefits of civilization. Technical and educational support —according to plan but not always reality—accompanied the transition to insure success. The results were disastrous. Indians lost land, tribal government weakened, and social problems worsened as Indians became wards of the federal government in the late nineteenth century.

Canada

Still under British control in the first half of the nineteenth century, Canada relied on the military to form alliances and treaties favorable to British objectives. It also hoped to place Indians on reserves (reservations) and make them conform economically and culturally to British behavior. As the century unfolded, Canada had even less respect for the idea of the sovereignty of Indian nations than the United States. Treaties thus played a less significant role.

The rise of the Métis population complicated Indian issues in Canada. By the middle of the nineteenth century, they had such a strong sense of identity that they longed for a Métis nation centered in the Red River Valley of Manitoba. With the impending transfer of land of the Hudson's Bay Company to the nation of Canada, the Métis feared that they would lose their own lands. Led by Louis Riel, they rebelled in 1869-70 and again in 1885. The rebellions reflected their growing nationalism and the growing marginalization of both Métis and Indians. With the fur trade in decline and the buffalo gone, agriculture was their only hope. As in the United States, Indians received very little good land and had inadequate support for creating prosperous agricultural communities. The result was impoverishment.

Indians had no say in the legislation that ended up controlling their future. The *British North America Act* of 1867 gave the federal government the power to regulate Indian life but said nothing else about Indian peoples. The first comprehensive legislation was the *Indian Act* of 1876. This and subsequent amendments to it gave the federal government broad legislative responsibility to control Indian peoples. It had the ultimate power over Indian lands and the political life of Indian groups. Its objective, as in the United States, was assimilation of Indians in Canadian society.

Under the *Indian Act* the government entered into treaties that interfered with many aspects of Indian life. The implications of these treaties expanded in 1870 when the government acquired the land previously owned by the Hudson's Bay Company. This was a vast territory that enlarged the power and responsibility of the government over Indians. In a series of treaties known as the "numbered treaties" (Treaty No. 1 in 1871 to Treaty No. 11 in 1921), Canada pursued its policy of assimilation. It offered money, land, and citizenship to Indians who left their tribes. Those who remained had access to reserves, or lands specifically designated for use by Indians, as well as educational and technical assistance and financial payments. Often these reserves, with their boundaries and borders, were ill-suited for agriculture and inhibited the traditional migratory lifestyle of many Indians. The numbered treaties continue to surface in Canadian politics. As recently as 2002, a federal judge in Alberta ruled that Indians covered under Treaty No. 8 are exempt from sales and income taxes whether or not they live on a reserve. The Federal Court of Appeal overturned the decision, however, stating that the exemption did not apply to Indians residing outside the reserve.

As in the United States, the cultural survival of Indians was in doubt, particularly as the government moved to suppress traditional rituals such as the potlatch (accumulation and distribution or destruction of wealth) and the Sun Dance (dances that invoked supernatural forces) that long had been important to Indian culture. Legal, social, and economic changes led many late nineteenth-century observers to agree that "most of the natives, surrounded by the rising tide, half-bastardised and debased, are being slowly but surely absorbed in the general population of the country... Conforming even in their political and municipal institutions to the practices of their Canadian neighbors, they will soon have retained no distinctive characters, except perhaps the vague memories of their forefathers" (Reclus 1886-95, 1:420).

The strength of Indian cultures belied such negative predictions. Unwittingly, late nineteenth and early twentieth-century policies in the United States and Canada did much to sustain Indian culture. By insuring the political and economic marginalization of Indians, they indirectly helped to protect their culture. Isolation and poverty acted as walls around reservations, protecting languages, rituals, and social relationships.

Mexico

After independence Mexico eliminated many colonial practices and customs that had defined Indian life for 300 years. No longer did Indians have to pay tribute, nor did they have recourse to the special courts and laws that had existed for them under Spanish rule. Under the first constitution of the Mexican republic, Indians became citizens along with other Mexicans. They did not have legally recognized tribes or reservations comparable to those in the United States and Canada. Instead, even in the remote deserts of the northwest and the jungles of the south, they lived in villages that had broadly similar forms of organization, regardless of ethnic or linguistic background. All Mexicans, in other words, lived according to the same laws and under similar officials. While laws eliminated some of the colonial-era protections that Indians enjoyed, they did not change their marginal position in society. A social structure that dominated and exploited Indians continued and led to many rebellions throughout the nineteenth century.

The Constitution of 1857 dealt a particularly sharp blow to Indian culture. Culminating the liberal drive to overthrow the communal landholding system of the colonial period, the Constitution strove to deprive the Catholic Church, Mexican towns, and Indian villages of the land that they held in common. Liberalism stressed the centrality of private property for the creation of a modern economy and hoped to break up lands held in common. The *Dawes Act* in the United States relied on the same principle. Indians suffered the most as they lost control over their land. Estimates vary, but Indian communities probably lost some 10 million hectares of land in the late nineteenth and early twentieth century. At the same time, new demands for agricultural products ushered in an unprecedented era of commercial agriculture and new demands for labor. Without land in their villages, Indians turned to haciendas and plantations for employment or migrated to the cities.

Few stepped forward to defend the Indians, capitulating instead, as they did in the United States and Canada, to assimilationist efforts. Assist the Indians in abandoning their languages and customs, provide them with land to work, and encourage their biological and cultural interaction with other Mexicans — these policies would eventually solve the "Indian problem" in Mexico.

The Mexican Revolution of 1910 changed the course of Indian history. Led by Emiliano Zapata, Indians in the state of Morelos rose up in arms to demand land. In 1911, they proclaimed the Plan of Ayala, which had as its theme "land, liberty, justice, and law." The demand for land became the battle cry of many Indians as they joined rebel leaders from Chiapas to Chihuahua. Success came in the form of Article 27 of the Constitution of 1917, which provided the basis for the agrarian policy of modern Mexico. The state now assumed the responsibility for distributing land to the poor, not for defrauding them. Indian communities found a new source of strength in the agrarian ideology of the revolution.

Modern Relations in North America

Indigenismo

Twentieth-century Mexican history is closely intertwined with Indians. After the Revolution a movement known as *indigenismo* emerged as a main theme of political and cultural life. Three goals drove indigenismo from the 1920s onward. First, it sought the rediscovery of the glory and triumph of the Indian past. Throughout Latin America, intellectuals and artists rescued the Indian past, giving it the attention that it deserved by studying Indian languages, music, art, and religion. Second, it created programs to improve the material conditions of Indian life. The government launched "cultural missions" in the 1920s to send teams of educators, nurses, and agronomists to the remote corners of the nation to help Indians. Third, indigenismo revived the old goal of assimilation. Division had too long characterized Mexican life. The barriers between Indians and the rest of Mexico must be overcome to integrate Indians into national life. While there was respect for the uniqueness of Indians and the plurality of cultures, the driving force still remained the physical and cultural blending of Indians into the Mexican nation. *Mestizaje*, the process of racial and cultural mixing, remained the principal social ideology in Mexico.

Lázaro Cárdenas gave new direction to indigenismo by reinvigorating Article 27 of the Constitution. He emphasized the redistribution of land in the form of the *ejido*, the traditional form of communal landholding of Indian villages. The loss of communal lands in the past had culturally and materially impoverished Indians, forcing them to the margins of society. Restoration of community lands held out the promise of a more prosperous future for them.

Mexico did not propose to set land aside in reservations and reserves similar to those in the United States and Canada. Instead, it revived the system of communal landholdings so important to the Indian past. Under the system, Indians had access to land through the ejido, now a legally constituted entity that received its land from the state. The ejido again became a cultural and economic cornerstone of village life. Politically, most of the ejidos had their centers in Indian villages or *municipios*, and coexisted or cojoined with village political organizations. This municipal political organization imposed uniformity on Indian life not found in the United States and Canada. Only the Lacandones in Chiapas and the Seris in Sonora fell outside of the municipio system. Beneath this uniformity was great diversity as traditional political practices common to individual groups continued alongside of municipio politics. Since President Carlos Salinas's agrarian reforms of 1992, the ejido has experienced tremendous change, now that rural peoples, including Indians and mestizos, can sell, rent, or trade their assigned portion of the communal lands. For example, it is quite common to find Mixtec-speaking mestizos from Oaxaca working in the vineyards of western New York because of the social and economic transformations that have taken place in rural Mexico.

To add a social complement to agrarian reform, Cárdenas created the *Departamento de Asuntos Indígenas* (Department of Indian Affairs) in 1936, which emphasized education, health, and the material conditions of Indian life. At another level he helped to create the *Instituto Indigenista Interamericano* (Interamerican Indian Institute) in 1940 that addressed questions surrounding the past and future of Indians. Under Cárdenas, Mexico became one of the leading nations in the Americas for promoting the well-being of Indians.

A subsequent institutional development was the formation of the *Instituto Nacional Indigenista* (National Indian Institute) in 1948 under the leadership of Alfonso Caso. Assimilation still remained the objective, but Caso also emphasized integrated development, coordinated with state and national agencies. The concept of integrated development viewed all elements of the Indian community as interrelated; one could not be changed without influencing and affecting the others. By taking this approach to development, Indian problems would no longer be viewed in isolation, separate from national development goals.

A new direction in policy emerged during the 1960s that led to the acceptance of the reality of cultural pluralism in Mexico. In place of forced assimilation, policies now advocated unity through diversity, expressed through an emphasis on bilingual education and cultural preservation. A 1991 amendment to the Constitution confirmed the new direction by declaring Mexico a "multi-ethnic" nation. Economic development was still paramount, but now Indians played decisive roles. "Ethnodevelopment" became a common term. It stressed the autonomy, independence, and rights of Indian peoples to determine their own futures. From the municipality to the nation, Indians, according to the new theories, should design their own programs. Rather than passive recipients of assistance, Indians became the promoters of their own well-being. This did not mean that the Mexican nation abandoned the mestizaje of the 1920s; it could not, given the racial and cultural predominance of the mestizo. It did, though, adjust its policies to recognize and support the distinctiveness of its many ethnic minorities.

Policy Shifts in the United States

Indian policy in the United States underwent changes during the interwar years. The increasing outrage over the failed policies of the late nineteenth century led to new ones, particularly the granting of the franchise in 1924 and the *Indian Reorganization Act* of 1934. The act provided the basis for a new self-determination of Indian tribes as a transition to the fuller incorporation of Indians into the political and economic life of the nation. At its political core, the act encouraged the creation of representative tribal government less dependent on the Bureau of Indian Affairs. For example, Indian tribes could determine who was a tribal member and who could receive a business license on the reservation. The act also stopped the sale of reservation lands, thus insuring the future survival of the tribes. The act did not solve the problems of Indians, but it was a step in the restoration of autonomy to Indian nations.

Passage of legislation collectively referred to as the *Termination Laws* (1953-62) represented another critical shift in Indian policy. The arguments for and against the legislation summarized much of contemporary thinking about Indians in the United States. Advocates argued for the elimination of the special status of Indians, which in turn would lead to their accelerated integration into the social mainstream. This as well would free Indian lands for development and reduce the responsibilities of the federal government. Opponents insisted that Indians had a special place within society and that the federal government must honor its commitment to recognize and support tribal cultures and governments. In the end, termination affected only about 3 per cent of Indians, but concerns over its effects led to declining enthusiasm and the end of government endorsement.

In the 1960s new, more militant Indian organizations emerged that demanded respect for their culture and a more sympathetic federal government. The American Indian Movement (formed in 1968) was the most vocal of these. It was a part of a Pan Indian movement that included representation from Canada and several Latin American countries and had its origins in the early twentieth century. More than any others, two events in the United States dramatized the new militancy of Indians and awakened society to their grievances. From 1969 to 1972 Indians occupied Alcatraz Island in San Francisco Bay, claiming ownership of the island with plans to use it as a cultural center. The second famous incident occurred in 1973 when Indians took over the town of Wounded Knee, South Dakota. The symbolism of place was important. Wounded Knee was the site of the massacre in 1890 that has often been cited as the end of the resistance of Plains Indians to the advance of U.S. society. Wounded Knee would now symbolize a beginning as well as an end.

Meanwhile, laws became more sympathetic to the Indian cause. The *Indian Civil Rights Act* of 1968 guaranteed Indians the civil rights accorded to all citizens, while also recognizing the legality of Indian tribal law on the reservations. President Richard Nixon reversed the *Termination Laws* of the 1950s, and the government once again endorsed a special status for Indians. The new legislation represented the final reversal of the assimilationist policy evident since the late eighteenth century. The government recognized the tribes as sovereign entities, capable of negotiating with the federal government and of governing themselves. Yet they were still not independent nations. As in the past, they continue to have a special status as wards of the federal government. The government recognizes their sovereignty and tribal law, as long as they do not violate treaties and federal law. Due to this relationship, much in the federal political affairs of Indians remains undefined and subject to court action. The one exception may be the 1990 *Native American Grave Protection and Repatriation Act*, or NAGPRA, which instituted major changes in the way human remains and funerary items are handled by government agencies and archaeologists on public lands. As a legal expression of cultural sensitivity to historical Indian burial sites, NAGPRA has pushed government agencies, scholars, and tribal communities to work together despite their competing interests. While some scholars want unfettered access to human relics and burial sites, most appreciate the general desire among indigenous peoples to maintain their ancestors in a manner appropriate to tribal custom.

Another wrinkle in the relationship between Indians and the U.S. government has been the rapid growth of Indian-owned casinos throughout the United States. Congress established the legal framework for Indian gaming in 1988, and since then more than 400 casinos and gambling facilities operated by 223 Indian tribes in 28 states have appeared. This phenomenal growth has engendered conflict between tribal and state and local governments, as the former asserts tribal sovereignty over gaming issues while the latter seeks new ways to generate revenue. In 2006 the U.S. Court of Appeals for the District of Columbia issued a highly anticipated ruling on tribal sovereignty and Indian gaming. The court decided that the federal government cannot regulate the ways in which Indian casinos run their biggest money-making games, such as black jack and slot machines. In effect, the decision stymied federal efforts to regulate the ever growing $22 billion tribal gaming industry. While tribes can still open casinos after having negotiated a "compact" with their state governor, the federal government's regulatory role has been severely limited.

Canadian Variations
During the early twentieth century, assimilation remained the primary goal of Canadian Indian policy. Enfranchisement represented the method. In its specific political meaning, enfranchisement conveys the right to vote; in the history of Canadian Indian policy, enfranchisement specified that Indians relinquish their status as Indians and forfeit the right to live on reserves and receive special government benefits. Mostly a voluntary program, enfranchisement in the 1930s and 1940s did little to alleviate the problems of Indians. Political enfranchisement, or the right to vote, did not come to all Indians in Canada until 1960.

As in the United States, the decade of the 1960s led to a growing demand for the special rights of Indians, including the right of self-government. As Indians became more assertive, often with the broad support of Canadian public opinion, the issue came to a head with government policy recommendations in 1969, which in effect called for the abolition of the *Indian Act* as well as provincial control of Indian policy. Jean Chrétien, as Minister of the Department of Indian Affairs and Northern Development, proposed the elimination of the special rights of Status Indians and the return of legal ownership of lands to Indians. Until that time the Crown held reserve lands in trust. Indians opposed the recommendations and demanded a continuation of their special status within Canada, arguing that the government should honor the commitments made under previous treaties. They had just begun to make progress in receiving support for their claims and felt betrayed by the government.

Fundamental principles clashed over the plan. Chrétien and Prime Minister Trudeau argued that Indians should participate freely and independently as individuals within Canadian society. Indians responded that they had been long ignored and exploited by the government. In addition, they asserted that they were the true founding peoples of Canada and thus deserved recognition equal to that accorded the French and English. As Canadian politics unfolded in the subsequent decades, the special position of Indians received increasing government support.

The *Canada Act* of 1982 finally guaranteed that Aboriginal groups had an "inherent right to self government" and accepted them along with the federal and provincial as one of the three levels of government. To define more precisely what this meant, Indians mobilized their resources. Four organizations joined the struggle for Indian rights: the Assembly of First Nations, the Native Council of Canada, the Métis National Council, and the Inuit Committee on National Issues. They argued during the Meech Lake talks (1987-90) about the validity of including the First Nations as one of the founding nations of Canada, along with the English and French. Failure to do this contributed to the failure of the Meech Lake Accord. The Charlottetown Accord finally and definitively agreed to the right of self-government. What all of this means in a practical sense is still in the process of evolution as Indians struggle to gain control over social services, transportation, economic activities, and other areas of tribal life.

Many of the undecided issues relate to land claims. Fewer than 100 of the over 600 land claims filed since 1982 had been resolved by 1995. The largest include the claims of 17,500 Inuit to 2 million square kilometers in the central and eastern Northwest Territories; the 15,000 Montagnais to 700,000 square kilometers in Quebec and Labrador; the 2,500 Dene/Métis to 282,000 square kilometers north of Great Slave Lake; and the 2,000 Gwich'in to 60,000 square kilometers in the Mackenzie Delta. According to some estimates, these and other land claims represent close to 50 per cent of the national territory of Canada. In the case of the Inuit, the land claims relate directly to issues of governance. As mentioned in a previous chapter, the creation of Nunavut in effect created an autonomous Indian territorial government. Efforts to create Denendeh, an Indian-controlled counterpart to Nunavut in the western half of the Northwest Territories, have not been as successful.

Quebec also deserves mention. Indian life in the province has been influenced by the massive James Bay hydro-electric project and by the Quebec drive for sovereignty. The James Bay project has altered the environment of thousands of square kilometers of land on the eastern side of James Bay, affecting especially the Cree and Inuit. Rivers have been rerouted, lands flooded, dams and spillways built, and enormous subterranean power stations constructed. If the master plan is fully implemented, reservoirs totaling almost 12,000 square kilometers (half the size of Lake Ontario) will have been filled with water.

To ensure continuation of Indian rights, the James Bay Agreement was signed in 1975. After years of negotiations, the agreement reserved land for Indians; promised hunting, fishing, and trapping rights; guaranteed self-government; and assured monetary payments. Despite the thoroughness of the negotiations, dissatisfaction emerged soon after. For critics, the James Bay project symbolizes (unfairly it should be added from the point of view of the Quebec government) the disregard for indigenous rights and the environment.

In Quebec, Indians also react to the emphasis on the French origins of Canada. They argue that Quebec nationalism has not respected the rights of English-speaking Québécois, much less the rights of indigenous peoples and other minorities. Indians fear that increased autonomy for Quebec will lead to decreased autonomy for Indians. They depend on the influence of the federal government for their rights.

Anticipating the Future

Conquest, disease, displacement, forced labor, and the onslaught of industrialization and vigorous efforts at assimilation have not defeated North American Indians. It is a remarkable story of survival and recently of growth. After centuries of decline, the population and the political and cultural strength of Indians are on the increase. Demands for cultural recognition are being met, as old stereotypes compete with a new appreciation of the complexity and intrinsic value of Indian culture.

Demands for "self-government" are also being met, though slowly and unevenly. Issues surrounding self-government involve ownership and use of land, provision and control over health and education services, passing and enforcing laws, and economic development. Indian tribes in the United States have made the most progress, since they are recognized as "dependent sovereign nations" and have substantial control over tribal life. Canadian Indians continue the process of negotiations and have made progress in wresting more power from the federal government. Mexican Indians, lacking designated reservations, have the least independence, but in areas where they dominate numerically they have control of municipal government. They also have become active partners in creating programs for their future. Economic gains have come slower than cultural and political ones. Indian peoples suffer the highest levels of poverty, disease, and illiteracy in North America. The challenge for the future is to improve the quality of life and at the same time preserve Indian culture.

By the 1990s, Indians in Canada and the United States shared many of the same political and economic objectives, namely, self-determination, tribal sovereignty, and a self-sufficiency fostered by participation in the global marketplace. Whether it is proceeds from timber, coal, or fishing industries, or profits garnered from casinos, Indians look for ways to reduce poverty and invest in their communities. For example, members of the Tohono O'Odham nation in southern Arizona receive a stipend from the tribal government every other year as long as the tribe earns sufficient profits from its casinos. Such payments can be as high as $2,000 (U.S.), and tribal members who reside south of the international border also are eligible to receive the stipend. At the same time, however, despite these economic successes, many indigenous groups maintain political pressure on government agencies as well as the court systems in both countries to ensure equitable treatment. As Roger Nichols has demonstrated in his book, *Indians in the United States and Canada*, there are striking similarities in the recent positions of indigenous peoples. In both countries, Indian groups work hard to keep their concerns in the news; many non-Indian Canadians and Americans now recognize the value of Indian culture and traditions. Moreover, large numbers of Indians have moved off the reservations and reserves and into the cities during the past 50 years. In the United States, for example, over one-half of the recognized Indians now live somewhere other than on the reservations. In Canada, employment opportunities, access to education, and better health care in towns and cities also attract reserve Indians. In both countries, however, Indians remain the poorest members of society (Nichols 1998, 321-22).

In Mexico, the Zapatista Rebellion of 1994 exposed the structural poverty of Indian communities as well as the incongruence of government policy. The ruling party's embrace of the neo-liberal model of economic development in the 1980s and 1990s fashioned a re-allocation of the national income, and indigenous peoples soon found broken the implicit moral contract that they had forged with the Mexican government after the Mexican Revolution of 1910. High infant mortality rates, low life expectancy, poorly funded schools, and wide-spread malnutrition permeated Indian communities from Chiapas in the south to Chihuahua in the north. While the Zapatista Rebellion never yielded any major military victory for Subcomandante Marcos and his peasant army, it has raised greater awareness of issues affecting Mexico's Indian population. For his part, President Vicente Fox, unable to break the military stalemate that had befuddled his predecessors, began to address these issues upon taking office in late 2000. He established a new cabinet post to handle discrimination cases, and he chose an Otomí Indian to head the Office of Indian Affairs. At the behest of the new president, the Mexican Congress debated an Indian rights bill, but hardliners in the PRI and PAN, unable to reconcile Indian demands for greater autonomy with their own assimilationist policies, delayed the bill until a weakened version was finally passed in the spring of 2001. If the 2006 presidential campaign is any indication of how the next Mexican president will prioritize issues affecting indigenous peoples, the marginalized status of Mexican Indians will continue for years to come.

The social complexity of Indian North America encapsulates the convergence and divergence that have shaped the continent for centuries. Indigenous societies and the natural resources that sustained their cultures structured European colonialism from the very beginning. French explorers established a trading post empire in the northern tier of the continent (Saint Lawrence Valley) whose survival depended on the local Indian population and its willingness to exchange beaver pelts for iron goods. A web of commerce developed that pushed the French and their Indian allies westward into the Great Lakes region. Many English settlers, on the other hand, arrived at North America's northeastern and mid-Atlantic seaboards as farmers with an eye toward creating a rural society that mirrored the one they left behind, albeit buttressed by mercantile interests and trade. In the initial stages of cross-cultural and material exchanges, the various Indian communities began their relationship with these farmers and merchants from a position of strength. By the end of the seventeenth century, however, warfare, disease, and displacement forced them into a state of dependence and subservience (Nichols 1998, 60). Spaniards, however, simultaneously created a territorial empire and settler colony in the southern tier of the continent, employing (and often coercing) Indian labor to extract precious metals, till the fields, and render tribute to the Spanish Crown. Pre-Columbian patterns of state formation among the different Indian societies afforded Spaniards the opportunity to graft their colonial enterprise onto these earlier structures.

The nineteenth century witnessed the establishment of national boundaries that ignored the much longer presence of Indian society in North America. Expansionist politics, population growth among non-Indian groups, and the demands of the Industrial Revolution encouraged the displacement of so many Indians that cultural survival was in doubt. Much of the twentieth century, and certainly the first decades of the twenty-first century have shown, however, that cultural resilience and revitalization are durable and complementary features of Indian North America. While the dominant culture in Canada, Mexico, and the United States often portrays indigenous peoples as static and timeless, fixed in a romantic, ahistorical rendering of the past, Indians themselves confront the many challenges to their physical livelihoods — including endemic poverty, alcoholism and diabetes, chronic unemployment, and the commodification of their natural and cultural resources — with a strong sense of identity and cultural persistence. World-renowned flutist R. Carlos Nakai, an Indian of Navajo-Ute heritage, put it best: "The tradition of being a native person isn't tied to what happened in the 1700s or the 1800s, but what's going on with us right now…." (Quoted in Simonelli 1992, 18).

CHAPTER 7
IMMIGRATION

Two broad currents of immigration have influenced the historical development of North America since the sixteenth century. The first and most pronounced was the arrival of people from Europe and Africa and then the rest of the world. Immigrants continue to arrive daily, bringing their culture and dreams with them. Second was the movement of people within North America, migrating from the central valleys of Mexico to the northern deserts, the seaboard English colonies to the Appalachian highlands and beyond, and the St. Lawrence River to the interior of the continent.

The movement of peoples within North America had deep roots in the pre-Columbian period as indigenous peoples followed ancient trade routes and searched for water sources and food. During the seventeenth and eighteenth centuries, it reflected first the material and political realities of colonial life and later the challenges of independence and the business of forging nation-states in the nineteenth and twentieth centuries. As this chapter demonstrates, the ebb and flow of peoples across political borders in search of economic security, personal liberty, or political freedom simultaneously facilitate and complicate the integration of North America.

Early Immigration

New Spain

Despite New Spain's long history of immigration, it was less influenced by immigration after the early years of colonization than the British colonies to the north. "Immigrant" is seldom used to describe the early arrivals to the Spanish colony of New Spain. Instead, they are referred to as *conquistadores*, conquerors who came to plunder and enrich themselves before returning to Spain. While there were conquerors, especially in the 1520s and 1530s, most newcomers arrived in search of a better life, bringing their skills, dreams, and families with them. Already by the end of the sixteenth century, one-third of the immigrants to Mexico were women.

Particular historical characteristics in New Spain influenced how many immigrants came, what they expected, and the type of life they found. The large sedentary

Indian populations in the center of the colony and the silver mines of the north lured immigrants with the promise of a courtly seigneurial life. Reality was different. After the first years of conquest, few found mineral riches or Indians to work for them. Most of the valuable, arable land was already in private hands, the Indian population had dramatically declined, and few new mines were discovered. Spanish immigrants (maybe 300,000 until 1810) thus filled a wide range of agricultural, artisan, mercantile, and administrative positions. In 1793 when there was an attempt at a count of the population, 70,000 *peninsulares* (Spaniards born in Europe) and 1,024,000 *creoles* (Spaniards born in Mexico) lived in New Spain along with 1,231,000 *mestizos*, those of mixed Indian and European ancestry who usually worked at the lower edges of the occupational hierarchy.

Large numbers of enslaved Africans—perhaps as many as 200,000 during the entire colonial period—arrived too, albeit against their will. They came as auxiliaries to Spaniards in the first stages of conquest and colonization, occupying intermediate positions between Spaniards and Indians. They worked as foremen and artisans, helping to build the new society. As sugar plantations developed, more slaves worked in the tropical coastal regions and lowland valleys. Never large, the African population mixed with the Spanish and Indian, forming the Mexican mulatto population. On the eve of independence in 1810, the colony had a mulatto (*Afromestizo*) population of 624,461, but it had only about 10,000 blacks.

Other races and ethnic groups also came. Asians arrived with the Manila Galleons on their return trip from the Philippines. Some non-Spanish Europeans slipped in but never in numbers large enough to influence the ethnic and cultural contours of society. Spanish policy was exclusive and restrictive, favoring Spaniards above all others. It was generally very successful. Spain never had to resort to the policies of France and England of promising land as an incentive or sending criminals and indentured servants to colonize New Spain.

After Indians and mestizos, Spaniards were always the most numerous group in colonial Mexico. They mixed with but remained separate by culture and social position from Indians, Africans, and mestizos, enjoying privileges of rank not granted to other groups. From the earliest years of settlement, a hierarchy based on race and culture divided the colony.

New France

Far fewer immigrants went to New France, despite the efforts of French mercantilist policies. By 1759 only 8,527 had arrived, and over 1,700 of them had come in the previous ten years. New France offered some of the harshest conditions in all of North America, discouraging immigrants from selecting it as their new home. Of those who did decide to go, most were single young men from northwestern France. Since only about one-sixth of the immigrants were women, France sponsored special trips for women, paying their transport and at times their dowries. Called the *filles du roi* (the daughters of the king), they were marriageable women who came from many different backgrounds. This and other population schemes had limited success, leaving Quebec always on the periphery of empire, less important to France and less attractive for immigrants than the French possessions in the Caribbean. Very simply, sugar plantations promised more opportunities for wealth and a desirable life style than the fur trade in Quebec. At the time of the fall of Quebec City to the British in 1759, New France still had a population of only about 70,000.

English Colonies

The founding of Jamestown initiated the movement of English settlers to the mid-Atlantic region of North America. Many of these came as indentured servants who agreed to work from four to eight years in return for passage and the promise of land. By 1688, the population of the 13 colonies had reached close to 200,000. These immigrants, whether free or indentured, established the English language, laws, and institutions that would prevail in the future. By the end of the seventeenth century, Dutch and German immigrants arrived in increasing numbers, followed by many Swiss, Irish, and Scandinavians. Always more open than the Spanish colonies to the south and more attractive than the French one to the north, the seaboard colonies experienced rapid population growth in the eighteenth century. By 1790, residents of English descent still predominated, but over 40 per cent (out of a total population of 3,929,625) of the population came from other areas. This contrasts with Canada, where only 8 per cent of the residents were non-English or non-French. The United States, more than its neighbors, was already a country of great ethnic, cultural, and linguistic diversity.

Slavery

Slavery was found throughout North America, but was concentrated in the Chesapeake Region, the southeastern United States, and the Gulf Coast of Mexico. Most deeply entrenched in the United States where it helped to define the social and economic life of the South, slavery gradually replaced the system of bound servitude that Africans first experienced in Virginia in 1619. The rise in tobacco and other plantation crops increased the demand for labor and gave rise to the slave trade. Influenced at different times by all the major colonial powers, the trade transported slaves from West Africa to ports as diverse as Veracruz (Mexico), Charleston (South Carolina), and Newport (Rhode Island). By 1790, 697,624 slaves lived in the United States, alongside of 59,557 free blacks, and 3,172,444 whites. Slavery continued to expand in the early nineteenth century, accompanying the rise of cotton across the southern United States and into Texas.

The U.S. Congress abolished the importation of slaves in 1808, but a substantial contraband trade continued. More important was the internal slave trade, which moved large numbers of slaves from the mid-Atlantic states to the new cotton lands in the South. By 1860 the slave population had grown to 3,953,760. It underpinned Southern society and would only be eradicated through war.

Mexico also had an enslaved African population, whose origins date to the early sixteenth century when they were brought by Spaniards to help in the settlement of Mexico. Africans participated in a wide range of economic activities in Mexico but gradually became concentrated in the plantations of the tropical coastal zones. In comparison to the United States, there was a stronger tendency for Africans to mix with European and Indian groups and more opportunities for manumission. These conditions, along with a decline in the slave trade, led to a decline in slavery just as it was expanding in the United States. In 1793, official counts listed only 6,100 blacks in Mexico, a very small number compared to the 369,790 mulattos listed in the same census.

In Canada, African slavery was economically and socially less significant than in the United States or Mexico, primarily a result of the lack of plantation economies. Indian slavery, however, was a frequent practice, especially among the French who called their slaves *panis*, after the Pawnee Indians whom they stereotyped as easier to control than other Indians.

Slavery, regardless of time, place, or extent, was never a static institution in North America. From the earliest years, *cimarrones*, or runaway Africans, challenged the system and went to the extent of creating their own communities. The most famous challenge to slavery was the Underground Railroad, a network of safe houses and way stations that transported slaves from southern to northern states and on to Canada. Most active between 1850 and 1860, the Underground Railroad helped to move thousands of slaves to Canada, which by that time was widely acknowledged as a refuge for escaped slaves.

Movement in the North

Two countercurrents of internal migration influenced the British and French possessions in the north. The process began with the Treaty of Utrecht (1713), which led to British control over most of Acadia. After the treaty, the Acadians, mainly French-speaking Roman Catholics, tried to maintain a position of neutrality and survive in the thumb of land between the French in Quebec and the British in New England. They were successful until the 1750s, when they were expelled. Known as *le grand dérangement*—the great exodus—the process lasted from 1755 to 1763, scattering 10,000 exiles throughout North America, some as far south as Louisiana. There they sank their culture deep into the swamps and bayous of the Gulf Coast, eventually becoming known as "Cajuns."

As the Acadians went south, British settlers went north. Britain offered an attractive colonization scheme, including land and the right to elect political representatives. The combination of Acadians moving south, thereby freeing land for new settlers, and attractive incentives offered by the British government prompted the movement of thousands of migrants north. With war and then independence in the United States, there was another outburst of northward migration. Many "Loyalists," or colonists who sided with Britain, opted to leave rather than change political allegiance. While the majority went to the Maritime provinces (30,000), about 10,000 migrated to Quebec, opting first for the commercial centers of Montreal and Quebec City and then the open lands to the south that would eventually become Upper Canada and then Ontario. The northern shores of Lakes Ontario and Erie were easily accessible to Loyalists and other immigrants coming from New York and Pennsylvania. By the time of the *Constitutional Act* of 1791, English-speaking settlers dominated the south. The decades immediately following the American Revolution witnessed an intense movement of loyalists and American settlers criss-crossing the political border that separated British North America and the newly independent U.S. republic. Commerce and economic security were common threads that linked the two groups despite differences in political allegiance.

The First Wave of Immigration

Historians often speak of "waves" of immigration, metaphorically emphasizing massive rises and falls in the numbers and origins of immigrants through time. The metaphor is a good one as long as it does not minimize the almost continuous stream of immigration that began with the first years of colonization. For simplicity, it is possible to think of three major waves of immigration after the independence of the United States, each succeeding one larger and more instrumental in changing the contours of society than the previous one. The first wave, unleashed by famine and political turmoil in Europe, lasted from the 1830s to the mid-1850s. German, Scandinavian, and especially Irish immigrants rode the crest of the wave. Famine years in Ireland began in 1817 and culminated in the Great Famine of 1845, driving many to seek refuge wherever they could. The total number of immigrants was staggering: 500,000 came in the 1830s, 1,500,000 in the 1840s, and 2,500,000 in the 1850s. They everywhere contributed to the growth of the economy, laboring in field and factory, building tunnels and canals, opening shops, cleaning streets, and settling new farm lands as far west as Wisconsin and Minnesota.

The Irish, in particular, faced difficulties in the new land. Arriving without money, often sick and poorly clothed, they struggled to survive, finding comfort and solidarity in their Roman Catholicism. Despite the obstacles, they, like so many immigrant groups before and after them, found jobs, built communities, and turned to politics to further their interests. Their increasing numbers and power triggered a reaction known as nativism, an anti-foreign sentiment that has periodically emerged in the United States. Based on a perception of U.S. culture as Protestant, English, and democratic, nativists lashed out at immigrants who differed from their perceived ideal. Organizations such as the Native American Association (1837), the Native American Party (1845), and the American (Know-Nothing) Party (1854) agitated to restrict the rights of Catholics and to limit immigration. Although no longer organizing political parties, nativists remain part of the political landscape in the United States.

Canada experienced a similar wave of immigration, only on a smaller scale. Before the middle of the century, most came from Ireland (upwards of 500,000 by the 1850s), slowly filling the cities and providing labor for the new industries. As in the United States, they worked in many different occupations and soon became a cultural and political force in their new homes. Also as in the United States, two groups of Irish immigrants came, Catholics and Protestants. In the case of Canada, still a British colony, the political divisions existing in Ireland were potentially more divisive than in the United States. Irish Protestants had less difficulty adjusting to the new land, since they shared a common political and often religious and cultural tradition with British Canada. In contrast, the Irish Catholics, insistent on an independent Ireland, provoked more fear and suspicion. Despite the cries of alarm directed toward the political and cultural threat of the Irish, they seldom reached the strident pitch of those in the United States. While the Irish predominated during this early wave, immigrants from many different lands arrived in both the United States and Canada.

Mexico and Texas

Mexico inherited a different past with a more restrictive social structure and immigration policy. Immigrants in the nineteenth century viewed Mexico as a less attractive opportunity than the United States, Canada, or countries in the far south of South America. The luster of Mexico as a land of great wealth and opportunity had long since tarnished. In the cities there was little work, the fault of delayed industrialization. Factories, railroads, and mines offered some new opportunities in the late nineteenth century but never to the same extent as in the United States and Canada. In the countryside, Indian communities and haciendas already claimed the best lands. Land policies tended to favor the large corporation, not the small homesteader. A few groups did arrive to fill narrow niches. About 300 Cornish miners followed British investors as early as 1824; French immigrants from the Barcelonette Valley founded a few communities; Spaniards who were expelled after independence soon returned to go into textile production. Despite efforts to attract immigrants, Mexico was unsuccessful. One count lists only 5,412 foreigners living in Mexico in 1852. In that same year, 371,603 immigrants arrived in the United States.

Mexico's one success was also its failure. It continued a policy of settling the northern frontier that had started in the seventeenth century and then gained momentum in the eighteenth. Colonization became imperative with the independence of the United States and its expansion westward. In 1821, just before the independence of Mexico, the Spanish government gave Moses Austin a grant of land for colonizing Texas. His son, Stephen F. Austin, continued and expanded the efforts. The old Spanish colonial provision of favoring the Catholic Church remained, and the charter specified that the immigrants be Catholic. A new colonization law opened Texas to even more immigrants, and in the late 1820s and early 1830s thousands poured in, turning the old mission communities into thriving towns. These new settlers remained culturally much closer to the United States than to Mexico and resisted the renewed efforts at Mexican centralization in the 1830s.

By 1830 much had changed. Mexico forbade the introduction of slaves into Texas and then closed it to immigration. Yet immigrants kept coming, and by 1835 there were 30,000 in Texas, compared to a local Mexican population of 7,800. Rebellion began in 1835, and by 1836 Mexico had lost Texas, a casualty of its failure to integrate the region into its new political structure. Despite the loss, Mexican culture survived in the new state, often forced to the margins of social and political life but always resilient in the face of efforts to suppress it.

The Second Wave of Immigration

The pace of immigration quickened in the late nineteenth century, leading to a second wave of immigration, larger and different in origins than the first. While Canada and Mexico continued to receive immigrants during this second wave, numerically speaking at least, the story reflects the growth of their middle neighbor. From 1865 to 1910, around 25 million immigrants selected the United States as their new home. Immigrants still came from the British Isles, Germany, and Scandinavia, but during the 1880s a shift occurred towards more immigration from the Mediterranean, Eastern Europe, Russia, and the Balkans. To give just a couple of examples: from 1810 to 1900, 1,040,479 Italians arrived in the United States; from 1900 to 1910, the number doubled to 2,045,877. During the same two time periods, the number of Austrian immigrants increased from 1,027,195 to 2,145,266; the number of Russians from 761,742 to 1,597,306; the number of Turks from 5,824 to 79,976. The numbers and origins of the new immigrants had a profound impact on the United States.

As before, immigrants provided the muscle for the continued economic expansion of the country. From the warehouses of Baltimore to the steel mills of Pittsburgh to the slaughterhouses of Chicago, the new immigrants worked to build a new life for themselves and at the same time influenced the communities in which they settled. It was this influence that provoked a reaction. Fear of the immigrant — of strange languages, religions, and appearances — triggered a reaction similar to the nativism of the pre-Civil War period.

Immigrants were soon identified with the social and economic problems of the cities. Unemployment, poverty, illiteracy, crime — all seemed rampant in the large cities in the United States. Critics pointed to immigrants with their different cultures as the culprits. For many, they represented a threat to the way of life of the country. Increasing concern over immigration erupted into racist and in some cases exclusionary policies in the late nineteenth century.

The reaction was first directed against those who appeared the most different.

Pressure against Chinese immigration began in the far west with their arrival to help build the transcontinental railroad in the 1850s and 1860s. Never welcomed, the Chinese worked and lived on the periphery, suffering hostility and discrimination. Legislation soon legalized the attitudes of hatred and finally culminated in the *Chinese Exclusion Act* of 1882 that prohibited Chinese laborers from entering the country (that same year a head tax of 50 cents was placed on all immigrants; it was raised to $4 in 1907). Variations of the law continued until 1943, when Chinese immigrants were again allowed into the country.

Japanese immigrants suffered a similar fate, only later. Japanese immigration began in earnest in the 1890s and peaked in 1910 as 129,797 arrived. By that year, hostility against the Japanese had already led to the "Gentlemen's Agreement" of 1907-08, whereby Japan agreed to stop the flow of immigrants. In the 1924 *Immigration Act*, Japanese immigrants were excluded from the United States.

Hostile sentiment against the new immigrant was widespread and led to growing local, state, and national measures. World War I provoked a particularly sharp reaction. Immigrants from enemy nations were no longer seen as simply an economic or cultural threat; they represented a potentially subversive force that might undermine the security of the United States. Feared most intently were the new ideologues of change, the communists and anarchists (usually associated with new immigrants from the Mediterranean or Russia) who sought to abolish government in violent fashion.

Legislation was now more encompassing. A 1917 literacy requirement gave immigration authorities wide discretion in determining who could read and thus qualify for admission. This was followed in 1921 by the *Emergency Quota Act*, which limited the number of immigrants to 3 per cent of the total number of that country in the United States according to the 1910 census. The maximum quota was 357,000. In 1924, the *National Origins Act* further restricted immigration, reducing the quota to 2 per cent of the total number registered in the 1890 census and reducing the maximum quota to 150,000. While this law did not go into effect until 1929, the door against the new immigrant had been shut. From a policy of encouraging immigration and depending on it for economic growth to a restrictive, discriminatory policy had taken less than 50 years.

Canada

Canada also experienced unprecedented increases in immigration during this period as a result of an aggressive policy of national expansion and integration. The National Policy had as one of its primary goals the peopling of the Prairies. By the end of the century, the government was actively recruiting immigrants and assisting their movement west. It had more success in the 1890s than before because land in the United States was less available, which encouraged more immigration to the open lands of Canada. The new immigrants came from many countries, but 88 per cent of Canadians still claimed French or British origins in 1901.

Canada clearly favored some immigrant groups over others. The most desirable came from the British Isles and the United States, then Western Europe, Eastern Europe, and the Mediterranean. Ethnically and culturally, it favored white Protestants and only reluctantly admitted Jews, Africans, and Asians. As in the United States, Asian immigration was most pronounced in the west, though many Chinese migrated east to work on the railroads. Nativism reared its head and led to policies and practices that restricted unwanted immigrants and made life uncomfortable for many who had already arrived. Canada initiated specific restrictive policies in 1884, when it levied a head tax on every Chinese immigrant. Later laws raised the tax and in 1923 eliminated Chinese immigration, a policy that remained in force until 1947.

The legacy of nativism made it easier for Canada to prompt discriminatory behavior against Germans during World War I. A law passed in 1917 actually disenfranchised some citizens who had been born in countries that were part of the Central Powers, who had spoken the language of that country, and who had not become a citizen of Canada before 1902. Germans suffered the most from these practices, and many left the country. One group of German Mennonites, about 6,000 strong, left their homes in Saskatchewan and Manitoba and migrated to Chihuahua, Mexico, where they established farming communities in the 1920s.

Mexico

Despite its efforts, Mexico attracted few immigrants during the period of Porfirio Díaz. Only 116,000 foreigners resided in Mexico in 1910, most coming from the United States, Spain, China, and Britain, and most living in the northern states, where they worked in the rapidly developing agriculture and mining sectors. Mexico always expressed ambivalence toward foreigners, recruiting them on the one hand and fearing and admonishing them on the other. By the outbreak of the Revolution of 1910, a strong anti-foreign sentiment ran through Mexico.

The Chinese experienced the harshest discrimination. The number of Chinese immigrants increased as the *Chinese Exclusion Act* in the United States diverted migration from there to Mexico. They settled in northwest Mexico, especially in Baja California and Sonora, where they worked in commercial enterprises, railroads, and mines. Sentiments against the Chinese and other immigrants intensified during the revolution and the 1920s, leading some states to pass segregation and anti-miscegenation laws. By 1927, 24,218 Chinese lived in the country, making them the second largest immigrant group after Spaniards. They suffered insults, the loss of property, beatings, and murder. The onset of the Great Depression resulted in heightened persecution and intense efforts to expel the Chinese from the country.

Spaniards during the 1930s enjoyed the opposite treatment. During the Spanish Civil War, President Lázaro Cárdenas of Mexico sent supplies and financial support to the Republicans (those who resisted the uprising led by General Francisco Franco). After their defeat, he supported their efforts to immigrate to Mexico. In

1939, 6,236 Spaniards (out of a total immigrant population of 7,097) immigrated to Mexico. The numbers declined in subsequent years, but refugees from the Spanish Civil War continued to arrive during the 1940s. Many of them became leading cultural and intellectual figures in Mexico.

Internal Changes

Two powerful movements, both with their origins deep in the past and both converging on the United States, gained momentum in the late nineteenth century. First was the movement of Mexicans north, which traces its origins to the seventeenth and eighteenth centuries when Spaniards settled in Texas, New Mexico, Arizona, and California. Second was the movement of French Canadians south, also with its origins in the seventeenth and eighteenth centuries. Strong historical and cultural ties, not to mention the search for economic security, encouraged these French Canadians to migrate to territory within the United States. There was continual movement both ways across the long stretch of the U.S.-Canada border. Some progressive-minded politicians recognized the connections. Henry Cabot Lodge, a U.S. senator from Massachusetts, remarked in 1908 that French Canadians "are hardly to be classed as immigrants in the accepted sense. They represent one of the oldest settlements on this continent. They have been, in the broad sense, Americans for generations, and their coming to the United States is merely a movement of Americans across an imaginary line, from one part of America to another" (Robitaille 1941, 265). Many did not agree, and French Canadians and Mexicans often experienced as harsh a reaction as any other immigrant group.

Mexico's loss of much of its north to the United States did not stop the migration. Just the opposite occurred, as more and more Mexicans sought opportunity and refuge in the north, imprinting a Hispanic stamp on the region that survived later overlays of northern European immigration. Traditional push and pull factors were at work. Overpopulation, unemployment, and political repression, combined with the convenience of location and accessibility, the cultural similarity, and the opportunity for work pushed Mexicans to look to the north. They found work in the railroads (the largest early employer), the expanding factories, and the emerging agricultural regions of the Rio Grande Valley of Texas and the Imperial and San Joaquin Valleys of California. Estimates suggest that up to 1 million Mexican immigrants lived in the United States in 1930.

The cultural complexity of the region increased as the new arrivals built on and around what was already there. In California, the old *californios*, descendants of early Spanish immigrants, were overwhelmed by the new arrivals. In New Mexico, the *hispanos* survived and strengthened their culture. In Texas, where the most intense early immigration occurred, the *tejanos* accommodated and adapted to the new waves of immigration from the south. All Spanish-heritage groups experienced discrimination and racism and were unable to take their cultural survival for granted.

Despite resistance, the preservation of Mexican culture was assured along the border by 1900. Organizations such as the *Sociedad México-Tejano* strengthened the commitment to cultural preservation. More important was the continual movement back and forth across the border until the Great Depression of the 1930s, when widespread unemployment prompted the U.S. government to force some 400,000 Mexicans to return to Mexico between 1929 and 1937. Lives were disrupted, but Mexican culture remained strong along the border.

The second major internal movement involved the immigration of 700,000 to 1 million French Canadians to the United States between 1850 and 1930. The population of Quebec had expanded rapidly in the nineteenth century, leading to exhaustion of the narrow stretch of soil along the St. Lawrence River. Decreasing opportunities at home were offset by the rapid rise of the textile industry in New England and the demand for workers. The migration to New England was so extensive that some towns took on decidedly French characteristics. Newspapers, clubs, and churches expressed and reaffirmed the culture of Quebec. Cultural preservation societies such as the *Union Saint-Jean-Baptiste d'Amérique* insured that French was spoken and traditional customs maintained. They were similar to the tejano societies in providing a bridge to the homeland.

The strength and extent of the Quebec presence in New England provoked a reaction. A widely quoted editorial in *The New York Times* warned that:

> Quebec is transferred bodily to Manchester and Fall River and Lowell. Not only does the French curé follow the French peasantry to their new homes, but he takes with him the parish church, the ample clerical residence, the convent for the sisters, and the parochial school for the education of the children. He also perpetuates the French ideas and aspirations through the French language, and places all the obstacles possible in the way of assimilation of these people to our American life and thought. There is something still more important in this transplantation. These people are in New England as an organized body, whose motto is *Notre religion, notre langue, et nos moeurs* [Our religion, our language, and our customs]. This body is ruled by a principle directly opposite to that which has made New England what it is. (*The New York Times*, 6 June 1892)

The Québécois also had deep fears, only in their case directed at the growing strength of the United States. Politicians and journalists such as Henri Bourassa put it best when they worried about the "universal contagion of American ideals, morals and mentality" that undermined traditional life in Quebec (Lanctot 1941, 299).

With the onset of the Great Depression, the Canadians were treated like the Mexicans and sent home in large numbers. Even before then, many had returned home, encouraged by a provincial government that saw their importance in defending Quebec culture against the increasing strength of Anglo Canada. These reversals did not interrupt the pattern of Mexican and Canadian immigration that had been firmly established during the early decades of the century. By the 1930s, all Canadians represented one-third of the total number of immigrants to the United States.

World War II

As millions of men and women joined the war effort, either in the armed forces or the war industries, the demand for labor increased. The United States looked south again and recruited *braceros* (laborers) through a program that lasted with variations from 1942 to 1964. Braceros were Mexican workers who came under special provisions to work in agriculture and the railroads, usually with contracts that guaranteed wages comparable to those received by U.S. citizens in the same jobs. About 4.6 million Mexicans entered the United States during this period, while about 5 million were returned as illegal immigrants. "Operation Wetback" was the most notorious repatriation program, when well over 1 million workers were returned to Mexico in 1954 and 1955.

Texas, because of its reputation for mistreating Mexicans, did not receive bracero workers. Yet it was not Texas but California that had the most widely publicized incident involving Mexicans during the war years. Mexican youths known as *pachucos* formed gangs. When the gangs clashed, then as now, they made the news. The pachucos were easily distinguishable because of their attire, the "zoot suits." A well-dressed zoot-suiter wore a broad brimmed hat, a tee-shirt, a droopy jacket with wide shoulders, and the characteristic ballooning pants that bunched at the ankles. In 1943 a clash between pachucos in zoot suits and military service men in Los Angeles was depicted as a riot, causing increased fear of Mexican immigrants. While national attention was riveted on the so-called riots, 250,000 Mexicans were serving in the U.S. armed forces to support the war effort, 1,000 of whom received the Purple Heart.

The Japanese faced a more intense and focused form of discrimination during World War II. Between 1942 and 1944, 117,000 Japanese and their descendants, about two-thirds of them U.S. citizens, were forced into retention camps, often in the mountain states of the west. The specific order said that anyone with one-eighth Japanese ancestry was subject to removal. Many Japanese immigrants, unlike the Chinese, had turned to the land and become successful farmers, growing fruits and vegetables for the expanding urban markets of the west coast. As a result of the internment, they often lost their land and property. The Japanese were casualties of the war and of the intense anti-Asian attitudes that had grown with increased Asian immigration.

Canada and Mexico took similar actions, making anti-Asian discrimination continental in scope. Mexico acted the quickest of all three countries, ordering the removal of Japanese from coastal areas on 11 December 1941, only four days after the Japanese attack on Pearl Harbor. Building on the discrimination directed at the Japanese and on fears of a coastal invasion, both countries forced persons of Japanese origin, whether citizens or not, into camps away from the coast. They had the same difficulty in regaining their property as the Japanese in the United States.

Canada and Mexico also interned Germans and Italians, essentially treating them the same as the Japanese. The United States only interred Japanese, leading to the argument that it was motivated more by racism than by security interests.

The Third Wave of Immigration

Several global processes interacted to create a third wave of immigration after World War II. The war itself caused massive dislocations, sending refugees to wherever they could find a home. After the war, the clash between the United States and the Soviet Union created a climate of global political instability. The Korean War (1950-53) and the Vietnam War (1954-73) produced unrest that sent large numbers of refugees to the United States. The *Refugee Relief Act* of 1953 began the process, providing 209,000 special visas beyond the number normally allotted by immigration legislation. Generally speaking, however, changes in postwar immigration policy in the United States were contested in a variety of ways and from a variety of view points, including big labor, race, competing models of economic development, and Cold War politics.

In the new nation-states in Africa and Asia, internal struggles for political and economic power also created instability and added to the flow of immigration. The same struggles occurred in Latin America. Wars in El Salvador and Nicaragua were the longest and most violent, but many Latin American nations experienced prolonged crises through the 1980s. Authoritarian regimes and warring factions, whether professing communism or democracy, drove millions into exile. All occurred against a backdrop of a rapidly increasing global population and unprecedented expectations for economic and social change. For those facing poverty and repression, the United States and Canada, as in the past, represented an opportunity to create a new future. Thus, millions became a part of the third wave that is still transforming the face of North America.

Legal changes allowed for the third wave. In the United States, the old *National Origins Act* gave way to the *Immigration and Nationality Act* of 1965 (implemented 1968). It imposed a ceiling of 170,000 immigrants from countries outside of the Western Hemisphere, with a maximum of 20,000 from any one country; from within the Americas, it allowed up to 120,000 immigrants. The new law eliminated the quotas of the old system, allowing Asians and Africans equal footing with Europeans in applying for admission. In 1965, 90 per cent of immigrants came from Europe; in 1985, that had dropped to 10 per cent. A new *Immigration Act*, passed in 1990, lifted the ceiling to 700,000 for three years and then dropped it to 675,000.

Hispanics and Asians represented much of the new immigration. Hispanic, a controversial term used by the government to describe Spanish-speaking peoples living in the United States, hides great complexity and cultural diversity. Some activists and scholars prefer the term *latino* because it implies a cultural affinity to Latin America. Mexicans, Cubans, Puerto Ricans, El Salvadoreans, and Nicaraguans are all Hispanic or Latino. They share a common language, but their cultural and historical backgrounds are often very different. Mexicans formed the largest immigrant group, followed by Puerto Ricans and Cubans. Cuban immigration was the most recent. Under the Cuban Refugee Program, hundreds of thousands immigrated after 1961. In 1980, the Mariel boatlift brought 125,000 more, many of them emptied from Cuban prisons. By 1990, the population of Cuban origin or descent numbered around 1 million, most of them living in southern Florida.

The number of Hispanics living in the United States jumped from 3 million in 1960 to almost 40 million in 2003. More than one in eight people living in the United States are of Hispanic origins, making Hispanics the largest ethnic minority. The numbers do not include the very substantial undocumented Hispanic immigrant population living in the United States. Estimates in 2006 generally suggest that there are between 10 and 12 million undocumented immigrants, most of them coming from Mexico (57 per cent of the total) as well as from El Salvador, Guatemala, Canada, and Haiti. As the number of undocumented workers grew in the 1980s, so did concern over their social and economic impact. The result was the *Immigration Reform and Control Act* of 1986, a complicated piece of legislation that granted amnesty and the possibility of legal residence to illegal immigrants who had been in the country since 1982. Its most important provision called for sanctions against employers who hired undocumented immigrants. In effect, employers now had responsibility for enforcing immigration law. The result of the act was that 3 million illegal residents applied for legal status. Employee sanctions, however, did not work, and the flow of undocumented workers continued. California again led the way in attempting to restrict immigration with Proposition 187, passed in 1994. It restricted undocumented workers from attending school and from receiving all but emergency health care services. The legality of the proposition was tested in the courts, leaving the question of undocumented immigrants as one of the unresolved political questions of the twenty-first century.

The massive protests in favor of immigration reform that broke out throughout the United States in early 2006 suggest that undocumented workers are embracing activism and protest as a way to blunt the anti-immigrant bashing that takes place in certain political and social sectors. Each chamber of the U.S. Congress has its own particular view of the issue, with the House of Representatives seeking to curtail immigration and declare illegal border crossings a felony, while the Senate favors a guest-worker program and the gradual legalization of undocumented workers. Security concerns in light of 9/11, however, have stalled the passage of substantial immigration reform despite efforts by President George W. Bush to prod the Congress into action. In 2006, the Congress passed legislation, with President Bush's signature, that mandates the construction of a wall to prevent Mexican workers from crossing the border without valid papers. Although the measure passed during the 2006 mid-term election campaign, when incumbents wanted to take a hard stand on undocumented workers, the legislation remains unfunded. The standard political cartoon in U.S. newspapers shows Mexican workers coming across the border to build the fence, while U.S. Border Patrol agents, dressed in uniforms made in Mexico, stand aside.

Asian immigration has also increased rapidly in recent years, more than doubling from 1.5 per cent of the total population in 1980 to 3.6 per cent (10.2 million) in 1995. Along with large numbers of Chinese and Japanese, came Korean, Vietnamese, Cambodian, Thai, and Indian immigrants, each with their own language and history. No longer isolated and confined to "Chinatowns" and "Little Tokyos," Asian immigrants increasingly have made important contributions to the political and cultural life of the United States.

Canada also accepted the third wave of immigrants by dropping most of its restrictive and quota policies. In the new *Immigration Act* of 1976 (implemented in 1978), it spelled out its immigration objectives, stressing economic development, family reunification, and refugee assistance. There was, however, a particularly Canadian twist to the policy since the provinces and the federal government had a dual responsibility for immigration. Quebec was the first province (1968) to form its own Department for Immigration, later called the Department of Cultural Communities and Immigration. It sought French-speaking immigrants and helped to integrate the arrivals into the Quebec community. Immigration, in other words, had the specific objective of widening the French language base and strengthening the political unity of the province. In the recent past, Canada has maintained a nondiscriminatory immigration policy, drawing about one-third of its immigrants from the Americas, another third from Europe, and another third from Africa and Asia. In this new wave, China has played the lead role. In 2005, immigrants from China accounted for 16 per cent of new immigrants to Canada and 33 per cent of Canada's top Asian source countries. Immigration from India, Canada's second largest source country since 1995, increased 30 per cent from 2004. The Philippines continued to be the third largest source of immigrants in 2005, increasing 32 per cent from the previous year. In the census of 2001, 13.4 per cent of Canadian residents declared an Asian, African, or Latin American background, which still leaves Canada primarily a country of European origins despite its progressive immigration policy.

A national poll commissioned in 2007 by Citizenship and Immigration Canada, the administrative arm of the Canadian government's immigration policy, revealed, however, just how nuanced the immigration debate has become in that country. Among those who were polled, a majority of Canadians believed that the deportation of any immigrant whose visa had expired or who had entered the country illegally was acceptable policy. Nearly two-thirds of the respondents expressed negative sentiment toward those immigrants who flouted Canadian immigration laws. A slight majority also believed that the presence of family members in Canada would not alter their feelings about the deportation of immigrants who had over-stayed their visas. On the other hand, the survey showed that Canadians identified many positive aspects of immigration, including cultural diversity and an increase in skilled laborers. Those polled also pointed to the negative dimensions of immigration, particularly the spread of cultural enclaves throughout Canada with little effort to integrate fully into society.

Mexico also experienced the third wave as refugees struggled through the mountainous regions of the deep south. Fleeing civil unrest in Guatemala, El Salvador, and Honduras in the 1970s and 1980s, hundreds of thousands came to settle in Mexico or to head north to the United States. Estimates suggested that the total Central American population in Mexico in 1990 was as high as 400,000. In an effort to stem the flow of refugees, the Mexican government deported 110,000 residents to Central America from 1988 to 1989. Evidence also suggests that Mexico joined with the United States in "Operation Hold the Line" to stop Central Americans from illegally entering the United States. With few exceptions, the number of deportations has steadily increased each year since the 1990s. In 2004 and 2005, for example, the yearly average exceeded 200,000, although the figure reflects only those who failed to make it to the United States and perhaps were deported from Mexico on multiple occasions.

Mexico also attracts residents from the United States, mainly retirees looking to stretch their pensions. Most live in the coastal communities of Baja California or in the interior cities of Guadalajara, San Miguel de Allende, and Cuernavaca. Attracted by climate, surroundings, and low prices, an estimated 150,000-200,000 U.S. citizens were living in Mexico in 2005.

Interpretations

Supporters and detractors argue over the impact of immigration on social, economic, and political life. Recent discussions in the United States have been particularly heated and are related to interpretations of multiculturalism and the future of the nation. In a photographic essay published in 1945, Wallace Stegner summarized the traditional viewpoint in the United States:

> The problem of the populations of America, the problem of making one nation from the many races and creeds and kinds, one culture from all the European, Indian, African, and Asiatic cultures that the promise of freedom has drawn to our shores, comes to a head in our time. Its solution is the absolutely essential first step of a process which is historically inevitable, but which can be materially hastened by the efforts of any American with the imagination and the good will to work at it. (Stegner 1945, 15)

"One nation" and "one culture" out of many has long been the ideal in the United States. The notion of the "melting pot"—the mixing and blending of diverse cultures to create a new culture—best represents traditional thinking. This was expressed in the political ideology that guided the independence movement and the foundation of the republic. Rather than a nation built on preference and privilege, the United States would emphasize equality before the law and the opportunity for social and economic progress for all people. As new immigrants arrived, they made their own contributions to the melting pot, but they also assimilated the basic beliefs and values of the dominant culture.

Proponents of the view of assimilation gave a twist to the melting pot idea. Not all cultures contributed evenly to the new culture. Instead they accepted (or should accept) the base culture established by English immigration in the seventeenth and eighteenth centuries. Later immigrants became "Americanized," giving up their language and customs to participate as quickly and fully as they could in the new society. This was the belief that long held sway in the United States.

Challenges to the interpretations of the melting pot and assimilation began in earnest during the 1960s. American Indians, African Americans, and Hispanics, all residents of the country for a long time, defied the idea of the melting pot, arguing that it had always excluded them. They argued that the dominant Anglo culture had used the melting pot as a method of manipulating and controlling the less powerful in the country. The third wave of immigration after World War II contributed to the new emphasis on cultural distinctiveness and preservation. Many of the new immigrants refused to relinquish their culture and instead demanded policies that protected it. The result has been an increasing recognition of the uniqueness and value of the different cultures that exist in the United States. Terms such as cultural pluralism, cultural mosaic, and multiculturalism express the reality of a more heterogeneous country.

The implications of cultural pluralism in the United States are not entirely clear. The language issue is an example. Cultures maintain their strength through continued use of language. Immigrants, whether speaking Spanish, Thai, or Farsi, have the right to use that language. Does that right extend to the schools, workplace, and government? The wide-ranging debate on the "English-language only" movement does not yield a clear answer. At another level, there is growing fear over the "Balkanization" of the United States and the threat of the tribal-like violence that has engulfed the region of the ex-Soviet Union and parts of Eastern Europe, Africa, and the Middle East. Alarmists point to this disintegration and fear the same in the United States. Those who wish can carry the argument further and foresee a threat to the survival of the country as immigrant groups, especially Hispanics in the southwest, dominate counties, states, and entire regions. The fear is that culture, language, and ethnicity will lead to demands for political autonomy.

The perspective of numbers is useful in this context. Despite the rhetoric and fear, the United States in 2000 was still 75 per cent white (not including Hispanics), though this was down from 80 per cent in 1980. It was also still an overwhelmingly English-speaking one, though the number of non-English speaking residents increased from 14 per cent to 18 per cent of the total population over five years of age from 1990 to 2000. The largest number spoke Spanish (29.1 million), representing a 60 per cent increase from 1990. Many other languages (Mon-Khmer, Miao, Syriac, French Creole, to mention just a few), however, have increased as fast as the more common languages, such as Spanish, Chinese, Korean, Vietnamese, or Arabic. All reflect the shifts in immigration patterns that began with the third wave.

Canada is different. Historical interpretations emphasize the importance of the English and French traditions. There were two founding cultures, not one. The different languages, laws, and cultures of the English and the French became a part of the practices and policies of Canada. Canada has in this context always been bicultural. Respondents to the 2001 census were allowed to choose any ethnic category that applied, however, and many people chose several ethnic groups. The most popular choice was "Canadian," which represented 39.4 per cent of the respondents, while 20 per cent chose English and 15.7 per cent chose French. Since the 1960s, multiculturalism has slowly eroded Canada's bicultural policy.

Multiculturalism owes its origins to the new immigration after World War II and also in an indirect way to the official bicultural policy of Canada. The 1963 Royal Commission on Bilingualism and Biculturalism confirmed the dual nature of Canadian society and explored ways for the peaceful coexistence of these groups. Quebec had little interest in biculturalism within the province, insisting instead on the French language as a method of assuring its distinctiveness. In the hopes of easing the political crisis emerging over cultural issues, the *Official Languages Act* of 1969 proclaimed English and French as the languages of Canada and recognized the rights of minority language communities. As the previous discussion of Quebec politics made clear, the act did not resolve the language issues for Quebec or the nation. The increasing number of immigrants who spoke neither English nor French found little solace in the act. As new immigrants arrived, they challenged "monoculturalism" in Quebec and the official bicultural policy of Canada, demanding in its place a broader policy of multiculturalism. In 1971, the federal government endorsed a national multicultural policy that recognized and supported the many different ethnic communities in Canada, not just the French and English. Controversial from the beginning, the new multicultural emphasis nevertheless signaled that Canada had moved far beyond the binational ideas of earlier years. Canada has not yet solved all of the problems springing from multiculturalism, but many observers argue that it has made more progress than the United States.

Mexico's historical experience led in another direction. Recent demands for recognition of Indian cultures have created an interest in a certain type of multiculturalism; fusion, however, and not separation has characterized Mexican history. Biologically and culturally there has been a greater fusion of Indians, Europeans, and Africans than in the United States and Canada. The result was the emergence of the mestizo. Recent estimates assert that 70-80 per cent of the Mexican population is mestizo. Once relegated to a position of cultural and biological inferiority, the mestizo was elevated in the twentieth century to the "Cosmic Race," combining the best of all the contributing races and offering a solution to the cultural and racial problems of the world. Popularized by José Vasconcelos, the concept of the "Cosmic Race" can be seen as a metaphor for what is happening in North America. The sociologist James W. Russell in his study *After the Fifth Sun* perceptively emphasized that the largest minority in North America is not one racial type but a mixture of the four major racial groups.

Language politics underscore the cultural consensus in Mexico. While there is increasing agitation for recognition and support of indigenous languages, there is agreement that Spanish is the national language. When Mexico hosted the "First International Congress of the Spanish Language" in 1997, participants expressed concerns over the purity of the language, not over its primacy. Academics and government officials in central Mexico have long criticized the infusion of English words and the creation of new ones, referred to as "Spanglish" along the northern border. Like English-language only advocates in the United States, some defenders of Spanish in Mexico worry about the political implications of the "degeneration" of the national language.

Despite the mixture of races and cultures, group identity has increased rather than decreased in North America. The third wave of immigration, the demands of indigenous groups and African Americans, and the general reaction to the standardization of urban industrial life have all helped to strengthen racial and ethnic identification. As the twenty-first century unfolds, citizens and residents in all three countries of North America continue to search for cultural paradigms that respect diversity and at the same time strengthen national unity. Moreover, immigration in the post-World War II period contributed to the regional identities noted in Chapter 3. The ebb and flow of peoples, goods, and services from the Pacific Rim, for example, created a strong Asian presence in the northwestern U.S. and southwestern Canadian corridors that took many forms, including urban and rural laborers, investment capital, and technology transfers. In the Canadian context, these regional identities will become more complex and less predictable in terms of the traditional perceptions of Canadian integration, especially as this third wave of immigration continues from the Pacific Rim and South Asia. In its *Annual Report to Parliament on Immigration* in 2007, the Ministry of Citizenship and Immigration plans to integrate at least 250,000 immigrants, investing $1.3 billion (Canadian) over a five-year period to help settle these newcomers and $342 million each year thereafter to ensure their formal integration into Canadian society.

In the context of U.S.-Mexico relations, the debate remains contentious and rancorous, with proponents of immigration emphasizing the benefits while opponents stress the security risks and economic costs. Neither Mexico nor the United States, the two countries in North America affected most by immigration, are candid about its structural causes. Mexico tends to put the blame on the ever-increasing demand in the United States for labor to satisfy U.S. consumer needs, while the United States points to wide-spread corruption and economic inefficiency in the Mexican system. Both arguments contain kernels of truth, of course, but so long as Mexicans perceive an economic benefit to coming north, with or without the appropriate paperwork, the 1,900-mile border will remain but a brief stumbling block in their efforts to secure their physical livelihood and that of their families. Fence or no fence, wall or no wall, Mexicans will continue to come to the United States, and U.S. companies will continue to find ways to hire them, notwithstanding efforts underway in various states (Arizona, Oklahoma, Missouri, to name just a few) to crack down on undocumented workers. In 2007 alone, 43 states passed 182 laws related to immigration, most of which restrict access to public benefits and housing, penalize employers, and compete with federal immigration laws. State governments point to federal inertia on the issue to support the frenetic pace of legislation.

If recent events and political commentary are indicative of patterns in government policy, the United States will try to structure the immigration debate around its post-9/11 security concerns. Canada will increase efforts to attract skilled workers to meet the growing needs of its diversified economy, and Mexico will continue its historical struggle to create sufficient employment opportunities at home while defending the rights and dignity of those who have crossed the international border in search of economic security.

CHAPTER 8
LABOR AND CLASS

L abor relationships evolve from cultural practices and economic transformations. In North America during the early years of settlement, natural resources and the size of the Indian population helped to determine the type of economic activities undertaken, which in turn provided the context for the type of work available and the way in which workers interacted with the owners of the resources. With the advent of industrialization, social and class relationships entered a new era dominated by the rise of labor organizations, big business, and strong flows of investment capital. The strength and vitality of labor unions, usually the result of decades of struggle, were challenged by new technological and managerial changes in the late twentieth and early twenty-first centuries.

Interestingly enough, despite the emergence of political borders and national identities in the modern history of North America, working-class ideologies, forged as they often were by immigrants bringing new ideas with them, had a transnational rhythm that followed the flows of investment capital across international boundaries. Labor and capital, therefore, shared something in common: urban and rural workers in Canada, Mexico, and the United States confronted the rapid expansion of the capitalist model of economic development with a series of strategies that included organizing workers, the use of strikes, negotiation, and accommodation, not to mention violent resistance. To be sure, while specific events reflected local circumstances mixed with national concerns, we can still discern a broader continental sensibility to labor issues and class consciousness. As this chapter shows, labor and class reflect the many ways that convergence and divergence have shaped North America.

Colonial and Rural Labor

Labor and Conquest

From the beginning, New Spain differed from its northern neighbors because of the size and density of the Indian population. As mentioned in Chapter 6, some estimates of the population run as high as 25-30 million. Even if just half that size, the population represented a large, concentrated labor pool for Spaniards. They built their empire on the backs of Indian labor, just as the Aztecs had done before them.

Labor relations reflected conquest society. The first arrivals had control over the largest Indians groups and used this control to enhance their economic, political, and social position. They used the *encomienda* and *repartimiento* with particular skill. The encomienda granted Spaniards the right to exact labor and tribute from Indians. It built on earlier patterns of dominance that extended back to the reconquest of Spain from the Muslims, when Spanish lords received the right to control newly reconquered lands and take labor and tribute from the conquered. The Aztecs before the Spaniards also had compulsory practices that forced subjugated peoples to provide labor and tribute to their masters. With these antecedents, the encomienda spread quickly in densely populated central areas, offering an ideal instrument for a few colonists to realize their aristocratic pretensions.

As the Indian population declined and the Spanish population increased, new demands for labor arose, eventually leading to the decline of the encomienda. In its place came the repartimiento, another forced labor arrangement. The repartimiento required a percentage of male residents of villages to join labor teams for several weeks a year. Widely practiced in the late sixteenth and seventeenth centuries, the repartimiento provided labor for cities, farms, and mines.

Concomitant with these formal labor systems were informal ones. Most emphasized but still not entirely understood is debt peonage, a practice whereby workers, usually rural laborers known as *peones*, entered into contracts with employers. The employers advanced wages to the workers, who became trapped in a cycle of indebtedness that was at times passed on to the next generation. Exactly how this system worked varied from region to region and time period to time period. Where there was a scarcity of labor, in the north of Mexico for example, the bargaining position of labor was stronger than in the center and south with its dense Indian populations. The point deserves emphasis. While general conditions of servitude prevailed in rural labor arrangements, there was diversity and variation. Free contract laborers, small and medium-sized property owners, workers on community lands, renters, lessees, day laborers, and many others tilled the soil of rural Mexico.

This complexity was matched in urban Mexico. Compared to the English and French colonies, Mexico was an urban land replete with cathedrals, government palaces, large residences, factories, and shops. This was also true before the conquest. In Tenochtitlán alone, with its vast population, residents labored at hundreds of different occupations, many of them such as the feather workers and chocolate makers which were exotic to Europeans. When Spaniards arrived, they added their own occupational complexity to that of the Indians. The conquistadores were essentially colonists who worked as bakers, tailors, coopers, silversmiths, hatters, at hundreds of other occupations.

Although Mexico was then a land of great complexity, this complexity seldom translated into openness and opportunity. Each occupation conveyed status and position in society. Indians, blacks, and mestizos usually occupied the lowest rungs of the occupational ladder, relegated to positions of inferiority. Even in the guilds the same racial hierarchy prevailed. There were always exceptions, but labor arrangements in Mexico emphasized subordination, dependency, and control, all of which hindered the emergence of an independent labor force.

Labor in the Northern Forests

New France lacked the economic and cultural diversity of Mexico. From the beginning, it was on the periphery of European colonization in North America, dependent for its livelihood on fishing, furs, and forestry. Trapping and trading more than any other activity gave identity to the early colony. The *coureurs de bois*, called "wood-runners" by the English and "bush-lopers" by the Dutch, often followed well-established Indian trading routes, traveling into the interior of the continent to obtain furs and then trading them to merchant companies in Montreal. As the trade became more competitive and restricted, the *voyageur* appeared. He was the trader who had specific contracts with Montreal merchants; in the eighteenth century, the term came to include the merchant capitalist as well as the adventurer trading with the Indians. The coureurs de bois and voyageur are the stuff of legend in Canadian history, providing inspiration for generations of poets and artists.

Another colorful worker in Quebec was the *draveur* or woodsman, who continued his dangerous work into the twentieth century. Woodsmen went into the forest in late autumn before the heavy snows, spent the winter felling and preparing trees, and then with the spring thaws rode the logs down the rivers to the mills. Without doubt it was one of the most dangerous occupations in North America, one that bred a unique culture and folklore, much like that of the coureur de bois.

The small agricultural communities along the St. Lawrence River provided the staples for the early colony. Peasant farmers, first known as *censitaires* (a term that originally referred to the one-one hundredth of the crop that was given as the tithe) and then later simply as *habitants*, gradually acquired ownership of the land. As part of their responsibilities, the farmers had to pay yearly dues to the feudal lord. They also participated in the *corvée*, a system of forced labor that helped to build the roads and bridges vital to the economy and defense of the regime. The corvée grew out of the feudal tradition in France where the lord had the right to exact labor and tribute from the peasant. In this sense it was similar to the Mexican repartimiento. It differed in its less onerous labor demands (only about two days a year) and in the lack of social stigma associated with it. The habitants, ethnically and culturally French, enjoyed many rights and privileges in the new society in contrast to Mexican repartimiento workers, members of a subordinate, racially different group relegated to an inferior position in society. Slaves, indentured servants, and convict laborers also lived in New France, but they were numerically much less important than in the English and Spanish colonies.

As the colony grew, led by the cities of Montreal and Quebec, the range of occupations broadened. Merchants, bureaucrats, clergy, and artisans became familiar members of society. Quebec was never as simple or as undeveloped as it has often been portrayed. It had its dynamic, entrepreneurial elements that contributed to and benefited from the Atlantic economy. It never, though, reached the same level of economic complexity as the Spanish and English colonies. Location and a small population held it back.

Labor Along the Seaboard

The first settlers in Jamestown in 1607 and Plymouth in 1620 came as workers and as shareholders in the companies that brought them. Through shareholding they expected to profit when the companies were dissolved and the proceeds distributed. Soon they acquired rights to the land that they worked and the ability to profit directly from their labor, with no obligations comparable to the censitaires in Quebec. Thus was born a tradition that came to characterize the English colonies — the small, independent freeholder working to better himself and his family.

For most early workers the desire to own land or to work on their own account was not easily realized. They volunteered as indentured servants, bound under contract to work for an employer for several years in return for passage and future opportunities. Some estimates put the number of voluntary servants as high as 75 per cent of total immigration before 1776. Involuntary workers also came. Forced to work to pay off their sentence, many were hardened criminals, sentenced to death. Contract labor continued through much of the nineteenth century as many workers were lured to the United States with prepaid passages and then forced to repay the costs through payroll deductions. This type of contract labor was finally eliminated in 1885.

As discussed in the chapter on immigration, African slavery soon became the most pervasive form of bound labor in the southern colonies. Initially, small numbers of slaves worked alongside indentured servants and free workers. While most were field hands, there were always many skilled slaves who worked at different occupations. From its modest beginnings in the seventeenth century in the Chesapeake Bay region, slavery expanded rapidly as plantation agriculture spread across the south. Rice, tobacco, indigo, sugar cane, and above all cotton depended on slave labor. As cotton spread across the South, slavery became entrenched in Alabama, Mississippi, Louisiana, and East Texas. By the 1850s cotton was king, as the South produced 60 per cent of the world supply of cotton. Cotton supported the local economies, provided fiber for the expanding textile industry of New England, and was the major export item of the United States. Upper-class white society in the South depended on African slaves to work the cotton fields and run the household.

The social system of the South was as dependent on slavery as the economic system. At the top, a small group of planters, owning 20 slaves and more, exerted the most influence on society. They owned the largest estates and controlled the most wealth. They used their power to influence the political system at the local and national level. Their principal objective was to insure favorable prices for their products and to maintain the slave system. Beneath the planter class, the owners of medium and small farms also hoped to own slaves, but most of them did not. Only about 25 per cent of landowners had the resources to buy slaves. Most nevertheless (along with many northerners) believed in the inferiority of African Americans and helped to perpetuate the slave system.

The Other Side of Rural Labor

Images of the yeoman farmer contrast with the history of bound and enslaved labor. Agricultural lore in the United States portrays the yeoman or small farmer as the very essence of the culture of the country, a free and independent farmer who lived close to nature, produced primarily for his family, and lived a simple and moral life that was uncorrupted by the greed and power of the city. Widely popularized by Thomas Jefferson, the yeoman was an ideal citizen, the backbone of the early democracy. This image of the yeoman persisted in U.S. history, even as farming became more mechanized and commercialized. It also persisted in the face of slavery, and of indentured servants and tenants who worked in rural areas.

The romanticized image of the yeoman finds parallels in some interpretations of the habitant in New France. Family, religion, and community were the pillars around which he built his life. Sturdy and hail, he built a new civilization in a harsh and unrelenting environment. He soon came to personify the essence of Quebec—Catholic, conservative, and the defender of highly valued traditional beliefs.

Very different are portrayals of the peon or *campesino*, Mexico's most common rural worker. If there is an archetypical Mexican laborer it is the campesino, working for others or for himself to meet basic subsistence needs and struggling to maintain or regain control over his land. Generally, though, he was viewed as exploited, abused, and confined to an inferior social and economic position. Very damning were comments about his productivity in comparison to rural workers in the United States or Europe. Foreign workers produced five or even ten times more than Mexican workers; thus, Mexico had to convince foreign workers to immigrate. Political rhetoric in the twentieth century has attempted to correct these historical stereotypes of the campesino but without success. Less emphasized in Mexican history, although now receiving more attention from historians, the *ranchero*, or the small farmer or rancher, was more common in the north and west than the center and the south. Descriptions of the ranchero emphasize qualities of independence and freedom, comparable to those of the yeoman in the United States. Importantly, the ranchero emerged in a region of labor shortage, while the campesino was more common in heavily populated regions.

Continued Rural Arrangements

Mexico remained primarily an agricultural country after independence. In many regions production expanded rapidly in the late nineteenth century as the country provided goods for the new global economy. The Laguna region of southern Coahuila was a particularly dynamic zone of agricultural and related industrial activity based on an increased demand for cotton. The new cities of Torreón (1883) and Gómez Palacio (1884) offered the chance for high wages and social mobility, opportunities common to new economic frontiers. Labor benefited in the Laguna and in a few other regions, but overall an independent agricultural working-class did not emerge. Rural workers encountered hardship, not opportunity. From the henequen plantations of Yucatán to the maize farms of the central valleys, low wages and oppressive local political systems bound workers to an increasingly exploitive economic system and to very low standards of living. Rural conflicts and rebellions often broke out but did not lead to improvement in the quality of life. Successful organization of rural workers had to await the changes brought by the Mexican Revolution of 1910.

The United States and Canada also remained primarily rural and agricultural, but the conditions of labor differed from those in Mexico. The great divide in the United States was the slave labor system that prevailed in the plantation belt from Maryland to Texas. Even after slavery, rural conditions in the South had characteristics of servitude similar to Mexico. The black freedmen along with many white workers entered into sharecropping arrangements with former plantation owners. The owner provided land, seed, tools; the worker had his labor and, if fortunate, a mule or two. Owner and worker then divided the crop. When they had to turn to merchants or financiers for money, they had to mortgage the crop, a practice known as the crop-lien system. Outside of the South, free landowners were more characteristic. They depended on wage and migrant labor, but a permanent class of indentured or bound rural workers was not common in the rest of the United States or Canada.

After the Civil War in the United States, small- and medium-sized farmers began to organize to further their interests. In 1867 they formed the Patrons of Husbandry, usually known as the Grangers, to push for lower freight rates and an end to monopolies. Farmers' political parties had similar objectives. Rural political protest accelerated in the 1890s as farmers suffered from the decline of prices and decreasing control over their financial futures. Discontented rural, southern, and small business interests coalesced in the Populist Party in the election of 1892. Defeat in the election did not spell the end of farmers' political activity, which continued in the twentieth century.

In Canada rural labor followed a pattern similar to that in the United States. Farmers in the Prairies and the west organized to protest against the new industrial policies of the nation, arguing that the policies penalized them while they benefited the rich industrialists of the St. Lawrence and Great Lakes region. As their numbers and economic power grew, farmers contended for power on two main levels. First, at the local level, they pushed for better roads, schools, and health facilities, goals that would improve rural life. Second, they demanded policy changes at the provincial and national level in the hopes of lowering freight rates and tariffs. They formed into organizations known as the Territorial Grain Grower's Association, Farmers' Institutes, the Grange, and others that led to the success of the Progressive Party in the 1921 federal election. The party called for free trade, a graduated income tax, and nationalization of the railways.

Labor and Industrial Transformation

In the late nineteenth century, North America entered into a new phase of its economic development as industry began to overtake agriculture. The center of the change was a rectangle that ran from Boston south to Baltimore, then fanned west to Pittsburgh and Chicago on the northern line and Cincinnati and St. Louis on the southern. Here coalesced all the ingredients necessary for industrialization: abundant natural resources, especially coal and petroleum; good transportation on rivers, canals, and railroads; new technologies that reduced the cost of production; capital from home and abroad as investors sought to profit from the new changes; cheap and willing labor from the millions of new immigrants; and business acumen from the new entrepreneurs. These new captains of industry became synonymous with the age. Often called "robber barons," they were portrayed as the opposite of the yeoman farmer. Seen as greedy, scheming, and ruthless, they rose to heights of wealth and power only dreamed of before the Civil War.

Within this milieu labor history began to change. Before, individuals had worked alone or in small groups. As members of a family, a partnership, or a small company, they established a personal relationship with their employer. While wages and conditions might not have been ideal, workers at least knew their bosses as they negotiated for improvements in their working conditions. As larger and larger businesses emerged and the corporate form of business organization led to more impersonal working relationships, workers became members of a class. The new industrial capitalism demanded more from the men, women, and children working in the factories. Long, hard, and unsafe work, much of it repetitive, was the fate of the new industrial working class. Sixty-hour — in some industries 72-hour — work weeks faced workers as they struggled for survival.

The modern labor movement emerged in response to these new conditions. Workers performing the same tasks identified with each other, not with their particular employer or place of employment. They had similar interests that were defined by their position in the production process. Since they were powerless to negotiate individually with their employers, they joined together hoping to improve their working conditions. At first, these were small, local organizations. Later they developed into regional and national bodies. For the purposes of our analytical narrative, we are emphasizing the organization of workers and the rise of unions rather than positing a general discussion of labor. Historians make distinctions between unions and labor; we should not conflate the two. Plenty of urban and rural workers throughout the continent had and continue to have economic and social relationships with corporations, small businesses, banks and credit institutions, non-governmental organizations, and the public sector without union mediation. On the other hand, the evolution of organized labor in the nineteenth and twentieth centuries reveals patterns of social and economic change that transcended the nation-state with a continental character to them.

The formation of national labor unions propelled workers to a new level of energy and strength. The Noble Order of the Knights of Labor, organized as a secret society in 1869, posed an early challenge to industry. Distinguished by its partly successful efforts to recruit women and blacks and by its promotion of social reforms, most noticeably the formation of worker-owned enterprises, the Knights had a short but influential history. The establishment of the American Federation of Labor in 1881, led by Samuel Gompers, had more lasting consequences for the labor movement. Gompers envisioned a movement that asked more from the system, not changes to the system. Not so with the Industrial Workers of the World established in Chicago in 1905. This movement brought together unskilled workers from many different industries and regions and advocated the abolition of the wage system. They believed that capitalism must be overthrown and society restructured in order to satisfy human needs. Fear of the violence associated with the movement alienated many and elicited repressive measures from the government, leading to its demise after World War I. By that time the American Federation of Labor was the undisputed leader among national organizations.

As the unions grew so did clashes between labor and industry, some of them ending in bloodshed and death. The Haymarket Square Strike in Chicago (1886) was part of a national strike for an eight-hour day. Seven policemen died and scores of workers were injured. The Homestead Strike, another violent confrontation, pitted workers at the Carnegie Steel plant outside of Pittsburgh against the Pinkerton Detective Agency in 1892. Strikes had become one of the most powerful weapons of labor in its struggles to improve its position in the changing economy. Meanwhile, big business often had an ally in the U.S. government; both public discourse and corporate rhetoric equated labor unions with socialism and other European ideologies that immigrants brought with them across the Atlantic Ocean. Immigrants, once again, were seen as provocateurs whose Old World ideologies threatened the established order and instigated violence.

Canadian Variations

Canada followed a similar path toward labor organization, though with less radicalism and violence. A pivotal development was the Toronto printers' strike of 1872. In response to the strike, Prime Minister Macdonald issued the *Trade Unions Act*, which allowed for strikes but required that unions be financially responsible for their actions. The early appearance of the Knights of Labor in 1881 gave the labor movement a wider social vision with its commitment to creating a more just and equitable nation, not just improving the condition of the worker. As in the United States, the Knights had little lasting influence. The first national organization with staying power was the Trades and Labor Congress of Canada, formed in 1883. It developed under the strong influence of the American Federation of Labor in the United States, essentially espousing its views of craft organization, strikes, and limited political participation. Militant labor activity fell to the Canadian arm of the Industrial Workers of the World. As in the United States, it advocated a more aggressive attack on the capitalist system. It was particularly active in the far west, with its new immigrant population working in mines, forests, and railroads. The Winnipeg General Strike of 1919 crowned the trend toward the increasing militancy and solidarity of labor. The strike shut down Winnipeg and only ended with the violent intervention of the Royal North-West Mounted Police. A later alternative to the Trades and Labor Congress was the All-Canadian Congress of Labour, formed in 1926. Focusing on industrial unionism and wary of U.S. influence, it had difficulty competing with the Trades and Labor Congress.

Quebec experienced a slow but steady growth of organized labor. The number of unions in the province increased from 22 in 1880 to 491 in 1931, with a membership of over 72,000 workers. Despite the growth, this represented only about 10 per cent of all wage earners in that year. An important influence on labor organization in Quebec was the role of the Catholic Church. The Vatican responded to the increasing social problems of industrialization by issuing the papal encyclical *Rerum Novarum* in 1891, which called for more attention to the working classes and new programs of social assistance for the poor, all predicated on a commitment to traditional morality and social stability. As a result, the church in Quebec encouraged the formation of labor unions, but these seldom took a radical stance. Instead, the church-supported unions hoped to stave off the influence of the more radical international unions such as the Knights of Labor, which appeared to represent the dual threats of socialism and foreign influence.

Mexican Difficulties

In Mexico the slower rate of industrialization and the authoritarian government of Porfirio Díaz impeded the emergence of organized labor. As an ally of foreign and domestic capitalists, the Díaz government used its power to halt the growth of organized labor. Hired thugs and government troops rebuffed efforts of workers to organize in mines and textile factories. Violence at the Cananea copper mine in northern Sonora in 1906 symbolized the collaboration of the Mexican government and foreign capitalists at the expense of workers. Striking for wages comparable to those of U.S. citizens working in the mine, workers were gunned down by Arizona

Rangers brought in by the governor of Sonora. Strikes in textiles plants contributed to the unrest. The Río Blanco strike in the state of Puebla was the most violent, as over 100 workers lost their lives.

The halting efforts at organization accelerated with the Revolution of 1910. In the revolutionary fervor, the *Casa del Obrero Mundial* (House of the Workers of the World), a radical anarcho-syndicalist movement, was established in 1912. It claimed a national following and supported Venustiano Carranza's army in 1915. With passage of the Constitution of 1917, labor finally achieved formal recognition in Mexico. Article 123 provided the juridical basis for labor organization and stipulated an eight-hour work day and a minimum wage. In 1918 Luis Morones helped to form the *Confederación Regional Obrera Mexicana* (Regional Confederation of Mexican Workers) which reigned until the 1930s. Labor was finally poised to become a more powerful voice in Mexican politics.

The Great Depression

Unemployment and poverty spread with startling rapidity in the 1930s, provoking widespread criticism of capitalism and government social policies. Critics lashed out at the greed and callousness of industrial leaders, but this did not affect the underlying dynamics of the Great Depression. Prices spiraled downward as the economy contracted, quickly leading to widespread unemployment. At the height of the Great Depression, approximately 25 per cent of workers in the United States and Canada lost their jobs. Millions of others worked at less than a subsistence wage and struggled to survive. Mexico also suffered but probably less so since more of its workers continued working in subsistence rural activities. While workers faced hard times in fields and factories, they made great strides in labor organization and legislation to protect their interests. The 1930s marked a significant transition for labor in all three countries and helped to establish a new relationship between labor and industry.

Mexico

Lázaro Cárdenas came to the presidency in 1934 committed to realizing the social goals of the Constitution of 1917. Article 123 had 31 major divisions that covered wages, hours of work, working conditions, and the right to strike. Both urban and rural workers benefited. The formation of the *Confederación de Trabajadores de México* (Confederation of Mexican Workers) in 1936 under the direction of Vicente Lombardo Toledano was a triumph for urban labor. Membership grew to about one million by 1940, despite the widespread unemployment and the large number of self-employed workers. The union had a favored position under Cárdenas, who saw it as essential to his government. A cozy relationship developed between government and labor, each supportive of the other. Cárdenas's support of the petroleum workers in their confrontation with British and U.S. oil companies was an affirmation of his willingness to use the presidency to further the interests of labor.

Cárdenas also supported the establishment of the *Confederación Nacional de Campesinos* (National Confederation of Farm Workers). Nothing distinguishes Mexican labor history more than the political rhetoric aimed at the campesinos. They became part of the popular consciousness of the revolution, and consequently Mexican politicians gave them unprecedented attention. The social goals of the revolution demanded that the peasant, so long exploited in Mexican history, have access to land.

As with industrial workers, Cárdenas emerged as the patron of the campesino. He identified with them and began to redistribute land, mainly in the form of the *ejido*, the communal lands that had their origins in the old village tradition of Mexico and were legally constituted during the colonial period. Workers in the ejidos worked the land cooperatively or, more frequently, as individual farmers with control over their own plots of land. The ideal of land for those who tilled it remained a part of public discussion but was less and less a priority. National policy began to argue that the social goals of the revolution could be achieved through economic development and redistributive social policies. This did not satisfy landless workers. The cry for land reached revolutionary levels again in the 1960s, when a struggle broke out in Chihuahua in 1964-65. This was ruthlessly suppressed by the Gustavo Díaz Ordaz administration, which effectively signaled an end to the struggle for land. Rural workers subsequently placed more emphasis on improvements in rural conditions than on acquiring land.

By the 1990s government policy had come almost full circle. Rather than emphasizing the need to create more ejidos, thereby providing land to the rural poor, it promoted the break-up of the ejido. Increased efficiency and productivity, not land ownership for the poor, were the main goals. When President Carlos Salinas assumed the presidency in 1988 he began to criticize the ejido as an archaic relic of Mexico's revolutionary past. Inefficient and unproductive, the ejido, according to the president, was the cause of rural poverty and agrarian uncertainty. Salinas used the ejido to explain why rural income was only one-third that of the rest of Mexico. He introduced amendments to the Constitution of 1917, specifically reforms of Article 27, which had defined Mexican agrarian policy for 70 years. These changes allowed for the private ownership of lands that had once been owned communally. Rural peasants received title to their land and in turn could sell, rent, or trade their parcels. The lure of quick cash or the pull of employment opportunities in the United States pushed some campesinos to sell their lands to large landowners.

Economic setbacks in the 1970s and 1980s derailed organized labor. Indeed, since the election of President Manuel Ávila Camacho in 1940, Mexican presidents have cooled in their enthusiasm for unions, attacking labor leaders and implying that organized labor was an enemy rather than a partner in the restructuring of the Mexican state. Unions fought harder and harder for fewer successes. One significant recent success was the petroleum workers union's ability to stall President Ernesto Zedillo's plans to privatize Petróleos Mexicanos in 1996.

Even the few successes lose significance in the context of corruption and manipulation by the government. Labor seldom acted independently of the government; its modest gains usually served to strengthen the government as much as labor. In addition, organized labor never mobilized a large enough percentage of the work force to become an independent power. In all three countries individual proprietors, working alone or with family members, worked without the aid of unions. Mexico, because of its slower pace of industrialization, had the highest percentage of independent, self-employed workers (in 2004 about 25 per cent, compared to less than 10 per cent in Canada and the United States). These workers, however, are under increasing attack. As in the United States and Canada, the chain supermarkets, discount stores, and pharmacies crush independent proprietors, presenting new challenges and opportunities for organized labor. Mexico also has a much higher percentage of the labor force in agriculture: 18 per cent in 2003, compared to 2.7 per cent in the United States (1988) and 4.7 per cent in Canada (1991). With the break-up of the ejido, the mechanization of agriculture, and the end of high tariffs to protect basic Mexican staples such as corn, beans, and milk, this, too, is undergoing rapid change.

United States

In the United States workers turned to the federal government and demanded reforms to counter the worst effects of the Great Depression. To support the farmer, the government passed the *Agricultural Adjustment Act* in 1933 in the hopes of raising agricultural prices. The essential concept was parity, or a return of farmers' incomes to what they had been between 1909 and 1914, a time of reasonably good prices for farm products. The act, prompted in part by the devastating "dust bowl" years of 1933 and 1934, led to a decrease in production and an increase in income. Temporary and migrant rural workers—*braceros*—faced a more difficult and prolonged struggle to achieve government recognition and support. Their early protests and attempts to organize between 1942 and 1964 had little effect but did establish the momentum for new movements. Finally, under César Chávez, the United Farm Worker's Union achieved success by signing an agreement with California grape growers in 1970.

To support urban labor, the government authored the *National Industrial Recovery Act* in 1933, a complex law that hoped to stimulate production and thus lead to more employment. Section 7a of the act gave labor the right to collective bargaining. The act also led to legislation that guaranteed minimum wages, regulated the hours of the work week, and banned child labor. When this legislation was challenged, it was replaced by the *National Labor Relations Act* of 1935, also known as the *Wagner Act*. The last great achievement of labor during the New Deal, the *Wagner Act* assured government protection of unions and the right to collective bargaining.

Labor benefited from other government activities. The Public Works Administration of 1933 funded jobs building dams, roads, bridges, schools, and other public works. The Civilian Conservation Corps, also started in 1933, gave work to men in the parks and forests of the nation, planting trees, building roads, and clearing brush. The Works Project Administration (1935) created jobs in the same fashion, emphasizing construction projects but also supporting service and the arts. Beneficiaries now taught classes and wrote books in addition to building bridges.

New initiatives by labor leaders also changed the direction of labor history. John L. Lewis argued for unionization based on industries, not on crafts. In 1935 he formed the Committee for Industrial Organization, which soon became the Congress of Industrial Organization. This in turn strengthened the United Auto Workers, the United Steel Workers, and the United Mine Workers, some of the most powerful labor organizations in the country. In 1955, the Congress of Industrial Organization joined the American Federation of Labor to form the AFL-CIO, which remains as the main national labor organization in the United States.

Canada

On the eve of the Great Depression, labor in Canada had not yet achieved the same level of organizational strength that it had in the United States. A slower pace of industrialization and an excessive concentration of power in a few industries limited the opportunities for unionization. When the Great Depression hit Canada, it gave new incentives to labor organization and demands for government support.

Government responded, but less rapidly and less extensively than in the United States. It set up unemployment relief camps between 1932 and 1936 that gave employment to over 170,000 workers. More important was the drive to create national unemployment insurance. Prime Minister R.B. Bennett had tried to implement it in 1935, but success did not come until 1940. Another achievement was the passage of legislation in 1944 (*Privy Council Act 1003*) that guaranteed the rights of workers to unionize and required employers to accept the unions.

As in the United States, industrial unionism made headway in the 1930s. Automobile, steel, and rubber workers formed unions around their industries, not their crafts. These unions merged with the All-Canadian Congress of Labour to form the Canadian Congress of Labour in 1940. The old Trades and Labour Congress (the crafts unions) continued as a competitor until 1956, when both merged to form the Canadian Labour Congress. These organizational changes took place as the number of unionized workers rose from 400,000 to 1,000,000 during the 1940s, a reflection of the postwar industrial boom and of more favorable labor legislation.

The organization of public-employee workers that began in the 1960s represented another significant development in the history of Canadian labor. Responding to the rapid growth in government employment, civil servants, teachers, and other public service employees started to unionize. In the 1970s they achieved many of the rights to bargain and strike that their counterparts in the private sector had achieved in the 1930s and 1940s. Quebec's public employees also organized in the 1960s and 1970s. As they grew in power, they emphasized the uniqueness of Quebec and its special political role within Canadian Confederation.

The rise of the public employee union in recent years is one explanation for the higher rate of worker participation in unions in Canada than in the United States. Another is more favorable government legislation. In 1990, 36.2 per cent of the non-agricultural wage earners in Canada belonged to unions, compared to only 16.1 per cent in the United States. In 1940, the percentage was 22.5 in the United States compared to 16.3 in Canada. Despite the successes, unions in Canada as in the United States face increasing difficulties. Changing economic and political realities continue to undermine their membership and influence.

Recent Years

Several interconnected forces influenced the well-being of labor in the late twentieth century. Perhaps the most important were the new technologies present in every field of production, distribution, and consumption. Automation and information technologies driven by the computer created changes as fundamental as those launched by the industrial revolution. The speed with which the new technologies spread surpassed anything seen in the past. Cellular phones, computers, and fax machines only became common in the industrial centers of North America in the 1980s; by the late 1990s they were found in the most remote corners of the continent. The era of automation that was much predicted (and feared by labor) in the 1960s was in every field. New jobs had been created, but many had been lost.

It is too early to predict the net effect on employment of the current changes, but there are ominous signs. One is the "down-sizing" that is occurring throughout North America, even in Mexico, where unemployment continues as one of the most severe social problems in the country. Another difficulty is that management has become more unsympathetic to workers and uses lay-offs as a way to reduce costs and reduce wages. Still another problem is the "temping" of the labor force. Every branch of economic activity — from medicine and law to tourism and manufacturing — relies increasingly on temporary labor, further weakening efforts at organization. All is taking place within a cultural and political climate unsympathetic to labor, a climate that emphasizes featherbedding and inefficiencies rather than the rights of workers. The result is that both blue- and white-collar workers struggle not to lose ground.

The changing economic realities are altering the class structure of urban-industrial North America. Data on income reveal the inequalities. A small percentage of the population controls an increasingly large percentage of the wealth. Canada and the United States are remarkably similar. In 1990 the poorest 20 per cent in Canada received about 6 per cent of the wealth; the wealthiest 20 per cent received 40 per cent. By the late 1990s, Canadian families at the ninetieth percentile of income distribution had incomes about four times higher than those at the tenth percentile. While incomes among the wealthiest 20 per cent were rising by 10 per cent, total family income stagnated among the poorest 20 per cent of Canadian families between 1990 and 2000. Despite the widely heralded beliefs in the welfare state, Canada remains a stratified society. In the United States, the top-fifth of households have 14.3 times more income than the bottom fifth. The wealthy in the United States made many gains in the 1980s and 1990s, while those in Canada simply maintained their position. In Mexico, the inequalities were more glaring but not as extreme as political rhetoric in the United States suggested. In 1989 the bottom 20 per cent earned just less than 4 per cent; the top 20 per cent earned 55 per cent. As in the United States, the inequalities have become more extreme.

Increased international trade is touted as one of the solutions to the problems of unemployment. Mexico offers an example of the double-edged nature of the problem. The convergence of agricultural labor needs in the United States and overpopulation in Mexico has already been noted. Capital flows to the south now take advantage of cheap labor in Mexico instead of attracting workers to the United States. The *maquiladoras* are prominent examples. These are plants that assemble imported components (garments, electronics, and auto parts) and then export them to the United States. The duty paid in the United States is on the value added from the labor in Mexico. Since labor costs are very low, the assembled items enter the United States with low duties. It should be added that while labor costs are low, the quality of the labor is high. By the 1980s much of the negative appraisal of Mexican labor had been reversed. Whether in the technologically sophisticated automotive industry or in low technology assembly plants, the efficiency of Mexican labor has attracted the interest of international investors.

Wages in the maquiladoras reflect national and international asymmetries. Maquiladoras paid high wages compared to those in the center and the south of Mexico, helping to increase the traditional geographic and cultural divisions between the northern and southern parts of the country. A sharper asymmetry existed between the northern Mexican and southwestern U.S. border. Both sides of the border shared much, but not equality of wages. Compared to the United States, the Mexican border situation was deplorable. The low wages and the increased social and environmental problems associated with the rapid rise of maquiladoras sparked frustration on the U.S. side of the border. Yet border cities grew from the spending of the Mexican maquiladora workers. From San Ysidro to Brownsville, merchants came to depend on the spending of Mexican shoppers, who bought everything from groceries to stereos. Mexico found increased employment from the maquiladoras, but they did not lead to development, nor did they solve the problems of undocumented migration to the United States. Since women were preferred to men as employees in the maquiladoras, the men have had little alternative except to search for employment in the United States. The economic crisis of Mexico in the 1970s and 1980s accentuated these problems.

The United States has lost employment from the movement of jobs to Mexico and more importantly to Asia. Global trading has led to increased competition and in many industries a decline in the U.S. share of production. The automobile industry is telling. In 1950 the United States manufactured 76 per cent of automobiles in the world; in 1990 that had fallen to 20 per cent. With the decline went millions of jobs in steel, glass, rubber, and other industries. Recently, many of these high-paying jobs have gone to Mexico. According to those who argue the benefits of this movement, increased income leads to increased imports of goods from the United States, which in turn leads to increased employment. The devaluation of the Mexican peso in late 1994 blunted this prediction. As the value of the peso declined in comparison with the dollar, Mexicans could not purchase goods made in the United States. In sum, it is too early to predict the long-term impact on labor of the increasing economic integration of North America.

The overarching similarity in the modern history of labor in North America is the struggle to increase salaries and improve working conditions. Utopian and millenarian thinking found few supporters in mainstream labor movements. Radical efforts to overthrow the system occasionally erupted but had little lasting impact on capitalism. Workers have sought to take more from the system, not to change it. They chose unions as the most appropriate method to achieve the objectives of better wages and conditions.

Union activity followed deep structural changes in North America during the nineteenth century. With the advent of industrial capitalism, the condition of workers deteriorated. As they shared increasingly difficult but similar conditions, they organized to confront management. The size and strength of unions differed, depending on region and level of economic activity, but by the middle of the twentieth century they had made great strides. As the twentieth century drew to a close, unions weakened and represented fewer workers. The reasons are many: big and medium-sized businesses have employed legal strategies to keep out union organizers; the new labor force that emerged in the early 1990s comprises more and more women and young people whose employment often generates a second income for their households; these same workers also tend to accept lower wages; a marked shift in the global economy favors the technology and service sectors at the expense of industrial and manufacturing jobs, which historically had given organized labor its rather large membership; and, finally, brisk competition from foreign competitors and non-union companies offer consumers a bevy of products and goods at lower prices.

Nevertheless, organized labor in Canada, the United States, and Mexico continues to develop and push multiple political agendas that reflect the changing circumstances of urban and rural workers brought about by free trade agreements and globalization. For example, NAFTA has pushed millions of Mexican peasants out of the countryside and toward the United States. While many find employment—with or without green cards—in the cities and rural environs of the United States, they work without the protection or support of labor unions. Labor unions in the United States and Canada oppose free trade agreements with low-wage countries like Mexico or those in Central America and point to the disruptive effects that free trade has had on rural Mexico. From the perspective of organized labor, corporate capitalism seeks out lower wages in a very transnational way, taking jobs away from citizens and giving them to workers in other countries who labor under weakened or nonexistent worker protection laws, as our discussion of the maquiladoras has shown. Moreover, even favorable economic conditions can create hurdles for unions to overcome. In Canada, provincial governments have tried to meet the increased demand for labor in a variety of industries, particularly the construction sector. Alberta alone, for example, expects to create approximately 50,000 new jobs in construction between 2007 and 2012 (*Daily Commercial News* 5 November 2007). Flushed with profits from its oil industry and with its rapid growth in infrastructure, the province has sought to reform immigration policy in order to streamline rules for immigrants and temporary foreign workers. No doubt Canadian labor unions will press their concerns and try to shape government policy. In the future, whether unionized or not, workers throughout the continent face the challenge of creating new methods and strategies to overcome the inequalities of wealth in North America.

CHAPTER 9
TRADE AND TARIFFS

Long before the arrival of Europeans, trade helped to stimulate the economies of many indigenous societies. The latter created mechanisms to try and ensure favorable trade terms and at times resorted to military action to protect trading interests. Europeans did the same, building on traditions that had their origins in the Commercial Revolution of the twelfth and thirteenth centuries in the Mediterranean world. Christopher Columbus had trade in mind when he set sail in 1492. Spain, England, and France built their empires on commercial and mercantilist policies that sought maximum benefit for the mother country; the economic benefits often came at the expense of the colonies.

The nation-states that emerged in North America in the late eighteenth and early nineteenth centuries developed trade policies that mirrored their colonial experiences, with the tariff becoming their primary policy weapon. Moreover, new technologies facilitated the rapid spread of transportation networks throughout the continent, which in turn allowed big business to move their protected goods to emerging regional markets at a much quicker pace. Global economic downturns and political crises in the twentieth century, however, pushed Canada, Mexico, and the United States to rethink economic nationalism, as proponents of continental integration argued that government policies that encouraged transnational investment and commerce stimulated economic growth over the long haul. Detractors pointed to a series of economic asymmetries, rooted in the historical trajectories of each country, which promised to deepen social and material inequalities.

Early Patterns of Trade

Atlantic trade patterns connected North America, Europe, and Africa through a series of supply and demand linkages that persisted for several hundred years. These are often portrayed as a series of triangles — North America exporting natural resources, Europe manufactured goods, and Africa labor. This is essentially correct, but there were many variations that changed according to time and place. Rather than equilateral triangles with balanced trade flows, there were major (Veracruz,

Mexico, to Seville, Spain) and minor (Quebec City to Le Havre, France) trunk lines that connected many other routes.

The early history of Mexico set the tone for the commercial history of North America. Much publicized in Europe, the splendor and wealth of the Aztecs generated hopes of finding other rich empires. The discovery of silver at Zacatecas (1546-48) and other mines in the sixteenth century furthered Mexico's image as a land of great wealth. Silver became the most sought after resource, and for 300 years Mexico fueled the Spanish economy with it. This gave Spain a sense of wealth and power, but much of the silver was used to import manufactured goods from north of the Pyrenees and to pay for an increasingly large Spanish army. The luster of silver soon tarnished for Spain, but it has remained an important export for Mexico well into the twenty-first century.

Agricultural products fed Mexican trade as much as precious metals. Specialty items, such as cacao, used for the chocolate drinks that became fashionable in Europe in the seventeenth century, and cochineal, a red dye made from insects that live on cactus plants, dominated during the colonial period. Sugar and tobacco, then coffee, cotton, and cattle later came to dominate the export market.

In return for its exports, Mexico received manufactured goods (steel tools and weapons, food and drink, and expensive textiles). Trade grew rapidly in the sixteenth century, shrunk in the seventeenth, and then expanded again in the eighteenth century. Mexico also benefited from the Pacific trade. The Manila Galleons made the crossing from Acapulco to Manila, carrying silver in exchange for silks, spices, and precious stones.

Both France and England sought a Pacific trade similar to the Acapulco-Manila connection. The unsuccessful search for a "Northwest Passage" propelled much of the exploration of the northern part of the continent for two centuries, almost achieving a mythic status as men and ships battled the northern seas. Only in the middle of the nineteenth century, first with the clipper ships and then with the growth of San Francisco and Vancouver, did an active Pacific trade emerge in the United States and Canada.

The early English and French colonies had to settle for the Atlantic trade. New England exported fish and lumber, the middle colonies flour, and the southern colonies tobacco, rice, and indigo (blue dye). Exports went to the British West Indies and to England. In return came manufactured goods from the mother country and rum and molasses from the islands. Africa figured prominently in the trade, receiving manufactured goods from England and rum from the islands in return for the export of slaves. In these triangular relationships, the islands of the Caribbean always shone more brightly in the exchequer's eye than the mainland colonies. Rum and sugar excited investors and tax collectors more than lumber and flour.

In the far north, trade was initially more international. Spain, England, and France fished for cod in the Grand Banks southeast of Newfoundland before 1492.

Fish provided protein for the growing populations of Europe. Their hunger drove the initial colonization of the North Atlantic. Disputes over the fishing grounds led to endless conflicts, with England gaining early dominance over Newfoundland and France asserting control over the mainland.

With the settlement of Quebec, trade patterns took a different turn, literally following the trail of the beaver. European fashion helped to dictate the tempo of development. As broad-brimmed felt hats became more popular, the demand for imports increased, hastening the rise of the fur trade. The trade generated wealth, but it was a minor resource upon which to build a colony. Despite the best efforts to diversify the economy, the Quebec settlements remained small and marginal, exporting only limited amounts of food and lumber along with fur. It was a costly colony for France, not a source of wealth comparable to the English and Spanish colonies to the south.

Mercantilism

Spain, England, and France created complex institutions and policies to control the trade. These are generally labeled as mercantilism, a body of thought and practice that attempted to regulate the economic relationships between European countries and their American colonies. Three interrelated objectives shaped mercantilist policies. At its core, mercantilism aimed to increase the supply of precious metals for the colonizing power. "Bullionism" equated wealth with the store of precious metals and prompted nations to try and control the flow of gold and silver. A second objective sought to protect and promote domestic manufacturing and agricultural activities. As examples, England frowned on the import of woolen textiles from New England, and Spain discouraged the cultivation of olives and grapes in New Spain. European powers hoped that the successful implementation of these policies would further the third objective — political strength in Europe and in North America.

Spain led the way. To summarize, it tried to regulate the Atlantic trade by insisting that all commercial ships sail in *flotas*, convoys that carried bullion back to Spain. The ships could only stop at Veracruz in New Spain, Havana in Cuba, and Seville in Spain. Merchants in this trade clustered in *consulados* (merchant guilds), in Veracruz and Seville, preventing other cities from participating in the trade. In Seville, the *Casa de Contratación* (House of Trade) oversaw all, acting as an administrative and judicial body for activities related to trade.

England pursued a similar type of exclusivity, dictated in the *Navigation Acts*. Beginning in 1650, the acts covered a range of commercial activities, most designed to increase the wealth and power of English merchants and manufacturers. They prohibited foreign ships and merchants from trading with the colonies; insisted that all goods destined for the colonies leave from English ports; restricted the export of wool from the colonies; and limited the production of manufactured goods, such as hats. The mercantilist net was widely cast, but it did not control all economic activity. Local agriculture and manufacturing enterprises thrived despite the acts, producing goods in demand in other colonies. To satisfy this demand, a coastal trade sprang up, linking Boston, Newport, New York, Philadelphia, and Charleston. The extent of the trade — larger than in New Spain and New France — created a large domestic merchant class.

In New France mercantilism received a boost from the policies of Jean-Baptiste Colbert, appointed Minister of Marine by Louis XIV. Beginning in 1663, he hoped to diversify the economy of Quebec and encourage exports to France and to French possessions in the Caribbean. He appointed Jean Talon as Intendant, an office with broad administrative and judicial responsibilities. Specifically, Talon and his successors concentrated on the financial development of the colony. Although there was some economic diversification, New France never had the economic strength of the English or Spanish colonies. The triangular trade that did emerge linking Quebec, the Caribbean, and France did not offset the costs of maintaining the northern colony.

The assault on mercantilism began in the eighteenth century as some policy-makers advocated "free trade" as a method of promoting economic growth. By allowing the forces of supply and demand to dictate the economy, trade would expand and the economy would grow more rapidly. One of the foremost advocates of free trade was Adam Smith, whose *Wealth of Nations* (1776) became a widely cited justification for new economic policies. Spain had started to dismantle its mercantilist system long before. Gradually it opened more ports to trade with its colonies, abolished the old fleet system, and allowed new merchants to participate in trade. All culminated in Charles III's *Reglamento para el comercio libre* (Regulations for free trade) in 1778, which facilitated a rapid increase in commerce.

The United States broke from Britain before mercantilism came to an end. Canada, now including the former French colony of Quebec, remained the principal British colony in North America. The *Navigation Acts* still regulated trade, insisting that all commerce take place in British ships. Another series of laws known as the "Corn Laws" (1660-1846) also had an impact on Canada. This legislation hoped to protect English farmers by guaranteeing that their wheat had access to the domestic market. When wheat was scarce in Britain, the colonies (Canada) had a favored position in the market. This helped to give early stimulus to the production of Canadian wheat. While the United States and Mexico now had control over their trade actions, Canada still depended on Britain for guiding its trade policy.

Early National Goals

The United States was fortunate to emerge from the wars for independence with only modest debts. It paid these quickly and established a good credit rating. Attracted by the opportunities of the new market, foreign capital arrived early and expanded through much of the century. Transportation and industry benefited, but the United States remained primarily an agricultural country. In 1860 cotton still represented 54 per cent of all U.S. exports; manufactured goods lagged far behind at

12 per cent of the total. Agricultural exports continued to expand after the Civil War, but their relative importance declined in comparison to manufactured goods. By 1914, fully 60 per cent of exports were manufactured goods.

Tariffs helped to determine trade flows. Very early in the history of the country, the government passed the *Tariff Act* (4 July 1789). Section 1 summarized its purpose: "…it is necessary for the support of government, for the discharge of the debts of the United States, and the encouragement and protection of manufactures, that duties be laid on goods, wares and merchandise imported." The act was passed over opposition, thus beginning a debate that continues until today on the value of the tariff. Alexander Hamilton's *Report on Manufactures* (1791) became a sort of manifesto for the use of the tariff to protect nascent industries. This became more common for the young nation in the nineteenth century. Iron, lead, and textiles benefited greatly from the new legislation, setting off sectional disputes that inflamed politics.

The tariffs on manufactured goods helped the industrial regions of New England and the mid Atlantic states, while penalizing the agricultural south and west. Tariffs became so controversial and politicized that they received their own nicknames. Southern cotton planters who feared that they would pay higher prices for their manufactured goods while receiving lower prices for their products adamantly opposed tariffs. They labeled the tariff of 1828 the "Tariff of Abominations" and that of 1842 the "Black Tariff." These early arguments over tariffs point to their explosive potential as national issues. Politically, tariffs were like dry washes in the desert, usually barren and attracting little interest. Suddenly, they could swell and become powerful forces attracting the attention of all in their path.

Mexico did not have the good fortune of the United States. It entered its national period broke and entangled in foreign crises, though resolved to establish its credit worthiness and attract foreign investment. Enticed by the possibilities of renewed silver production, the British came first, as they did in most of Latin America. Yet foreign and internal conflicts continued to weaken the image of Mexico, undermining its economic objectives and frightening potential investors.

Within this context, tariffs assumed special significance. Debates on the tariff during the independence movement and the framing of the first constitution divided the nation. In very general terms, liberals embraced the doctrine of free trade, while conservatives opposed it. But this is too simple. Regional and economic differences influenced attitudes toward the tariff, as they did in the United States and Canada. Bureaucrats in Mexico City and Veracruz lived from collecting tariffs and thus supported them; import-export merchants in both cities depended on the flow of trade and thus opposed them. Manufacturers in cities such as Puebla could both support and oppose tariffs. Lucas Alamán, Mexico's leading conservative statesman, was one of the strongest advocates for a protective tariff for textiles. Textile production was the first step toward the development of a strong manufacturing base that would free Mexico from its traditional reliance on agriculture and mining. Manufacturers needed protection from cheaper imported textiles. At the same time they depended on imported raw materials and machinery. Thus, they could both oppose and support tariffs.

The *Tariff Act* of 1837 established a protective tariff against foreign imports and interior tariffs to protect one province from another. These inland tariffs, known as *aduanas secas*, continued to limit the movement of goods in Mexico until their final abolition in 1886. Even with the rise of liberals to power in the late 1850s, textiles still received some protection, provoking cries from merchants and artisans.

Liberalization of Trade

Protectionist sentiment declined in the middle of the century. Internationally, Britain led the way by starting to reduce tariffs in 1842 and repealing the *Navigation Acts* in 1849. Other countries followed, lowering their tariffs and attempting to attract more foreign capital. Trade in the United States grew quickly in the 1840s and 1850s, triggered by internal growth, westward expansion, and the absorption of lands taken from Mexico. Trade in Canada benefited directly from the *Canada Corn Act* of 1843, which allowed Canadian wheat into Britain for a very modest duty, regardless of the prices there. The result was a rapid increase in the export of Canadian wheat (tripling in the 1840s alone). When Britain repealed the *Corn Laws* in 1846 as part of its move toward trade liberalization, Canada lost its preferred place, but after a short disruption the expansion of the wheat trade continued. By 1860, the era of mercantilism finally ended as tariffs on many goods had been reduced or eliminated.

In their efforts to increase trade, Canada and the United States agreed to the Reciprocity Treaty of 1854, a major step in a long and complicated history, fraught with disruptions and disappointments but ultimately binding the two countries closely together. Though it only lasted until 1866, the treaty settled fishing disputes, permitted fishermen from each country access to the waters of the other, and lowered or eliminated tariffs on natural products. As a result, some 90 per cent of the trade between the two countries enjoyed duty free status. During this time Canada became the second most important trading partner of the United States (after Britain); it remained either first or second through the twentieth century.

Even before the treaty came to an end, protectionist sentiment was on the rise. In Canada the Galt-Cayley Tariff of 1859 sought to protect nascent manufacturing. In the United States the passage of the Morril Tariff in 1861, which eventually raised average duties to 47 per cent, undermined free trade and increased opposition to reciprocity with Canada. Mexico, while not a part of the agreement, had already raised its tariffs with the passage of the Juárez-Payne Tariff of 1856. Within this climate the Reciprocity Treaty was doomed.

Protection

The beginning of the National Policy in Canada (1879) marked another shift toward national protectionism. The National Policy, part of John A. Macdonald's platform to protect Canada's manufacturing base, imposed tariffs on imports that competed with domestic manufacturing and at the same time reduced duties on primary and partly manufactured goods coming into the country that would stimulate manufacturing. In this way, the prime minister sought to weaken Canada's economic dependence on the United States by encouraging the growth of manufacturing, which, in the late nineteenth century, was seen as the linchpin of a strong economy. Until 1879, raw materials, especially lumber, minerals, and grain, dominated trade. Wheat, more than any other commodity, sparked international trade in late nineteenth century. A wheat economy dominated Canada as farms spread across Manitoba, Saskatchewan, and Alberta. At the center was Winnipeg, the capital of the world wheat trade in the early twentieth century. The National Policy helped to curb this dependence on wheat. With the protection of tariffs, manufacturing spurted as refineries, mills, and factories started to produce everything from sugar to shoes. Infrastructure development was a part of the policy, witnessed in government support for a national railway and the settlement of the Prairies and British Columbia. All aimed to develop Canada economically and to assist it in the transition from a producer of primary products to a diversified economy with manufacturing at the center.

Through the National Policy, Canada advanced in its hopes of becoming a stronger, more integrated nation. Yet at the same time the policy accented regional frustrations and differences. The Maritime provinces lagged behind, and the Prairie provinces complained that the policy benefited the St. Lawrence region more than the rest of the country. Moreover, farmers in western Canada had to buy domestic machinery at higher prices while trying to sell their grains on the global market at competitive prices. Generally speaking, the National Policy caused a spike in prices for the average consumer, as people flocked to the cities searching for stable employment in companies that were slowly becoming monopolies, a harbinger of economic inefficiency.

Neither Mexico nor the United States had a policy similar to Canada's National Policy, but both countries aggressively sought to increase trade. In Mexico, the Romero Tariff of 1872 triggered the old debate of protectionism versus free trade. At the regional level, the rapidly growing northern states, with Monterrey at the economic center, wanted free trade in their own trade zone with the United States. The idea extended back to 1849 after the Mexican-American War, when Mexicans viewed increased trade as one method to shore up the northern frontier. In 1885 the Díaz administration created such a trade zone, stretching it from Matamoros to Tijuana. It lasted until 1905, when opposition from the interior brought it to an end.

Under the Díaz administration, production and trade jumped. Foreign investment was essential to the process. After nearly 50 years of turmoil and efforts to attract foreign investment, Mexico finally caught the eye of the international investment community. Mining led the way. Both gold and silver production increased many fold from 1876 to 1908, helping Mexico to finance its development projects. The figures are impressive. Gold production increased from one to 40 tons; silver from 607 to 2,305 tons. Gold and silver remained the staples of the export trade, but copper and petroleum production rose rapidly as well. Petroleum was the new industry. Successful drilling along the Gulf Coast from Tamaulipas to Tabasco helped to propel Mexico to the forefront of petroleum-producing countries by the beginning of the twentieth century.

Transportation and Economic Growth

Despite advances, transportation difficulties hindered Mexico's development efforts. Until the late nineteenth century, sea routes provided the main communication and transportation links with the United States. The ports of Veracruz and Tampico, with New Orleans the main destination, dominated the trade. Overland trade was more difficult. Earlier in the nineteenth century, traders pushed hard along the Santa Fe Trail from St. Louis, Missouri, to Santa Fe, New Mexico, to meet their Mexican counterparts. Before the Texas War they had already followed an even tougher route south along the old *Camino Real* (Royal Highway) to the cities of Durango and Monterrey.

In comparison, the United States and Canada benefited from a benign geography in the areas of densest population in the nineteenth century. Goods and people moved easily along the eastern seaboard between the seaports of Baltimore, New York, Boston, and Halifax, and from there up the St. Lawrence to Montreal. The rapidly growing regions along the southern shores of the Great Lakes also had easy access to Toronto and Ottawa through a combination of lake, canal, and highway transportation.

By the middle of the nineteenth century, railroads started to dominate continental transportation systems. They heralded another step in the mastery of the continent, a new age of prosperity built on steel and steam. Business interests and governments joined in all three countries to raise the capital to lay the tracks that would stimulate economic growth. The United States led the way in railway construction, overshadowing its neighbors to the north and south. Already by 1869 the United States had created a transcontinental rail system, joined at Promontory Point in Utah. The flurry of construction continued up until the 1930s, when the United States had over 400,000 kilometers of track in use, followed by Canada with 66,000, and Mexico with 23,000. By this time, most of the track had been laid, and in the case of the United States subsequent decades saw a decline in the economic significance of railways. By the late 1990s, the United States had only about 240,000 kilometers of track open, followed by Canada with 78,000, and Mexico with 24,000.

Canada was not far behind the United States in railway construction, and in 1885 the country rejoiced as the financier and politician Donald Smith drove the symbolic "Last Spike" that tied the transcontinental system together at Craigellachie,

British Columbia. With Canada's small population and economy (compared to the United States), the completion of the Canadian Pacific Railway represented an unparalleled achievement in the history of continental transportation. It helped to stimulate economic production and tie the recently created nation together.

Mexico lagged behind, but with the construction of railroads it did begin to overcome some of the transportation difficulties that had hindered economic development. The first step was the completion of the Veracruz-Mexico City route, which had been started in 1837 but remained incomplete until 1873. Major boosts in construction began in the 1870s and then accelerated under the Díaz regime. With the assistance of foreign capital, railroads eventually linked Mexico City to the United States through El Paso and Laredo, Texas, and Nogales, Arizona. As transportation costs declined, up to 15 times by some estimates, the Mexican economy gained momentum.

Improved transportation networks hastened continental integration and investments in mining, manufacturing, and agriculture. As a result, the economic domination and power of the United States extended quickly, both south and north. Mexican nationalist sentiment grew in response, leading to a growing anti-U.S. attitude. U.S. capital also flowed north. A highly symbolic example was Standard Oil's 1898 acquisition of Imperial Oil, Canada's largest oil company. U.S. investment expanded rapidly, noticeable in every sector of the Canadian economy. Canada in return found the United States its most important market for its exports.

Despite the similarities in the economic dependence of Mexico and Canada on the United States, there was one important difference. Canada never experienced an invasion by the United States for the sole purpose of defending economic interests. As previously mentioned, U.S. forces entered Mexico to end the Cananea strike and in the process helped to gun down Mexican workers. The memory of Cananea lived long after the event, as did other violent actions of the United States in Mexico.

Early Twentieth-Century Changes

The rise of corporate capitalism in the United States led to an increase in tariffs again. Big business was powerful, especially when formed into organizations called trusts that could dominate entire industries and influence governments. The *McKinley Tariff Act* of 1890 sought widespread protection of many industrial goods and agricultural products, including wheat, maize, and barley. Industrial production was on its way to surpassing agricultural production, and by 1914 manufactured goods represented 60 per cent of exports. By this time, sentiment had shifted again. Some politicians recognized tariffs as tools that the giant trusts used to exploit the public, which led to increased pressure for their reduction.

As elsewhere in North America, foreign investment, mainly from Britain and often in railroads, helped to stimulate growth. At the same time, U.S. international investment expanded, although on the eve of World War I the country was still a debtor nation. By the 1920s that had changed, and the United States had become the largest creditor nation in the world. Much of the investment went to Canada and Mexico.

By the early twentieth century, the interrelationship of the three economies guaranteed that changes in one would reverberate in the others. The economic crisis of 1907-08 in the United States sent the stock market reeling, which had the effect of reducing credit in Mexico and Canada. In Mexico, for example, fragile banks restricted and then called in loans, precipitating a series of crises and bankruptcies in the country. The newly developed agricultural and industrial north of Mexico faced harsh prospects as leading families could no longer receive credit. Compounding the crisis was the drop in U.S. demand for Mexican exports. As the upper and middle classes faced ruin, their enthusiasm for the Díaz regime waned, contributing to the eventual outbreak of the Mexican Revolution.

To increase trade with Canada, reciprocity was again proposed. The liberals in Canada had long campaigned for lower tariffs but had to wait for the election of Sir Wilfrid Laurier to advance their ideas. He and President William H. Taft in the United States agreed to a reciprocity treaty that went beyond that of 1854, but Laurier's defeat in 1911 brought an end to the plan. Nevertheless, a favorable climate for lower tariffs continued, building on the Payne-Aldrich Tariff of 1909 and the policies of President Woodrow Wilson.

At the same time that increased commercial activity tied Canada and Mexico more closely to the United States, those two countries began to fashion their own direct trade and investment linkages. Canadian trade initiatives to Latin America extended back to the 1860s, and by the turn of the century Canadian investors and entrepreneurs sought opportunities in Mexico. The Bank of Montreal established a branch in Mexico in 1906, followed by the Canadian Bank of Commerce in 1910. These banks helped in the purchase of utility and transportation companies such as the Mexico City Light and Power Company, the Yucatán Power Company, and the Mexican Northwestern Railway Company. The first years of the new century were still heady ones in Mexico as Canadian and other foreign investors envisioned a prosperous future. Their hopes and plans clashed with the reality of the Mexican Revolution, which ended this early stage of Canadian investment in Mexico.

The Great Depression and its Aftermath

Tariffs started to go up again in the 1920s, culminating in the Hawley-Smoot Tariff of 1930, the highest peacetime tariff in U.S. history. Over the loud objections of citizens and foreigners alike, President Herbert Hoover signed the tariff into law, which quickly exacerbated the downward economic trail of the Great Depression that had started in 1929. Foreign countries retaliated with their own protective tariffs. Canada signed a series of treaties known as the Ottawa Agreements (1932) designed to protect Britain and many of its dominions as trade continued to shrink. Initiated by Britain, the Ottawa Agreements modified the policies of free trade that extended back to the nineteenth century.

Canada benefited from the Ottawa Agreements, as it did from the 1934 passage of the *Reciprocal Trade Agreements Act* in the United States that authorized the president (without the approval of Congress) to negotiate reciprocal tariff reductions with foreign countries. This led to a downward movement in tariffs and the new *Reciprocal Trade Act* of 1936 that reduced tariffs between the United States and Canada. Changes in tariff policy, triggered by foreign policy and special economic interests, continued in the United States, but did not alter the trend toward more open trading policy.

Nationalists in both Canada and Mexico often interpreted the trade and treaty negotiations as examples of the increasing economic and political influence of the United States. The nationalism that had first stirred in the nineteenth century took definite shape in the interwar years and became a defining feature of the political landscape. Political independence, control over national resources, and industrialization fused together to influence domestic and international politics. Occasionally, these led to new calls for protectionism as economic nationalists in Mexico and Canada feared that free trade jeopardized domestic manufacturing. Without protection, markets would fill with cheaper imported goods, leading to unemployment and new forms of dependence on external producers. As manufacturing declined, the economies would again be restricted to the role of primary producers.

Mexico was particularly adamant in its opposition to the economic policies of the United States as it followed policies supporting its industrialization. In a backhanded way, the Great Depression helped. Mexico, since it exported less, had less foreign capital to import foreign goods, which gave domestic manufacturers more opportunities to capture local markets, a process referred to as import-substitution industrialization.

Nationalism did not prevent Mexico from signing the Reciprocal Trade Agreement (1942-50) with the United States. The treaty reduced or eliminated tariffs on Mexican mining and petroleum products exported to the United States and on manufactured goods exported to Mexico. Mexico benefited because wartime conditions limited the ability of the United States to export manufactured goods. The import-substitution industrialization that had started with the Great Depression continued into the 1940s.

After the war, U.S. goods flooded the Mexican market, leading to increased opposition to the treaty and its cancellation in 1950. The conflicting views had boiled over at the Chapultepec Conference in 1945. Formally called the Inter-American Conference on Problems of War and Peace, the conference studied the relationship between tariffs and development. The United States wanted a general lowering of tariffs throughout the Americas. Mexico opposed, seeing the policy as an instrument of continued U.S. domination of its economy. Mexico's new managerial and manufacturing groups were committed to the industrialization of the country and insisted on the need for tariffs to protect young factories and markets. Loud anti-U.S. rhetoric accompanied the careful calculations of the new industrialists and encouraged Mexico to follow an aggressive protectionist policy to support its industrialization objectives.

During the 1940s, the Mexican government used various mechanisms to protect and encourage industrialization, especially currency exchange controls, import licensing, and tariffs. During the 1940s and 1950s, the call for high tariffs attracted the most support. Materials necessary for industrialization entered Mexico easily, but finished goods and those that competed with Mexican manufacturers faced tariffs of 100 per cent and higher. Import licenses acted much like tariffs: goods complementing the industrialization process received licenses; competing goods did not. All helped to create an elaborate shield that protected Mexican industry and agriculture from competition from the United States. With these and other policies, Mexico aspired to become an industrialized nation.

Through import substitution, World War II, tariff jockeying, and other policies, Mexico entered a new stage of its economic development. Growth from the 1940s to 1960s reached such high levels that commentators called it the "the Mexican Miracle." With growth came changes in the structure of the economy. Minerals, which under the Díaz regime had accounted for more than 60 per cent of exports, continued to decline in relative importance. By 1950 they had dropped to 33 per cent of trade, while agriculture products accounted for 55 per cent. Cotton, coffee, and fish led the way. Imports also had changed. Capital goods (equipment, machinery, tools) far exceeded the so-called the consumption goods (foods, beverages, clothing) that had dominated imports in the past. More significant was the new place of high value manufactured goods, such as petrochemicals and electrical products, in Mexican exports.

Most of the trade was with the United States. Geography, investment patterns, and transportation had sealed the relationship since the late nineteenth century. While Mexico has been interpreted historically as a part of Latin America, its trading patterns have placed it squarely in North America. In 1950, it sent 74 per cent of its exports to and received 82 per cent of its imports from the United States. Canada was still only a modest Mexican trading partner, but the 1940s did see a substantial jump in trade between the two countries.

Canadians did not react as aggressively to the increasing economic power of the United States as the Mexicans, but economic nationalists did begin to call for changes in policy. They feared that Canada was becoming an economic dependency of the United States, vulnerable to its markets and to its increased investment in and ownership of Canadian natural resources and businesses. According to this view, the excessive U.S. control led to stunted and uneven development, more a reflection of U.S. needs than Canadian ones. This situation led to the 1955-57 Royal Commission on Canada's Economic Prospects, which urged an independent economic policy that emphasized planning for balanced growth. The creation of the Foreign Investment Review Agency in 1973, which had responsibility for reviewing foreign investment proposals to determine their impact on Canada, furthered the ambitions of economic nationalists. In 1985 the name of this agency changed to Investment Canada, a sure sign of the changing times. Efforts now focused on attracting foreign investment, not discouraging it.

Prelude to Free Trade

Support for economic integration increased at the national and international level, gradually overcoming the tradition of economic nationalism. The treaty that most influenced trade after World War II was the Geneva Agreement on Tariffs and Trade (GATT), signed in October 1947. Participating nations agreed to a reduction or elimination of tariffs on some 45,000 items and to "most favored nation status," which made every country the beneficiary of trade reductions made by other countries (many exemptions and escape clauses limited the treaty). GATT was an important step toward the long-sought goal of creating a new world economic order. The United States promoted GATT, hoping to gain increased access to world markets. Mexico opposed, viewing it as a threat to its attempt at industrialization. Only in the late 1980s did Mexico join. Canada was an original signatory to GATT, but it—and many other countries—only slowly lowered tariffs on selected goods. Evaluating the cumulative impact of these agreements is difficult. There is no doubt, however, that the trade of Canada, Mexico, and the United States has increased dramatically since GATT.

Mexico and Canada also took internal steps to increase their trade with the United States. In 1965, Mexico launched the Border Industrialization Program, which designated a 20-kilometer-wide strip south of the border exempt from import-export duties. At the same time, the United States changed its customs laws to allow for the import (with only a value added tax) of U.S. products that had been sent abroad for processing. This created the *maquiladora* assembly industries discussed in the previous chapter.

Canada took its own steps toward the liberalization of trade, pushed along by the "continental integrationist" arguments that had surfaced periodically since the nineteenth century. Advocates argued that economic integration was natural and necessary and could be achieved without sacrificing political goals. The weakening of protectionist sentiment led to two significant agreements in 1965. The Canada-United States Defense Production Sharing Arrangement called for free trade in military products, and the Canada-United States Automotive Products Agreement (Autopact) called for free trade in auto manufacturing (with many qualifications). These agreements bound the economies of Canada and the United States even closer than in the past.

Free Trade

The United States and Canada pushed ahead in the move toward free trade in the 1980s. For Canada the move was momentous, since it had relied on some type of protectionism since 1879. While there had been substantial progress under a century of protectionism, the costs had been high: an enormous national debt, decreasing efficiency, and increasing competition from foreign producers. Nevertheless, in its trade with the United States—Canada's largest trading partner—Canada enjoyed a surplus.

During the early 1980s Prime Minister Brian Mulroney, leader of the Progressive Conservative Party, led a movement that envisioned free trade as part of a general strategy for restructuring Canada. Free trade would lead to new economies of scale and increased competitiveness in Canadian industry. It would also prepare Canada to compete with the new and powerful regional trading blocs that had emerged. Caught between the Pacific Rim and the European Community and increasingly vulnerable to the economic strength of the United States, Canada needed free trade to survive and grow. After much negotiation, the Free Trade Agreement (FTA) finally went into effect in January 1989, with the objective of eliminating trade restrictions over a 10-year period. Agricultural goods, fish, and "cultural products" (films, music, books) sought and received exemption from the treaty. As a result of the FTA, tariffs started to go down and new binational committees went to work to settle trade disputes. The committees differed from those provided for by the GATT, since their recommendations for resolving disputes were binding.

Canadians interpreted the results of the FTA differently. Some saw it as disastrous and causing widespread unemployment. (A recession in Ontario aggravated the negative impact of the FTA in the early 1990s.) Others, particularly those in Quebec, saw it as an opportunity to strengthen their provincial economy. Despite disagreement over the results of the FTA, momentum gathered to broaden the pact to include Mexico and create the North American Free Trade Agreement (NAFTA).

In Canada numerous arguments supported NAFTA. It would eliminate tariffs on more goods, attract more capital, and resolve lingering trade disputes with the United States. In Mexico it would open a market of some 90 million consumers with a large and growing middle class. Telecommunications and banking attracted the most attention, but energy and raw materials also represented opportunities. As importantly, NAFTA would serve as a stepping stone to the broader Latin American market. Opponents argued that the agreement would cost jobs, further weakening Canadian industry. Ontario, the most industrialized province of Canada, was particularly adamant in its opposition. The Canadian Labour Congress along with the support of Bob Rae, the New Democratic premier of Ontario, led the opposition. In addition to the hard economic opposition, there was the festering fear that Canadian culture, already so vulnerable to the U.S. media, would lose more of its identity.

In contrast to the FTA, which had moved quietly through the U.S. political process, NAFTA prompted loud discussion in the United States during the 1992 presidential election (which was fought by Democrat Bill Clinton, Republican George H.W. Bush, and Independent Ross Perot). Both Democrats and Republicans, bolstered by big business, supported the treaty. Perot led the opposition. His speeches hammered at the asymmetry between the United States—a large, industrialized, global economic power—and Mexico, a Third World economy plagued by problems of poverty and slow growth. This stereotype of Mexico was misleading. The United States was the world's largest economy and Canada was the eighth largest. Not widely publicized or appreciated was the size and potential of the Mexican economy, the fourteenth largest in the world.

Specifically, opponents argued that there would be a rush of jobs to Mexico or, as Perot described it, "a big sucking sound" of jobs leaving the United States. Seldom did they discuss the broader historical issues of the loss of manufacturing jobs in the United States and the decline in real wages. Most of these jobs went to cheap labor markets in Asia, the Caribbean, and Mexico. Labor unions, threatened by downsizing and increased competition, saw NAFTA as another step in the loss of jobs. Small businesses, textile manufacturers, and fruit and vegetable growers also joined the opposition. Environmental critics who deplored the destruction of the environment along the border, especially in the Rio Grande Valley, joined the fight against the treaty. Northern environmental problems, such as Canadian asbestos mining and timbering practices, also aroused concern but seldom generated as much attention as the problems along the Mexico-U.S. border. Other opponents took the moral high ground, arguing that Mexico's closed political system and its failure to slow the drug trade were enough to derail NAFTA. In addition, they expressed alarm over an anticipated increase in the number of illegal immigrants that would result from the treaty. Trade and tariffs had once again become major issues in continental politics.

In contrast to previous treaties, discussion in Mexico centered on displaced workers, the environment, and political behavior, not on the actual tariffs. The ruling party in Mexico (PRI) and President Carlos Salinas de Gortari controlled the debate. While Salinas anticipated social and economic dislocations and admitted that NAFTA was not a quick fix for the economy, he stressed that it would thrust Mexico into the twenty-first century as a modern nation. Official political rhetoric emphasized the pride that Mexico felt as it negotiated as an equal with the United States. It withstood U.S. efforts to have Mexican petroleum, still controlled by the state agency Petróleos Mexicanos (PEMEX), included under the treaty. It also guaranteed that Mexican financial, telecommunications, and agricultural sectors would have time to adjust to the new economic realities. Other analysts emphasized that NAFTA would contribute to the growth of the middle class, thus leading to more pressure to liberalize the Mexican political system.

Voices of opposition centered on the fear of the increasing economic power and control of the United States. Mexico's dependent position in the hemisphere would continue, as the large transnational corporations used it as a source for cheap labor and a market for surplus production. Mexican industry could not compete with its more technologically sophisticated northern neighbors. Nor could agricultural production, especially the traditional maize agriculture of the campesino, equal that of the north. NAFTA would aggravate rural problems, enlarge the exodus to the cities, and as a result intensify urban problems. Mexico's traditional criticism and fear of the United States provided additional ammunition for the opposition. Historical memory remained strong in Mexico, and the annexations of the nineteenth century and the interventions of the early twentieth century sharpened nationalist sentiments and opposition to the treaty. Proponents overcame opponents in all three countries, and the treaty took effect on 1 January 1994. Its broad goal called for the integration of the economies of the United States, Canada, and Mexico. It would do so through the gradual elimination of trade restrictions and the development of new mechanisms to settle trade disputes. The treaty hoped to create a more integrated North American market that allowed for the easy movement of goods, services, and business and professional travelers. It did not create a North American common market with common tariffs for all countries. Mexico, the United States, and Canada continue to have trade agreements with other countries that are not bound by NAFTA.

The treaty confirmed the close relationship among the three countries and contributed to the already substantial trading networks in North America. In the 1990s, Canada remained the leading importer of U.S. goods, followed by Mexico, which overtook Japan as the second most important market for the United States. On the other side of the ledger, the United States continued to increase its imports from all three countries, with the largest increases coming from Mexico. Despite their importance, Mexico and Canada together still represented only about 21 and 11 per cent respectively of the total U.S. export market. In contrast, Canada sent 82 per cent of its exports to the United States, while Mexico sent 83 per cent. Mexican and Canadian trade are still small but growing incrementally.

Interest groups in all three countries present statistics to support particular points of view. In the United States, for example, critics point to the collapse of the Mexican peso in late 1994 to prove that the treaty was bad for the U.S. economy. With the devaluation of the peso, Mexican consumers had more difficulty purchasing U.S. goods, leading to increased unemployment. Aggravating the situation, U.S. consumers, faced with cheaper Mexican goods, increased consumption, and thus contributed to more unemployment (but more employment in Mexico). Such arguments are difficult to prove and tell little about the long-term prospects of the treaty. In addition, as in the past, unanticipated political problems tend to cloud the brightest of economic horizons. The Helms-Burton Bill (the *Cuban Liberty and Democratic Solidarity Act*, 1996) is a recent example that has produced a widespread, almost uniformly negative reaction in Canada and Mexico. Helms-Burton gave U.S. citizens the right to sue foreign nationals in U.S. courts if they invested in or profited from expropriated Cuban properties claimed by U.S. citizens. It also gave the State Department the authority to deny visas to the accused foreign nationals. Both Canada and Mexico, in addition to most European countries, have condemned the legislation and in some cases have threatened economic retaliation.

The U.S. and Canadian governments issued reports in 2004 to herald the ten-year

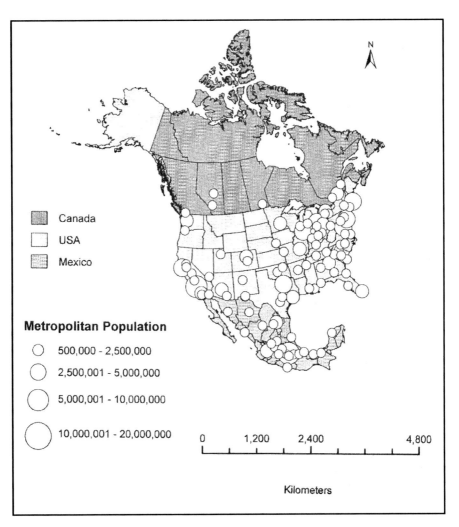

Map 5. Population Densities within NAFTA Countries.
From *NAFTA in the New Millennium* by Edward J. Chambers and Peter H. Smith. Copyright ©
2002. Reproduced by permission of the Center for U.S.-Mexican Studies and the University of
Alberta Press.

anniversary of NAFTA. Taken together, the reports examined the ways in which trade, investment, and employment have changed since the treaty took effect in 1994. Not surprisingly, both governments proclaimed NAFTA a success and looked for ways to improve the treaty by promoting competitiveness, monetary cooperation, and increased investment. In terms of exports the figures are striking. Between 1993 and 2003, U.S. export growth to NAFTA partners outpaced exports to the rest of the world. In all, American companies exported a total of $651 billion (U.S.) in 2003, including $83 billion to Mexico and $148 billion to Canada. As the U.S. report states, Mexico and Canada account for 36 per cent of total U.S. exports to the world. Trade between the United States and its NAFTA partners increased a stunning 111 per cent between 1993 and 2003, while total two-way trade between the United States and the rest of the world grew by only 79 per cent. Moreover, since NAFTA loosened decades-old restrictions on investments in Mexico, U.S. investment there ballooned by 242 per cent from 1994 to 2002, compared with 148 per cent growth in U.S. investment in the rest of the world. Conversely, Mexican investment in the United States increased 280 per cent from 1994 to 2002, while investment in the United States by non-NAFTA nations increased by 185 per cent (United States, Department of Commerce 2004).

In the services sector of the North American economy, the results also have been impressive. U.S. companies exported a total of $279 billion in services in 2002, up 63 per cent since 1993. This figure includes $24 billion in services to Canada and nearly $16 billion to Mexico. When combined, Canada and Mexico account for 14 per cent of total U.S. exports. Sales of services by U.S. subsidiaries in Canada increased 176 per cent from 1995 to 2001, to a total of $51 billion. American subsidiaries in Mexico also experienced high growth; in fact, sales of services more than tripled between 1995 and 2001, reaching almost $8 billion in 2002. Services industries employed 86 million American workers in 2002, an increase of 17 million workers in 1993. Moreover, services industries made up approximately 80 per cent of total U.S. private non-agricultural employment in 2002, which was an increase of 75 per cent from 1993.

The impact of NAFTA on skills and wages in Canada has been surprising. According to Wulong Gu and Lori Whewell, authors of the chapter on productivity growth in the Canadian report, Canada's very high rates of post-secondary educational attainment have not provided the kind of comparative advantage that Canadian NAFTA supporters would have liked. Canada's so-called "skill content" of exports was not that much different from that of imports, and only a bit higher than the business sector average (Canada, Ministry of Foreign Affairs and International Trade 2003, 2). One possible explanation is that the U.S. system of higher education provides a higher skills profile to its students, thus making them more attractive to high-tech firms in the global marketplace. On the other hand, increased reliance on the United States as an export market did not aggravate income disparity in Canada. The report challenged calls to diversify the country's export markets to ensure so-called income stability, arguing that sustained interference with free trade and the market system could actually lower incomes for Canadians without having any significant impact on income stability (Canada, Ministry of Foreign Affairs and International Trade 2003, 4-5).

The effects of NAFTA on Mexico have been substantial. Although the Mexican government has yet to issue a similar report, and several independent think-tanks have released contradictory findings, the World Bank argues that the treaty has facilitated economic development in Mexico. In its report, the World Bank says the Mexican labor market recovered quickly after the peso devaluation and economic crisis of 1994. When the peso lost more than one-third of its value, Mexicans pulled their money out of the country, and many banks were forced to close. Increased economic activity, linked to NAFTA according to the World Bank, has allowed unemployment and real wages to return to their pre-crisis level. Free trade, in particular, has pushed up the demand for a more skilled Mexican workforce, thus putting pressure on the federal and state governments to increase spending on education. The World Bank also noted that NAFTA has spurred productivity growth in Mexico. The country needed about one-half of the time to adapt to foreign technology as it did before the treaty took effect in 1994. Finally, the most controversial element of the World Bank's report is its assertion that NAFTA has not disrupted Mexican agriculture: "[NAFTA] has been quite positive for export agriculture, but it has probably had little impact on small farmers in the southern states (for example, Oaxaca, Chiapas, Guerrero)" (World Bank 2003).

Not surprisingly, competing reports contradict the World Bank's findings. The Carnegie Endowment for International Peace argues that while direct foreign investment in Mexico created 500,000 manufacturing jobs from 1994 to 2002, the country lost, at a minimum, 1.3 million jobs in the agricultural sector, where one-fifth of Mexicans still work. Moreover, the Carnegie study shows that real wages in Mexico are lower than they were in 1994 when NAFTA took effect. Some analysts point to the massive influx of Mexican migrant workers to the United States since 1994 as concrete evidence that NAFTA has turned the Mexican countryside upside-down. Since the treaty seeks to eliminate most, if not all of Mexico's agricultural tariffs, U.S. and Canadian agribusinesses can dump their produce, some of which is government subsidized, on the Mexican market. The effects on Mexican corn production have been devastating, as the amount of U.S. corn shipped to Mexico has increased fifteen-fold. In a similar vein, the amount of U.S. beef exported to Mexico has doubled, poultry has tripled, and pork exports have quintupled (Papademetriou 2003). Peasants growing corn on small plots of land in the Oaxacan countryside simply cannot compete with U.S. companies that employ the latest technologies and enjoy smooth access to financial institutions.

In 2007, Mexicans took to the streets of the federal capital to protest escalating corn prices, most dramatically felt by those who stood in long lines to buy tortillas, the basic staple of the Mexican diet. Nutritionally speaking, poorer Mexicans obtain more than 40 per cent of their protein from tortillas. The "corn polemic" that has developed in Mexico shows how interconnected the continent has become since the passage of NAFTA. Rising international corn prices reflect the intensity of the demand for the grain-based fuel ethanol. President George W. Bush, looking to break U.S. dependence on Middle Eastern sources of oil, has pushed what many analysts see as an ambitious goal for the United States: to produce 35 billion gallons of ethanol by 2017. To attain that goal, U.S. farmers will have to plant 90 million acres of corn by 2010 just to meet the growing demands of the ethanol industry. Before the ethanol boom took off, corn in Mexico was selling for $2 a bushel; when it reached over $4 a bushel in early 2007, the newly elected president Felipe Calderón, who had championed free trade during the 2006 campaign, negotiated with business leaders to cap tortilla prices at 35 cents a pound, which was less than half the highest reported rate. To meet the pressing material needs of so many Mexicans, Calderón put aside his free market ideals in favor of price controls. Moreover, the president also approved the importation of more than 800,000 tons of corn from the United States and other countries, a marked change from the previous administration.

In Vicente Fox's last year in office, he allowed Mexican agribusinesses to export 137,000 tons of corn in an effort to capitalize on the ethanol boom. In 2006, commercial corn production in Mexico had reached 24 million tons, the biggest yield in a decade. While 60 per cent of Mexican corn producers are subsistence farmers and, therefore, unlikely to benefit from the rising demand for ethanol, Mexican agribusiness was planning to expand its corn acreage by 4.3 million acres in 2007. If agribusiness achieves its stated goal, Mexico will have planted 25 million acres of corn by the time the last remaining tariffs and trade barriers are eliminated in 2008 under NAFTA.

The historical forces unleashed in the past 150 years leading to the increased integration of North American markets will be difficult to contain. With the United States at the center, trade between the countries increased rapidly after the middle of the nineteenth century. The Reciprocity Treaty between the United States and Canada signaled that most of the trade was to the north, but Mexico also gained dramatically in the late nineteenth century. By the early twentieth century, the relationship had been sealed. Momentum picked up after World War II as the economies became even more integrated. The 1960s trade pacts between the United States and Canada and Mexico's Border Industrialization Program were simply another step toward the formalization of continental trading agreements. These older pacts, and the free trade agreements that followed, acknowledged the increased movement of capital, technology, and labor in the North American marketplace. For the moment, the nineteenth-century geographers who argued that the force of mountains, plains, and coasts would lead to economic integration seem vindicated. Yet if past is prologue, protectionist measures may yet return, but they will face new difficulties trying to unhinge the economic linkages of the last 30 years.

CHAPTER 10
CHURCH, STATE, AND SOCIETY

Religion bridges culture, economy, and polity, touching on them in different ways as it influences the development of state and society. In North America it has traditionally been the most powerful voice expressing the moral beliefs of society. As an encompassing force, religion has both united and divided people, leading to widely held fundamental beliefs, while at the same time provoking rancor and discord. Religion's influence has waxed and waned through the centuries, but it has always been influential in North American political and social life.

Faith and theology, shaped as they are by more formal, institutional understandings of the sacred and profane, intersect with popular piety in ways that express the public and private attributes of religiosity in North America. Despite the increasing commercialization of the continent, which puts a high value on the production, marketing, and acquisition of consumer goods, and which seems to proselytize for new adherents with as much vigor as that of institutional religion, traditional faith and morals continue to provide the building blocks of community for millions of citizens of Mexico, Canada, and the United States. As this chapter shows, organized religion and religious belief distill the forces of convergence and divergence in complex and sometimes elusive fashion.

European Background

European and Indian religious beliefs and practices collided in the sixteenth century, leading to the at times fast and erratic, at other times slow and methodical displacement of Indian religions. The new religions, more so than the indigenous ones, have influenced social and economic life in North America. They have not, however, led to the elimination of indigenous religious practices, many of which continue today throughout the continent, both as vestiges of ancient practices and as living alternatives to the new religions introduced by Europeans.

Conflicts in sixteenth-century Europe provide the context for understanding much of North American religious history since the early years of colonization. Martin Luther's declarations in 1517 initiated disputes that engulfed the European continent by challenging the power of the papacy and the practice of selling indulgences.

He advocated "justification by faith," the idea that salvation came about primarily through acknowledging belief in Jesus Christ. Others soon followed, presenting theological alternatives to Catholicism. John Calvin, the French theologian, carried the ideas further, arguing predestination, the belief that God had already chosen the faithful and that there was nothing that good works could do to change what had already been predetermined. The faithful, though, could hope for a glimmer of their fate, *revealed* in the way that they lived their lives. Those who lived a morally accountable life were those most likely selected for heaven by God. The new theologies did not stand apart from politics in Europe and then in North America. A dramatic example from England was Henry VIII's failure to get the pope's approval for his divorce from Catherine of Aragon (his first wife) and the subsequent break with the papacy and the formation of the Church of England.

The theological and political movement that broke from Catholicism in the sixteenth century was known as the Reformation. Catholic regions reacted in a movement traditionally known as the Counter Reformation, now commonly referred to as the Catholic Reformation. Even before the Reformation, there was recognition of the need to reform the Catholic Church, especially those clergy who failed to live according to their vows. After the Council of Trent, a series of discussions that lasted from 1545 to 1563, Catholicism entered a period of renewal, commitment, and energy. Spain, the center of the Catholic Reformation and the inheritor of the Holy Roman Empire, embarked on its overseas adventures with a crusading zeal. After the initial voyages of Christopher Columbus, the Spanish Crown entered into negotiations with the pope, and the result was the *patronato real*, or royal patronage. In return for royal support of the church's endeavors in the New World, including the conversion of the Indian population, the pope, in effect, made the Spanish monarch the head of the church in Spain and throughout Spanish America. Colonists and Indians alike would come to know the authority of *las dos majestades*, or the two majesties of church and state.

Orthodoxy in New Spain

The Catholic Church accompanied Spanish colonization in North America, everywhere giving society the appearance of coherence and unity. Hernán Cortés proposed the formal missionary effort when he asked Emperor Charles V to send priests to begin the work of conversion. Twelve Franciscans arrived in 1524, followed by Dominicans, Augustinians, and then Jesuits. The large Indian population in central New Spain represented a challenge that early missionaries accepted with an enthusiasm and dedication characteristic of the Catholic Reformation.

As the missionary effort was just getting under way, an event occurred that had far reaching consequences for Mexico. According to traditional belief, a dark-skinned Virgin Mary appeared to a poor Indian, Juan Diego, in 1531 on a hill just outside of Mexico City. She asked him to build a place of worship in her name. She became known as the Virgin of Guadalupe, and the basilica built in her honor remains a major pilgrimage site in North America. The Virgin of Guadalupe personifies the particular religious heritage of Mexico. She is Mary, the Mother of God in the Western Christian tradition, and she is the dark-skinned patroness of the Indian, of the poor and the oppressed in Mexican history. When Mexico struck out for independence from Spain in 1810, the movement was led by a parish priest, Miguel Hidalgo, who carried the banner of the Virgin of Guadalupe to rally his Indian and mestizo parishioners. Her image is venerated in virtually every church, chapel, hermitage, and roadside shrine throughout the Mexican Republic, not to mention in those areas of the United States with a large Mexican population. Popes have declared her "Queen of Mexico" and "Empress of the Americas." When Vicente Fox entered the basilica in the aftermath of his electoral victory in 2000 to offer a prayer of thanksgiving to the Virgin, after decades of official anti-clericalism and hostility to public expressions of religiosity by politicians, he was neither reinventing the colonial marriage of church and state nor was he wearing his religion on his presidential sleeve; rather, Fox was merely expressing the same gesture of gratitude that many Mexicans had done and continue to do. This explains why so many viewed his public display as routine, ordinary, and quite unremarkable, notwithstanding the rants of Mexico's old-style, anticlerical politicians. True to form, upon leaving office in late 2006, Fox returned to the basilica in a final show of public obeisance.

The Virgin of Guadalupe became part and parcel of popular devotion in Mexico only in 1648, decades after formal evangelization had ended. Missionaries dominated the early history of the Mexican Church, establishing monasteries in the core cities of the realm and then later reaching out to the Indian communities through rural parishes. Faced with new cultures, the missionaries set about mastering languages, customs, and rituals to better understand their prospective converts. Given their limited numbers, they worked through Indian intermediaries, who were entrusted with maintaining the small local chapels that were linked to the monasteries, learned the prayers and rituals, and became extensions of the Spanish Catholic world.

On the periphery of the empire, the Franciscans and Jesuits built other missions in deserts, mountains, and along faraway coasts. Different from those in the center, these missions, many of them still standing today, combined religious, civil, and military functions to strengthen Spain's claim to its northern frontier. The most famous were the missions founded by the Jesuits in the Pimería Alta (southern Arizona and northern Sonora) and the Franciscans between San Diego and San Francisco, California. San Xavier del Bac in Tucson, Arizona, often called the White Dove of the Desert, remains the primary parish for many Tohono O'Odham and provides material testimony to the longevity of indigenous expressions of Catholicism in North America.

The results of the missionary effort are difficult to measure. Indian resistance, both physical and cultural, slowed the effort, as did noncompliance and the continued worship of traditional deities. In some regions of New Spain converts were left without priests or sacraments soon after baptism. In other regions a syncretic religion, one that combined Catholic and Indian elements, was the best that the missionary effort could achieve. Despite the problems, much had been accomplished in the eyes of the church. A vast and culturally complex land had become at least nominally Catholic in a very short period.

Conversion was only one purpose of the church. The other was to minister to the needs of the faithful, which required the formation of dioceses and parishes. Beginning in 1527, Spaniards created bishoprics in Tlaxcala and Mexico City; five others followed in the sixteenth century. These priests and bishops (the secular clergy) often fought with the Franciscans, Dominicans, and Jesuits (the regular clergy) over jurisdictions, tithes, and theological principles. They also fought with civilian authorities, each jealously guarding their rights and privileges.

By the second half of the eighteenth century, the church was under increasing attack by an expanding and centralizing state. In New Spain, the Jesuits suffered the most from the drive for centralization by the Spanish state. Fear of Jesuit wealth and power, not to mention the perception that the order was closely aligned with the pope, led to their expulsion from New Spain and the rest of Spanish America in 1767. The state also attacked the secular clergy, aiming primarily to divest them of their wealth. In the famous 1804 *Act of Consolidation* the state took over much of the church wealth that had been used to finance charitable activities. As a result of these issues, the church was the center of controversy on the eve of independence. Catholicism as a religion was not questioned, but the wealth and political influence of the church was. Anticlericalism, rather than anti-Catholicism, continued as a major theme of Mexican history in the nineteenth century.

Catholicism in the North

New France was also colonized by a Catholic power. As in New Spain, the church served as an instrument of colonization that furthered the growing imperial interests of France. These interests quickly came up against the hard reality of New France — a small, scattered Indian population and meager economic resources, problems that always hampered missionary activities and kept the church smaller than it was in New Spain.

Three Récollet (a branch of the Franciscans) priests started the missionary efforts in 1615, but their numbers were too small and the distances too great to have much of an impact. Jesuit priests arrived in 1625, initiating a new phase in the history of the church in New France. They focused on the Huron and established missions similar to those in Mexico, organizing the Indians into villages and trying to prevent trappers and settlers from entering the area. Ste-Marie among the Hurons was the largest and most famous of the missions. Located in what is now Ontario, it was a fortified agricultural center that at its peak housed 19 priests. Iroquois attacks from 1648 to 1650 disrupted life and led to the destruction of Ste-Marie. (Today it has been reconstructed as an historic site, much like many of the missions in the U.S. southwest). The failures did not prevent the Jesuits and the missionary effort, much less Catholicism, from becoming a part of the founding mythology of Quebec.

Beginning in 1659, the influence of the Jesuits was gradually eroded by the establishment and growth of an episcopal hierarchy and by the arrival of state officials. The true power of the church devolved to the *curé*, the parish priest. As the colony expanded, parish priests assumed more influence, often more than that of the local lord. Their support came from the tithe, officially a meager one-twenty-sixth of the wheat harvest (it was one-thirteenth in France) that seldom satisfied church needs. In the material realm, the church, like most other institutions in Quebec, was poor.

British success in the French and Indian War briefly curtailed the influence of Catholicism. After an attempt to anglicize the residents of Quebec, the British passed the *Quebec Act* in 1774, legally recognizing the validity of the Catholic Church, confirming its right to collect tithes and to own property, granting the citizens of Quebec the same political rights as British subjects, and insuring that Catholics could be represented in the governor's council of the province. This was a deliberate attempt to dissuade the colony from rebelling. With the guarantees of the act, Quebec had little enthusiasm for the revolutionary sentiments stirring in the British colonies to the south.

By this time, the clergy had successfully assumed a social as well as a religious role in rural Quebec. They stood as respected and needed members of the villages that dotted the Quebec countryside, contributing to the cohesion of rural life. This function assumed more importance after the political fall of New France. The church helped to defend the language and laws of Quebec under British rule, a task made easier by the lack of strong anticlerical sentiments in Quebec. The interests of the church and those of the political leadership became so intertwined that it was difficult to distinguish one from the other. These conditions helped to insure a powerful church in nineteenth-century Quebec.

Religious Pluralism in the British Colonies

In contrast to the religious unity of the Catholic colonies to the north and south, diversity and dissent marked the early religious heritage of the British colonies. The Puritans led the way, challenging the authority of the new Church of England and set out to create societies that emphasized direct communion with God. For them, the new Church of England (Anglican Church), established after the king's break with Roman Catholicism, did little to allow them freedom of worship. Too many trappings of Catholicism remained. They denied the need for the intermediaries of priests and the rituals of the established church. As they sought to "purify" the church, they faced more persecution. The most extreme group of Puritans became separatists and decided to break from the church rather than to try and reform it. The Pilgrims who arrived at Plymouth in 1620 belonged to this group. They entered into a covenant with God and with themselves, promising to build a better life by following carefully prescribed rules.

Another, larger group of Puritans arrived in 1630 to establish the Massachusetts Bay Company. They were not separatists from the Church of England, but they did assert that each congregation had the right to select its own minister and to worship in its own way. This was the beginning of the Congregationalist Church, which settlers from New England established in Nova Scotia and New Brunswick in the eighteenth century. From there Congregationalism spread, gaining most of its supporters in Ontario. The Congregationalist churches of New England and eastern Canada today are the offspring of the Puritan sects of the seventeenth century.

In Virginia, the Church of England was formally established and acknowledged by law as the colonial church. As colonization moved to the Carolinas and Georgia, the Church of England spread, but it never acquired the status that it had in Britain. Lax laws and splinter groups undermined its efforts at becoming the dominant church in the colonies. After the independence of the United States, the Episcopalian Church supplanted the Church of England; in Canada it survived and grew as the Anglican Church.

Catholicism also arrived early in the colonies, finding a home in Maryland, founded by the Calvert family in 1633 as a haven for Catholics. The *Toleration Act* of 1649 officially enshrined religious toleration and freedom, but this did not last, and Catholicism was later restricted in all of the colonies except Rhode Island and Pennsylvania. Intolerance also affected other groups. The Quakers, or the Society of Friends, was a separatist group that faced persecution in the homeland and the colonies. William Penn founded the colony of Pennsylvania as a refuge for Quakers in 1681. Outside of Pennsylvania and Rhode Island, Quakers faced persecution, as did several other religious groups. Both tolerance and intolerance had deep roots in the religious history of the colonies.

During this first century of colonization many other groups came: Baptists, who stressed adult rather than child baptism; Mennonites and Amish, who lived according to pacifism and German traditions; Lutherans, who followed the tenets laid down by Martin Luther; Presbyterians, who emphasized church rule by elders; and Jews, who adhered to the Old Testament. While it is difficult to summarize the beliefs of these and other groups, two general principles did emerge, albeit slowly and unevenly. First, most religions advocated the separation of church and state. The established Catholic Church in New Spain and New France and the Anglican Church in Britain smacked too much of the past. Individuals should have the right to worship according to their conscience. Second, and evolving more slowly and uncertainly, was the struggle for religious toleration. The extremism and exclusivity of the seventeenth century gradually gave way to more openness and acceptance in the eighteenth century.

This tolerance did not extend to Indian and African religious practices, usually condemned by Europeans. The Catholic Church in New Spain and New France tried to convert Indians, while most churches in the British colonies did not. The Puritans in mid-seventeenth century New England and the Moravians in mid-eighteenth century Pennsylvania were among the few who tried to establish Indian missions, but they had only modest success. Most churches also ignored the increasing African population. Except for the Society for the Propagation of the Gospel, an Anglican organization, there was little effort in the British colonies to convert Africans.

The cultural biases and discrimination against Indian and African religions did not prevent the new nation from pronouncing religious freedom as an official policy. The Constitution of the United States articulates these principles in Article VI and the First Amendment. Article VI states that "no religious Test shall ever be required as a qualification to any Office or public Trust under the United States." The First Amendment goes further: "Congress shall make no law respecting an establishment of religion, or prohibiting the free exercise thereof." The Constitution thus confirmed the separation of church and state, one of the great political principles of the United States.

The wars for independence had another impact on the religious history of the country. The divisions and factionalism that had characterized colonial religions lessened as colonials fought against the British. Colonial rule was the overriding enemy, not doctrinal differences among faiths. The result was an independent United States that had more religious unity (based on Protestantism, rather than Catholicism, Judaism, or Indian beliefs) than in the past.

The Church in Post-Colonial America

Mexican Issues

Deep and troubling disagreements splintered Mexico during the independence movement. Miguel Hidalgo and José María Morelos, both parish priests, led the fight and at the same time called for social improvements for the poor. Independence came but not social reform. Emperor Agustín Iturbide declared Catholicism the religion of the new nation and guaranteed the church the same privileges that it had enjoyed under Spain. Official support for the church collapsed in the face of growing liberal strength, leading to church-state relations characterized more by discord than harmony. The church sided with traditional and powerful groups in society and supported conservative governments as it did in Europe. Consequently, it was one of the most criticized institutions in the growing crossfire between conservatives and liberals.

The wealth of the church, estimated by some historians as 20 per cent of national wealth, headed a long list of controversial issues. A wealthy church alongside a poor state foretold of bitter struggles. Another controversy centered on the *fueros*, or the church's special charter of privileges. The church had its own courts, separate from those of the nation, a situation that became more intolerable as equality before the law emerged as one of the hallmarks of liberal rule. In general, liberal thinking viewed the church as impeding the development of Mexico and the creation of a modern state. With its emphasis on spiritual rather than material life, on acceptance of hardships as preparation for reward in the next life, and on submission to authority, the church stood with the conservative forces in society.

Attempts to reduce the power and wealth of the church started early. In 1833, Valentín Gómez Farías (vice-president to a semi-retired Antonio López de Santa Anna) secularized education, abolished the forced payment of the tithe, and turned over the Franciscan missions in California to the secular clergy. Conservatives reacted so intensely that most of the reforms were not enacted. Demanding *religión y fueros*, religion and special rights, they fought every effort to control the church. Nevertheless, the reformers gained momentum and promulgated more far-reaching reforms in the Constitution of 1857. It took the War of the Reform to bring the liberals to power, and when they arrived they attacked the church with a vengeance. They limited the jurisdiction of the special courts, sold church lands, outlawed wearing religious clothing in public, and prohibited religious oaths in civil ceremonies. In addition they declared freedom of religion in Mexico. As with so much of Mexican political history, there was a difference between law and reality, and many of the reforms failed to have an impact. The French intervention brought a respite for the church. So did the administration of Porfirio Díaz, an acknowledged liberal but one interested in developing and maintaining a working relationship with the church.

The crusade against the church culminated in the Mexican Revolution of 1910. Several articles of the Constitution of 1917 legalized reforms that had been advocated intermittently since the 1820s. Three had particular consequences for church and society. Article 3 prevented priests from participating in elementary education; Article 27 limited church ownership of land; and Article 130, the most comprehensive article regulating the church, forbade priests from voting or participating in politics. The Constitution included many other provisions that severely restricted the church in Mexico but did not yet bring an end to the century of factionalism over church-state relations.

Canadian Differences
Two religions rather than one shared the allegiance of Canadians. Catholicism, still the dominant religion, enjoyed renewal in the nineteenth century, partly because of its association with the struggle to insure the survival of Quebec culture. In response to the increasing number of English settlers, the Anglican Church, along with an increasing number of Protestant sects, also grew. The first Anglican bishop, appointed in 1787 in Nova Scotia, served all of Canada until the creation of the Diocese of Quebec in 1793. Subsequently, other dioceses formed as Anglicanism spread throughout Canada.

Education was a key issue in the nineteenth-century history of the church. The formation of the Province of Canada included provisions for Christian but not denominational education. In response, Quebec demanded that the state support Catholic as well as Protestant education. The result was that the state subsidized (and still does in some provinces) religious education, a practice different from the United States. Several political realities help to explain the difference. The Province of Canada (Quebec and Ontario) contained two primary religious groups, Catholics and Anglicans. To satisfy the minority group (Catholics in Ontario and Protestants in Quebec), the government called for state support of the minority educational group. Another reality was the tradition of church-state relations that extended as far back as the *Quebec Act* of 1774, which guaranteed the rights of Catholics in Quebec. Finally, in the mid years of the nineteenth century, there was still a strong belief in the interrelationship between religion and education in Canada.

The *British North America Act* of 1867 perpetuated the existing system but also opened the door for controversy. Under provisions of the act, the provinces had the authority to control education, but they had to respect the existing denominational schools. The result has been the development of a different perception of public education. In Canada, public (supported by the state) education was either separate (denominational) or common (non-denominational). Private education (not supported by the state) can be either. Sorting out the responsibilities of the provinces and the rights of different religions has led to many political battles in Canada.

Revivalism in the United States

In the United States, according to the Constitution, the state neither protected, nor supported, nor discriminated against religious belief and its expression in churches. This represented a confirmation of trends established during the seventeenth and eighteenth centuries. Even in colonies where the Church of England was the official church, there were many different denominations of Christianity. They depended on voluntary associations, expressions of religious convictions rather than of state support.

These convictions periodically burst forth into religious revivals that shook religious and social life. The first, spanning the middle years of the eighteenth century and emphasizing a rejuvenation of religious belief, was known as the Great Awakening. The first half of the nineteenth century was also a period of vigorous and emotional expressions of Christianity, which led to the Second Great Awakening, a movement that gained strength in the 1820s and 1830s as preachers exhorted their followers to seek a new, more intimate relationship with Jesus Christ. Appealing more to emotion than reason, these movements and their successors reflected a special type of Christianity in the colonies and then the United States. Emphasizing the Bible, conversion, and direct contact with Jesus Christ, the movements challenged the control of traditional denominations and created new ones.

Canadian evangelism also flowered in the late eighteenth and early nineteenth centuries, heightening the social appeal of religion and intensifying the competition for souls. Gathering strength in the 1770s, the Great Awakening in Canada drew its inspiration from local conditions, the colonies to the south, and England. It spread from Nova Scotia westward, influencing cultural life in much of English-speaking Canada. Regardless of the country, hucksters and showmen were always a part of this type of religious activity, whether in the eighteenth century or the 1920s or the 1980s. But there was something deeper — a profound dislike of religious formalism and hierarchy, a personal search for spiritual meaning, and an expression of moral righteousness — that spilled over into social and political life. While religion was not formally a part of the state, it informally influenced social and political behavior.

Reform

Religious renewal often had social implications. Even the eighteenth century revivals are best interpreted as one part of the unrest that changed political, intellectual, and social life in Western Europe and North America. The outbreaks of evangelical fervor in the nineteenth century continued the tradition as religious institutions reacted to the increasing problems associated with the economic transformations of the nineteenth century. The United States, undergoing an earlier and more intensive process of urbanization and industrialization, led the way. The list of social problems was long and daunting: crime, poverty, unemployment, illiteracy, violence, and alcohol abuse.

Attempts to control alcohol consumption offer a good example of the merging of religious belief and public policy. In Mexico the attempts extended back to the sixteenth century, when the rapid cultural changes accompanying the conquest led to increased alcohol abuse. *Pulque*, a fermented beverage made from the juice of the agave, a cactus common in Mexico, was the leading culprit according to reformers. Through the centuries, religious and political officials called for the control of pulque and other alcoholic beverages. By the late nineteenth century, pulque was likened to a scourge that afflicted the body and soul of Mexico. Indeed, alcoholism had become a severe problem in rural and urban Mexico. Efforts to root it out continued in the twentieth century.

Programs in Mexico lacked the organizational and political strength of those in the United States and Canada. The movement in the United States gathered strength as early as the 1840s and continued strong into the twentieth century. Led by the Women's Christian Temperance Union, which claimed 245,000 members in the early twentieth century, it successfully forced the passage of prohibition laws in 19 states by 1916. The final push for national legislation culminated in the passage of the Eighteenth Amendment in 1919 (repealed by the Twenty-First Amendment in 1933).

In Canada support for prohibition also gained strength in the nineteenth century. The Sons of Temperance Union joined the Women's Christian Temperance Union to fight alcohol on every front. Early success came with the passage of legislation in New Brunswick in 1855 that outlawed alcoholic beverages, although it was quickly repealed. The legislation was at least partly in response to the prohibition law that had been passed in the neighboring state of Maine in 1851. By the early twentieth century, several provinces had enacted prohibition, and in 1918 the national government, as a wartime measure, restricted the manufacture and importation of alcoholic beverages. A year later, it recanted and allowed the provinces to determine their own liquor laws.

Quebec was always a holdout against prohibition and formally rejected the national measure in 1919. Montreal, in particular, benefited from the rush of tourists from neighboring New York and Canadian dry provinces. Towns scattered along the U.S.-Mexico border also benefited in similar fashion. Despite the support for prohibition by many (Pancho Villa advocated prohibition in Chihuahua), Mexico never banned alcohol. Travel to the border towns of Tijuana and Ciudad Juárez increased in the 1920s as tourists came in search of liquor and night life. They returned smuggling bottles of liquor. The production of liquor in both Mexico and Canada increased in the 1920s to meet the demand in the United States.

The Social Gospel was the most comprehensive, religiously inspired reform movement of the late nineteenth century. According to the reformers, the gospel of Jesus Christ offered the best solution for the social problems of the day. Besides joining the temperance movement, the reformers built settlement houses, reformed school curricula, sponsored training programs, and organized to pass legislation to regulate everything from sanitation to child welfare. Reformist political movements in both Canada and the United States depended on the energy and enthusiasm of the promoters of the Social Gospel. While the movement would continue in different guises, it ebbed in the 1920s as postwar prosperity seemed to minimize social problems.

In Mexico and Quebec, social reformers drew inspiration from Catholic social thought, but they seldom achieved the success or notoriety of the advocates of the Social Gospel in the United States and English-speaking Canada. As discussed in Chapter 8, papal pronouncements recognized the building tensions in the new urban-industrial societies of the late nineteenth century and issued calls for assistance to workers and the poor. The pronouncements, though, were phrased within the Catholic tradition and seldom called for a radical restructuring of society.

Demands for social reform were only one part of a broader struggle that pitted fundamentalists against modernists. The modernists called for an adaptation of Christianity to the scientific and social changes of the late nineteenth and early twentieth century. Specifically, they argued for a more flexible Christianity that could adapt to the new scientific discoveries of the times. Life changed at a bewildering pace, undermining the traditional role of family and religion. A modern Christianity was especially necessary in education, where students could learn about the new scientific discoveries of the age. The fundamentalists continued to insist on a strict interpretation of the Bible as the only true means of organizing knowledge and life. In the United States, the conflict culminated in the 1925 "Scopes monkey trial," in which John T. Scopes, a teacher in Tennessee, was convicted of violating state law when he taught the biological principles of evolution. Despite a reversal of the conviction, fundamentalist views on science continued to influence textbook treatment of evolution well into the twentieth-first century, revealing the ongoing struggle between Christian fundamentalism and secular modernism.

New Directions

After the Revolution of 1910, the Mexican church struggled to survive under the limitations imposed by the Constitution of 1917. A brief accommodation lasted until 1926 when the Archbishop of Mexico City, José Mora y del Río, in an interview with the Mexican press, reacted to anticlerical measures by arguing that Catholics did not have to follow the Constitution. President Plutarco Elías Calles (1924-28) reacted with draconian measures, severely curtailing the activities of the church. On 31 July 1936, the Mexican church, with the blessings of the Vatican, declared a strike, as the clergy shut down churches and refused to administer the sacraments or even say Mass. When some of the faithful reacted with violence, a guerrilla war broke out that lasted until 1929. Known as the Cristero Rebellion because its adherents rallied around the cry, *Viva Cristo Rey* (Long Live Christ the King), it testified to the deep antagonisms still present in Mexico after the revolution. The effects of war reverberated as far north as Canada, where an outraged Bishop Michael Francis Fallon of London, Ontario, protested the religious persecution as well as his country's assistance to Mexico as it attempted to reorganize its national railway. Fallon described the Calles administration as a "gang of venal ruffians and treacherous assassins who have displaced civilization by savagery, and have destroyed the last vestige of civil and religious liberty in the Republic of Mexico" (Ogelsby 1976, 183).

After the war the church's uneasy relationship with the state continued. Under President Lázaro Cárdenas it faced new threats to its educational and moral goals of instilling Catholic values. Cárdenas emphasized a comprehensive program of educational, social, and economic reform that borrowed from socialist doctrines. Some Catholic conservatives joined the *sinarquistas*, a reactionary mass political movement sympathetic to Fascism in Europe. Others joined the new National Action Party, founded on Christian and capitalist principles. The extremism of the 1930s gave way to moderation in the 1940s. The church no longer faced persecution, but it was still limited in education, economics, politics, and in public religious displays. Only slowly did the strident anticlericalism of the past abate.

Catholicism survived as a powerful force in Quebec until the 1960s, when it rapidly lost power and influence. Some historians of Quebec label it a time of "*déclérisation*," or the diminishing presence of the church in education, society, and government. It did not come about through the radical anticlericalism that dominated Mexican history but through a rapid secularization that catapulted the state to the forefront of activities in the province. As provincial bureaucracies gained more influence during the 1960s, the church became more marginalized, losing its traditional power in many social services. More damaging was its loss of priests and parishioners. The number of priests in the province dropped from 8,400 in 1960 to 4,285 in 1981; parishioners stopped going to Mass; churches closed. The Quebec church, so long a pillar of society, had lost its privileged position in the province.

A significant early development in the rest of Canada was the formation of the United Church of Canada in 1925 through the union of the Presbyterian, Methodist, and Congregational churches. This was a major step toward ecumenism that continues until today. True to its original goals, the United Church remains active in missionary and social work. Its ecumenical goals have not been realized, but they have surpassed efforts in the United States.

The United States maintained its official separation of church and state, even as religion continued to display social and political strength. A symbolic act was the insertion of the words "under God" into the "Pledge of Allegiance" in 1954 so that it read "one nation, under God, indivisible." There was no established church in the United States, but Christianity in its many variations had become a deeply ingrained characteristic of national life. Many politicians defend the separation of church and state, and public schools forbid school prayer. At the same time, however, politicians regularly make public professions of their religious beliefs.

Christianity continued to splinter into many denominations and sects after World War I. Literally hundreds of Protestant denominations spread across the land, most of them failing to attract many members. In addition, many other religions practiced by immigrants continued to grow. Judaism received its strongest boost from the Eastern European and Russian immigration of the late nineteenth century. Buddhism, Confucianism, Taoism, and Hinduism spread with Asian immigrants. Islam arrived with immigrants from North Africa and the Middle East. Begrudgingly accepted at first, these religions have become widely accepted in the United States and Canada. In Mexico, the predominance of Catholicism, the small number of immigrants, and the strident anticlericalism of the state restricted religious diversity.

The growth of Christianity and other religions in the twentieth century occurred in the face of increasing secularization. Urbanization and industrialization led to new economic relationships that minimized the importance of God. Rapid economic growth in the interwar years laid the foundation for a new materialism that threatened the power of religion. The rise of science and the growing devotion to scientific explanations for life seemed to reduce the need for religious explanations. Intellectual and political currents did the same. Popular magazines periodically ran feature articles on "Does God Exist?" or "Is God Dead?"

Secular sentiments did not kill God. Instead, in the 1950s Christianity assumed even more power as preachers and priests used the new medium of television in addition to radio to spread the gospel. Billy Graham, the twentieth century's most

famous evangelist, was still preaching in 1998; Monsignor Fulton J. Sheen popularized the Catholic message; Martin Luther King Jr. headed the Civil Rights movement
and argued for non-violent methods to end racism. Hundreds of others achieved
regional and national stature as representatives of the mainline religions or of
smaller denominations.

Recent Controversies

In recent years religious figures and institutions in the United States continued to
speak out on political issues that had moral implications. While there was never
unanimity among Christian believers, many fundamentalists adhered to the tenets
of the Moral Majority, a religious-political movement of the 1970s and 1980s that
attempted to influence elections, laws, and legal decisions. The abortion issue com-
manded the most attention. In 1973 the Supreme Court ruling of *Roe v. Wade* overturned state laws forbidding abortions. Since that time, the abortion issue has
divided society. Alongside of it are many others. The 1962 decision of the Supreme
Court declaring prayer in public schools unconstitutional (*Engel v. Vitale*) still ran-
kles many.

Many other issues continue to frustrate church-state relations in the United
States. One is the *Native American Free Exercise of Religion Act.* Indians want protection of sacred sites, which are locations for religious ceremonies. The close relationship between place and ritual remains one of the characteristics of Indian religions.
They also want freedom for the Native American Church to use peyote in its ceremonies. The Native American Church was founded in 1918 and now has over
250,000 followers in the United States, Canada, and Mexico. Its ceremonies rely on
the use of peyote in practices that extend back for centuries. State laws are inconsis-
tent in allowing or forbidding its use. In addition, Indians argue for the right to use
eagle feathers, although the bird is protected under endangered species law in the
United States, and other items in religious ceremonies. Finally, they insist that Indian
prisoners have the same right to practice their religion as do members of Judeo-
Christian religions.

Canadian churches took stances on similar issues, usually siding with their U.S.
counterparts on matters of abortion and indigenous religions. There were differences, however. Canadian beliefs and sentiments were more muted and contained,
less likely to spill into the political realm and equate public policy with morality. The
strength of churches in Canada was dissipating rapidly, more so than in the United
States. Quebec's experience was the most extreme; as we have seen, the Catholic
Church lost its position of moral leadership and control over education and social
services. Churches in the United States, where church support had always been voluntary, co-existed more easily with the forces of secularization.

In Mexico the Catholic Church may be on the verge of reviving its political voice.
While Mexico was never a center of liberation theology, many religious leaders

throughout the country embraced the idea of the gospel as a call to improve the lives of the poor. Particularly in the depressed and heavily Indian states of the south, priests participated in political struggles for change. Despite localized efforts to initiate social justice, Mexicans were reminded on a much grander scale of the disparities of wealth in their society by the frequent visits of Pope John Paul II. He chose Mexico for his first overseas pastoral visit, visiting the city of Puebla in 1979 to attend a Latin American Episcopal Conference. The visit would become the first of five pastoral visits to Mexico, and each time the pope used the bully pulpit to address Mexico's most pressing social and economic issues. It was apparent even to the most casual observer that John Paul II was touched by Mexican displays of affection and religiosity. When he declared Juan Diego, the Indian to whom the Virgin of Guadalupe appeared, a saint, the pope assured himself a permanent place in the hearts of many Mexicans. John Paul combined the humility ascribed to Juan Diego with the motherly care of the Virgin to speak out against poverty and injustice.

At the national level, voices also began to challenge political corruption and social inequality. In late 1996, Archbishop Norberto Rivera Carrera (now Cardinal Rivera), in the tradition of his predecessor in the 1920s, declared that the church "can and should involve itself in politics, as did Jesus" (*The Washington Post*, 23 October 1996). Here was one of the leading prelates of the land openly challenging the power of the state. All was taking place within a new political atmosphere that had relaxed many of the constitutional restrictions on the church. When Carlos Salinas assumed the presidential office in 1988, he began a policy of engagement with the church by restoring diplomatic relations with the Vatican, relations that had been severed for 130 years. President Salinas also pushed for amendments to the Constitution's most anticlerical provisions. By the end of his administration in 1994, public religious celebrations were legalized, the Mexican Church could own property as well as run parochial schools, and the clergy could vote in elections. The election of Vicente Fox in 2000 was yet another step in the modern history of church-state relations in Mexico. National and international newspapers published front page pictures of the newly elected president receiving communion at Mass, another sure sign of the new accommodation between the church and state.

Throughout modern North American history, commentators have decried the decline of religious influence and the resulting social chaos and moral decay that such a decline precipitates. The great revivals from the eighteenth century onward attempted to rejuvenate Christianity and stem the tide of dissolution by arguing for social reform. Despite the fears of a godless society, religion was and is a powerful force in North American society. The continent-wide success of Mel Gibson's 2004 film, *The Passion of the Christ*, demonstrated that leisure time and religiosity are part of a broader cultural fabric that brings together families and neighborhoods, even if many in Hollywood are in denial. Popular religious sentiment is but one variable, however, to understanding North America. The Mexican Catholic Church is still adjusting to the economic and social transitions of the last two decades, but it is speaking out anew on national issues. The Catholic Church in Quebec has not recovered from the secularization of the 1960s, but Christians of many denominations throughout Canada quietly speak about national issues and provide a religious context for decision-making. In the United States, religion remains an unbreakable thread in the social and political fabric of the nation. Moral and political issues are closely intertwined, and churches speak loudly and with conviction about the appropriate course for the nation.

As the twenty-first century unfolds, the issues and problems will change and likely become more complex as religious diversity increases with the arrival of more immigrants. There is little doubt, however, that organized religion and its accompanying theology will continue to shape the beliefs and values of Mexicans, Canadians, and Americans, competing in the marketplace of ideas, which, in turn, imbues public discourse with a sensibility that is neither rigidly theocratic nor abrasively secular but rather illustrative of the multiple meanings that believers and non-believers attach to the role of religion and spirituality in society.

CHAPTER 11
STRUCTURES OF THE PAST

This chapter summarizes some of the fundamental differences and similarities in the historical development of North America. It emphasizes what might be called the structural features of the North American experience, those characteristics and patterns that endure for long periods of time. This approach has advantages and disadvantages. Historical abstractions conceal much of the diversity and richness of the past, much like the rounded hills and eroded ridges of the Appalachian Mountains hide the lives of the men and women living in the hollows and river valleys. These abstractions, however, can reveal broad patterns of change and continuity that are essential for interpreting North America as a whole.

A common assumption among many historians and their students is that the trifurcation of the North American past is somehow natural and timeless, that national histories provide a sufficient conceptual framework for explaining change over time. From the vantage point of the early twenty-first century, when more and more scholars are employing world history paradigms and interdisciplinary methodologies in their research and teaching, national histories, which often have been written without much regard to sustained contact and exchange with other cultures and societies, provide but one kind of narrative of the human experience. Our task has been to recast the narrative in a much larger context, that of the continent rather than just its constituent parts. To be sure, a continental understanding of North America includes a rigorous examination of the scholarship produced in Canada, Mexico, and the United States, which identifies and interprets what is considered unique and exceptional to the historical experiences of each nation-state. At the same time, however, the similarities and differences in historical trajectory point to the continental dimensions of political economy, cross-cultural contact and exchange, trade, and a consumer culture that creates demand for the material expressions of yet another age of globalization. Simultaneously complex and subtle, predictable and elusive, the forces of convergence and divergence test the ability of our continental approach to explain the history of North America in a persuasive and meaningful way.

Bedrock Features

Two fundamental characteristics deserve emphasis at the outset. First is the size and distribution of Indian peoples before the arrival of Europeans. The difference in the historical development of central and southern Mexico and the rest of North America derives in large part from the dense concentration of Indian peoples in the highland valleys of Mexico. The entire Spanish colonial enterprise in Mexico, from the cathedrals and government palaces of the cities to the mines and haciendas of the countryside, depended on the labor of Indians. With Indian labor, Spain was able to build a larger, more complex colonial world much more rapidly than England and France to the north.

The achievements of Spain came at a cost. Indians were subordinated to Spaniards and restricted to secondary roles in the new society. Little opportunity existed for them to improve their lives, although it would be incorrect to compare their situation to the one in India, where a rigid caste system separated people. Some mobility and flexibility existed, but overall colonial life controlled and dominated Indians. The political structure separated them from Spaniards and imposed special restrictions and burdens on them; the economic system exploited them; and prevailing social and cultural beliefs relegated them to an inferior position. Mexico carried this burden into the twenty-first century.

A second bedrock feature was the timing of colonization. Spain was caught between the medieval and modern worlds in the first years of the sixteenth century. Its most important legacy was the *reconquista*, the almost 800-year long process of "reconquering" the Iberian peninsula from Muslim control. As the reconquest unfolded, it helped to define the social and economic patterns that Spain introduced into Mexico. Status and wealth were equated with force of arms, the right to collect tribute, and control over vast estates. The ideal of the *señor*, or seigneurial lord, admired for his power as well as for his large farms, brocaded clothing, and ornate carriages, provided inspiration for the new immigrants who arrived from Spain.

At the same time Spaniards arrived full of a renaissance drive for knowledge, wealth, and power. They inherited many of the ideas of the modern world — business organization, accounting and insurance practices, new techniques in map-making and navigation, and the ability to diffuse knowledge quickly through the printing press. In this sense they were as modern as the English and French colonists who followed 100 years later. Yet their modernity always butted up against a past that lingered in their minds and actions. They strove to recreate as accurately as possible the life of the medieval lord with his titles and power based on the ownership of large landed estates and control over subordinates and retainers. The availability of a large Indian population to shoulder the burdens of building the new society helped them to accomplish their objectives. Although they arrived a century later, the plantation owners in the slave societies of the southern United States fit the same mold.

Despite these characteristics of Mexican history that give it a strong Latin

American texture, thick historical threads bound it to the north instead of the south. War, diplomacy, trade, transportation, immigration — all had more of a northern than a southern dynamic. Patterns of colonization and a shared frontier with the United States also linked it to the north.

The northern tier of Mexico with its small Indian population, harsh climate, and wide-open spaces developed a culture different from that of central Mexico or the slave societies of the south of the United States. More open, mobile, and egalitarian than the Mexican south, northern Mexico was a land of opportunity during much of its history. It shared an ethos closer to that emerging in the British colonies in the eighteenth century than central Mexico in the sixteenth century.

French Canada was in a slightly different position. The French created a seigneurial system reminiscent of the feudal past that called for the settlers to pay their lords rents and dues. These were usually modest and at times not paid. Indeed, the system often worked to the advantage of the settlers, since the lord had to provide them with expensive grist mills and ovens. Further weakening the system was the opportunity for settlers to leave their land and enter the world of the fur trade. The result was the failure of a rigid hierarchical feudal system to develop.

The early history of the colonies laid the foundation for many of the social and cultural differences found within North America. The meaning of race is an important example. In Canada race had little to do with genetic characteristics or physical difference. Instead, it emphasized the cultural and historical differences between English and French settlers. Historians wrote books and politicians gave speeches about the race question in Canada, many discussing the superiority of Anglo-Saxon political and economic institutions and the inferiority of French-Canadian ones. The French Canadians in turn expressed belief in their own superiority when they spoke of the future of their race in the face of the English domination of Canada.

Mexico with its large African and Indian population was racially more complex than Canada. Yet by the early nineteenth century, ideas about race had little to do with Africans and much to do with Indians and mestizos. The deep-seated practices of discrimination against Indians continued through the colonial period. Independence eliminated their legal inferiority but not the prejudice directed against them. The Revolution of 1910 further liberated them but still did not end their inferior position in society. The glorious portrayal of Indians in the great art of the post-revolutionary period did not change their miserable living conditions.

Mestizos represented another group in the racial complexity of Mexico. Mestizos were usually closer to the European than the Indian world, but they experienced discrimination as well during much of the colonial period. In the nineteenth and twentieth centuries they underwent a slow metamorphosis from marginality to centrality in the historical consciousness of Mexico. After the Revolution of 1910 mestizos were officially recognized as the core ethnic group of the Mexican nation, charged with the special mission of creating a new world of racial fusion and harmony. In the

1960s and 1970s, *la Raza* became something different still in the Latino community of the United States. It suggested a cultural and social unity for people of Latino (especially Mexican) descent in the United States. "La Raza" connoted pride and a commitment to political action to improve the social and economic condition of Latino peoples.

In the United States race and racism historically apply invariably to black and white relationships, although recent scholarship has tried to widen the scope of critical inquiry by evaluating the multilayered experiences of Hispanics, Indians, Asians, and those who identify themselves with a variety of racial and ethnic groups. Under slavery and then as free men and women, blacks suffered discrimination and segregation. Seldom did culture, wealth, or shades of color soften the blows of racism. In Mexico Indians could acquire a different status through education, wealth, power, and the process of becoming mestizos. Patterns of racism in the United States seldom allowed for this kind of flexibility. Born out of a slave system that grew rapidly in the first half of the nineteenth century, just as Mexico and Canada were abolishing slavery, racism provided the ideology to support plantation society. The Civil War changed that society in many ways but did not eliminate the racism that was so important to its survival.

Despite the burdens of racism, the English seaboard colonies were from the beginning more open, flexible, and promising of opportunity than bordering Spanish and French societies. Immigration policies and patterns were sure evidence of the differences. Quebec and Mexico remained almost exclusively French and Spanish, while the English colonies had immigrants from all of Europe in addition to England. Immigration continued to mark the difference after independence. The United States, endowed with great natural resources and a rapidly expanding economy, absorbed wave after wave of immigrants. Long before the Civil War its population dwarfed that of its neighbors, insuring it of a special place in the Americas. The belief in social mobility, that is, the ability to acquire wealth and status, has been a guiding principle in the social organization of the United States. It continues to attract immigrants.

Economic Structures

Theories of economic development offer other insights into the history of North America. Both Canada and Mexico initially grew from the export of primary products to Europe. The "staples theory" of development in Canada emphasizes the export of fish, fur, lumber, and then grain as the central economic activities that conditioned growth. In Mexico a similar idea, known as "dependency theory," emphasizes the export of silver and the lesser value commodities of cacao, tobacco, cochineal, and other products. In both countries, exports locked the economies into a dependent position in the international economy, a position both reflecting and reinforcing the dominant political and social institutions.

The theories are helpful and do set the Canadian and Mexican economies apart from the U.S. economy, which early on showed signs of diversity, complexity, and industrial strength. They do not, however, go far enough in explaining the different tempos of economic change and development. Despite its reliance on the export of staples, Canada, more specifically Ontario, emerged as a major industrial power with a rapidly increasing standard of living, while Mexico continued as an extractive and agricultural economy that repressed its workers. Economically Quebec was more similar to Mexico than to Anglo America. It continued to rely mainly on extractive industries and outside capital for its economic development.

Particular events and developments at just about every point in the history of North America are useful in explaining the difference. In the 1840s, for example, while Mexico struggled with the aftermath of the loss of Texas, conflicts with France, and internal instability, Canada made great economic strides. The export of staples, especially wheat, tripled during the 1840s, providing capital for development. Improvements in transportation came with the completion of the Welland Canal (connecting Lakes Erie and Ontario) and helped to move grain cheaply. At the same time, the population increased rapidly as immigrants arrived. Canada was now ready to break beyond the edge of the great shield and spill into the Prairie provinces, leading to another stage in development. Essentially the same was happening in the United States as agricultural and industrial manufacturing increased, transportation networks spread, and the population grew.

Mexico, on the other hand, was mired in a factionalism that prevented any uniform development strategies. Few immigrants came and foreign investment was limited as the country struggled to create order out of disorder. The end of the decade brought even more hardship as the Mexican-American War cost Mexico half of its national territory; the War of the Reform followed, and then the French intervention. These crises impeded Mexico's development efforts for almost another half-century. When growth accelerated toward the end of the century, it reinforced the export-oriented features of the economy and failed to create a modern industrial base.

Reform

One of the singular features in the political history of North America is the strength of reform movements in the United States and Canada and their weakness in Mexico. The differences are evident from the first years of settlement but most telling in the nineteenth and twentieth centuries. After independence in the early nineteenth century Mexican efforts at reform centered on reducing the power of the church and resolving conflicts among competing political factions. By mid-century reformers targeted the break-up of the land held by the church and Indian villages as the solution to the country's problems. The results triggered the War of the Reform in the late 1850s but did little to reform society. The reform did free some capital for economic development, but it did not create an open democratic society with new opportunities for Indians. After the reform movement of the 1850s, new programs to improve the condition of the poor, the educational system, and the effectiveness of government seldom gained enough momentum to alter the social and political structure. Very simply, Mexico's drive for reform was not as widespread and deeply rooted as that in Anglo-America in the nineteenth century.

The frustrated efforts at reform broke into revolutionary violence in 1910. First in an attempt at political reform and then in a series of economic and social convulsions that shook the nation, Mexicans attempted to create a new, more just society. The Constitution of 1917 advanced radical measures for improving the lives of urban and rural workers. In fact, it can be argued that the Mexican Constitution is the most progressive political document to have emerged from the continent in the twentieth century. The achievements of the Mexican Revolution and the Constitution of 1917, of course, have been much debated. Opinions differ, but the reality of Mexican society in the latter half of the twentieth century spoke for itself: corruption and excessive centralization in political life; widespread inequalities in the distribution of income; uneven regional growth; emergence of a so-called *narcocultura*, or drug-trafficking culture; and increasing pessimism about the future. Given this environment, the reforms initiated in the 1980s assumed more importance. The economic restructuring that started in the 1990s, as well as the stunning defeat of the ruling party (PRI) at the polls in 2000 and then again in 2006, hold out the promise of meaningful social changes in Mexico, but skeptics, disillusioned with past failures, lack confidence in the future. They point to the 2006 presidential election and its aftermath as additional evidence for their pessimism: followers of the PRD candidate, Andrés Manuel López Obrador, refused to acknowledge the PAN candidate Felipe Calderón's razor-thin victory despite international and domestic assurances that the election was clean. López Obrador declared himself the next president, even staging an inauguration ceremony and appointing a shadow government. While most Mexicans, including several prominent PRD leaders, distanced themselves from these tactics, they also had to contend simultaneously with a troublesome drug war that was causing much bloodshed in several Mexican states, particularly Michoacán and Nuevo León. The divisiveness of the 2006 election results, coupled with the expanding role of the Mexican military and federal police to combat the violent influence of the drug traffickers, suggests that continuity will continue to butt heads with efforts to nurture and sustain structural changes in Mexico's political economy.

The political history of the United States is different. In almost every decade since the late eighteenth century reform movements have affected life. The Great Awakening, the Second Great Awakening, the Abolitionists, the Temperance and Suffrage Movements, and the Social Gospel called for change in just about every corner of life. In more comprehensive ways, the Populist, Progressive, and New Deal political movements did the same, demanding modifications in government to address social, political, and economic inequalities. In the 1950s and 1960s other reform movements got their start—civil rights, women's rights, environmentalism, and gay rights—and other large and small-scale politically conscious groups shaped political life. The emergence of the religious right in the 1980s, as well as anti-immigration groups in the 1990s, shows that the more conservative elements in U.S. society also can mobilize their respective constituents to achieve stated goals. In other words, reform movements continue to influence the United States.

Canada's experience was more of a bimodal one. English Canada had a tradition similar to that of the United States, though the intensity and scope of reforms were generally milder and more restricted. One explanation is the influence of the Loyalists who moved to Canada from the United States during and after the revolt against Britain. They (along with the steady stream of immigrants from Britain) helped to impose a decidedly Tory cast to Canadian political history, conferring respect and power on the established political and religious institutions. Another explanation is the late, gradual, and peaceful independence of Canada. Even when independence came it was only partial. Britain retained treaty power and the final say in amending the Constitution.

Despite these limitations to reform, English Canada was far more reformist than Quebec. After the French defeat in 1759, traditional political and religious forces dug in and defended Quebec from British influence. The power of the Catholic Church was essential in the struggle to preserve the traditional culture. It assumed much more power than it did in Mexico, where it was under attack even before the wars for independence broke out in 1810. In Quebec, Catholicism shored up the French language, rural values, and a conservative political ideology that withstood many of the reforms affecting the rest of Canada. Even during the Great Depression of the 1930s, Quebec resisted the New Deal reforms influencing Canada and the United States. Instead, it stressed a provincial nativism, emphasizing order and hierarchy. Once again, a church allied with conservative political forces was at the center of upholding traditional society.

When change came it did so quickly. Reforms swept through much of Quebec during the *revolution tranquille* of the 1960s. Traditional values and ways of life gave way to a new secularism that reduced the power of the church. Quebec reconciled its urban and industrial reality with its rural agrarian past. It demanded and received new control over its economy and new independence in its political life. Conservative Prime Minister Stephen Harper's assertion in late 2006 that Quebec is a nation within a nation, supported as it was by a motion in the House of Commons, sustains the region's sense of distinctiveness. Many in the province, however, want to avoid abrasive tactics to express the point. Quebec in society, work, and politics has become much like the rest of Canada and the United States.

The Future
The forces of convergence continue to drive the integration of the continent. People,

culture, and goods and services move north and south at a dizzying pace, making the borders less significant in the development of each nation-state. As this interaction intensifies it produces reactions: increased immigration leads to cultural change and political movements; trade agreements create hardships and prompt demands for renegotiations; labor searches for new forms of organization to promote its interests; regions and localities assert their distinctiveness and demand more and more auton- omy; new continental organizations — education, environment, trade, defense, and others — arbitrate disputes and plan for the future.

These thrusts and parries have been a part of the past and will continue to influ- ence the future. They have not yet produced major political restructuring of the con- tinent. They are in a sense a continuation of the old continentalism of the nineteenth century, pushing for foreign investment, lower tariffs, and foreign trade. Mexico is very much a part of this new continentalism, whereas in the past it always had strong reservations about the political consequences of closer integration with the United States.

The new wave of continentalism will not necessarily lead to political changes, but the Quebec situation adds a new element of uncertainty. If Quebec does achieve sov- ereignty, the forces of political continentalism will be invigorated. The natural links between the Maritimes and New England, the Prairie provinces and the upper Midwest and Great Plains, and British Columbia and the state of Washington, cou- pled with the intense interaction that has taken place in the last 20 years, will most likely lead to discussions of new binational and trinational political arrangements.

The border between Mexico and the United States adds another element of insta- bility. It, more so than the Canadian border, has experienced intense economic and social change since the 1960s, including a constant influx of Spanish-speakers seek- ing employment, the establishment of *maquiladoras* in need of foreign investment, hybrid cultural forms, and the violence associated with drug trafficking. A part of this change has been the development of a culture that has claims to its own distinc- tiveness, different from those in central Mexico and the United States. U.S.-Mexico border culture, always in continuous formation, is the subject of much more com- mentary and debate than that along the northern border, although 9/11 has raised security concerns about the porous nature of the U.S.-Canadian border. The Canadian penchant for promoting multiculturalism within a framework sensitive to the political realities of a multilingual society adds another social dimension to northern border culture whose long-term effects are difficult to ascertain.

The political implications of these changes along the border remain elusive to define in any fixed and concrete way. A set of distinct educational, linguistic, health, security, environmental, and economic problems has emerged that seeks political expression in order to facilitate solutions amiable to the three nation-states of North America. There are many possibilities for political and economic realignments, some of which reflect post-9/11 security concerns while others conjure up bolder initiatives that go beyond free trade. The United States might embrace, for example, a huddled, go-it-alone foreign policy, one reminiscent of President George W. Bush's decision to invade Iraq without strong international support or consensus. The isolationist strain in this scenario pushes the United States to look inward in terms of labor, trade, and even culture, while the hawkish strain seeks to flex U.S. muscle to achieve policy objectives without regard to its effects on continentalism. Trinational cooperation and economic integration become part of a diplomatic lexicon that the U.S. political leadership occasionally employs when domestic politics permits it. Such rhetoric often gets used as a response to concerns about the explosive growth of Asian economies or the spread of Islamic terrorism. In other words, the broader question becomes: how can continental cooperation serve the interests of the nation-state?

Another possibility for realignment arises from increased Mexican migration north of the international border. This scenario exerts steady pressure on social relationships in the United States and Mexico (less so in Canada), not to mention the broad fiscal consequences for local and state governments, health care, and schools in the United States. The result is a sustained U.S. backlash against all things Mexican that revives age-old animosities and suspicions. Backlashes have happened before, but they always proved fleeting and reflected specific regional expressions of economic crises. The deportation of thousands of Mexicans in the 1930s is a good example, as state governments on the U.S. side of the border scrambled to halt the debilitating effects of the Great Depression on their respective populations. For Mexico's part, immigration has reduced demographic pressures at home—and the billions of dollars sent back as remittances fuel the Mexican economy—but the social costs of scattered families have yet to be calculated adequately. Anecdotal evidence suggests that an entire generation of children is growing up in rural Mexico without parents or, at the very least, without a father. The downward trend in Mexico's birth rate suggests, albeit hesitantly, that, within a generation, Mexico should be able to produce enough jobs to meet demand and thus limit the need to migrate north to the United States. Until then, however, Mexican patience with the harshness of U.S. immigration politics might thin sooner rather than later, jeopardizing binational cooperation and continued economic integration. A populist streak in politics, which dates to the nineteenth century and includes a dash of nativism, continues to find expression in the three nation-states of North America. It is not difficult to imagine Mexico, Canada, or the United States clamoring for disengagement and pull-back from even a diluted form of continentalism.

The creation of a new political entity, one that overlaps each side of the border, offers yet another possible realignment. Some variation of a common market appears the most likely, although plenty of opposition exists in the United States, Mexico, and Canada to such a formalized and structured arrangement. Moreover, the idea of an integrated political entity is sometimes discussed in relation to a North American common market. It would not be a sovereign body but a trinational organization (or several binational organizations) equipped with powers to represent and resolve the special problems of the border, not to mention deal with the continental dimensions of these very same problems (pollution, security, immigration, etc).

Such realignment inched closer to reality in March 2005 when Paul Martin, George W. Bush, and Vicente Fox met in Texas to discuss ways to increase continental cooperation and understanding in a variety of economic, diplomatic, and political areas. The three leaders put their respective executive imprimaturs on the Security and Prosperity Partnership of North America (SPP). The principal objective of SPP is to "increase and enhance prosperity...through greater cooperation and information sharing...the initiative is premised on our security and our economic prosperity being mutually reinforcing...[and that the three] nations are bound by a shared belief in freedom, economic opportunity, and strong democratic institutions" (http://www.spp.gov). It seems rather easy to assign the "shared belief in freedom" to President Bush's rhetoric since 9/11, and the "economic opportunity" phrase to Mexican president Vicente Fox, with Canadian Prime Minister Martin using each of the three points to satisfy particular constituencies. The mixing-and-matching of rhetorical style and word choice, however, tends to privilege the domestic politics of each country rather than the broader diplomatic significance of renewed continental cooperation, now called a partnership. In fact, Martin, Bush, and Fox identified a series of critical issues beyond the traditional free trade model that included energy security, emergency management, and avian and pandemic influenza, as well as the creation of a North American Competitiveness Council.

Reaction to the SPP was essentially the same in all three countries, as most Canadians, Mexicans, and Americans went about their busy lives without feeling the need to check their "North American" pulses. Here again a North American identity has not yet emerged, and given the historical longevity that patriotism (both of a negative and positive quality) has enjoyed, not to mention the pedagogical tendency to categorize the world into nation-states, it is not surprising at all that the SPP went unnoticed by the vast majority of North Americans. The exceptions, of course, are noteworthy. Diplomats and academics committed to creating and maintaining a continental framework of political and economic cooperation cheered the news. In fact, the SPP was a pleasant surprise to some NAFTA supporters, who had become disillusioned when President Bush suddenly shifted the gears of U.S. diplomacy to respond to 9/11. When Canada and Mexico refused to support the U.S. invasion of Iraq in March 2003, North America watchers across the continent held their breath as relations cooled between the three countries. As the war in Iraq turned ugly for the United States despite a quick military victory that toppled Saddam Hussein, President Bush's foreign policy team decided to return to the one regional partnership that had enjoyed both diplomatic and economic success.

In March 2006, the national leaders met in Cancún to discuss progress and to look for ways to strengthen the SPP. Although Stephen Harper had replaced Paul Martin as prime minister, there was no change of course in the Canadian sensibility toward continentalism. Some Canadians even worried that Harper's pro-U.S. leanings might have their country supporting Bush's unilateral foreign policy, something that has been seen as an affront to the continentalism forged in the late 1980s and 1990s. Even a cursory analysis suggests that Harper, who heads a minority government, cannot afford politically to establish the Canadian voice within a North American framework by echoing U.S. policy on every issue. For its part, Mexico under Vicente Fox also remained committed to moving the relationship forward, especially with the July 2006 presidential election looming. Fox had wanted to formalize his version of continentalism in more concrete fashion since taking office in December 2000, a continentalism that included increased U.S. and Canadian investment as well as an immigration accord with the United States. A North American partnership was a vital component to his agenda. Fox anticipated a tight presidential race, and he wanted to ensure that "North America" remained part and parcel of Mexican diplomacy and economic policy.

The other noteworthy response to the SPP was nationalist in tone, populist in sentiment, and at worst protectionist and xenophobic. While a minority of citizens in Canada, Mexico, and the United States embrace the response, it does reflect long-held suspicions toward any diplomatic agreement that emphasizes regional or global cooperation at the expense of sovereignty and the nation-state. In Canada and Mexico, this feeling resonates among those who fear the ill effects of "Americanization" and the unilateral style of U.S. foreign policy under George W. Bush. The occasional protest breaks out to express popular displeasure with the "middle neighbor." In the United States, on the other hand, those suspicious of a North American partnership do not have to attend meetings of the ultra-conservative John Birch Society to vent their fears of NAFTA, SPP, the United Nations, or any other so-called supranational body. They simply listen to talk radio in the morning or watch cable networks CNN and FOX in the evening. As recently as June 2006, Americans watching CNN heard Lou Dobbs, host of Lou Dobbs Tonight, declare that President Bush had signed an agreement (SPP) with Canada and Mexico that would effectively "end the United States as we know it, and he [Bush] took the step without approval from either the U.S. Congress or the people of the United States" (21 June 2006, CNN transcript). Moreover, undocumented workers are part of the equation, as Dobbs and others link border security with the ebb and flow of Mexicans who, without "green cards," are searching for employment to support their families. Often a sense of loss in terms of "national values" or the "rule of law" frames this suspicious response in the United States. Little or no value is seen in the creation of regional partnerships that transcend national borders, especially when these partnerships have the capacity to promote the very phenomena opposed in the first place: the northerly migration of Mexicans, supranational tribunals with the authority to review domestic legislation, the sharing of resources or information that might diminish the economic or military capability of the United States, and so on.

What to make of the minority view? Since all three nations of North America can find examples of the minority view in their respective national histories, it is part of a political dialogue that finds its origins in the end of colonialism and the emergence of the nation-state. In the American case, whether it was George Washington exhorting his countrymen to avoid "permanent alliances" or Thomas Jefferson stating "entangling alliances with none," the United States is often portrayed as isolationist until the twentieth century. Even U.S. participation in World Wars I and II had its critics and detractors. But the North American continent has always been part of U.S. political discourse, including its more belligerent elements when the United States invaded Canada and Mexico in the nineteenth century. Those now opposed to SPP because they see it as a harbinger for a continental union also tend to criticize American participation in the United Nations, World Trade Organization, and other global bodies. And while the SPP was the logical next step after NAFTA, particularly in light of continent-wide security concerns after 9/11, it contains no enforcement mechanisms that transgress national sovereignty. In other words, this new continental partnership emphasizes cooperation and mutual understanding in a variety of economic, diplomatic, and political areas, but it hardly lays the foundations for a North American Union. Neither a common market nor a common currency is part of the SPP vocabulary, nor has there been any discussion of a common foreign policy. Simply put, the SPP does not establish a European Union on the North American continent.

Cultural changes are both causes and effects of the emerging political contours of North America. There is increasing cultural complexity in North America, primarily the result of recent immigration. The United States and Canada are polyglot nations, cultural mosaics of startling complexity, where cultures mix but also stand apart and promote their uniqueness. Mexican culture is both expanding and contracting. Greater Mexico, meaning peoples of Mexican descent who treasure their language and customs, now extends into Canada. At the same time, the English language and every variant of U.S. consumerism and materialism — films, music, fast foods, dress styles — reach into every region of Mexico, competing hard with traditional Mexican culture. Even with these changes, it is hard to interpret the new consumerism as the foundation of an encompassing continental culture. Nevertheless, Mexico and Canada, more so than the United States, expend great energy in trying to protect their cultures. In the end, it is hard to argue that there is a North American culture or to find clear signs of one emerging.

More challenging for each country is to find a solution to the poverty that undermines society and produces widespread alienation. Mexico suffers the most from the burdens of the past and the political and economic problems of the present. Great regional, class, and ethnic disparities overshadow the many economic gains made since World War II and prevent Mexico from claiming the First World status that it so desperately seeks. Canada and the United States, so successful economically by most measures, have also failed to eliminate poverty and the social injustices that accompany it. Thick seams of poverty run from urban slums to agricultural villages, entrapping the elderly poor, inner-city youth, and migrant farm workers.

The history of North America gives rise to both optimism and pessimism. From the earliest years of European settlement, idealists have sought to improve the lives of the marginal and oppressed. Yet neither reformer, revolutionary, nor utopian dreamer has been able to overcome the problems of inequality. To be sure, progress has been made, but severe social problems remain. One significant difference between current efforts at reform and those of the past is the continental response to inequality and injustice. Whether describing the plight of Indians in Chiapas, migrant farm workers in California, or new immigrants to British Columbia, the problems and issues are large and complex enough that they now require continent-wide attention and a much broader response. North America watchers have long argued that a broader perspective, one unfettered by purely national concerns, generates innovative solutions to the problems of the continent, thus holding out the promise of a new era of political cooperation and economic integration. New eras often begin, however, when different answers emerge to older questions. For example, which line from Robert Frost's poem, "Mending Wall," speaks to a continental sensibility? Which line encapsulates the direction we think North American integration should take? "Something there is that doesn't love a wall," or "Good fences make good neighbors." How each of us responds to Frost's poetic language may, on some metaphysical plane, fashion a collective response that accommodates, rejects, or modifies continentalism. While many future historians will continue to study North America through the prism of the nation-state, by standing firmly on their side of the border and peering over the "good fence," others will cross disciplinary boundaries and scale "conceptual walls" in an effort to see the continent as a whole.

BIBLIOGRAPHY

The first section of the bibliography includes references to general works and monographs that introduce individual countries, continental perspectives, and sources cited in the text. The second section includes references to atlases, bibliographies, and statistical sources that are useful for further research. These latter items are often updated annually or biannually; those cited here were specifically used in the development of our narrative. We have added a third section on web resources for those interested in the federalist structures that govern the three nation-states examined in this book, as well as how those structures work together to solve problems or, depending on point of view, create new ones. Other web resources included here provide broader views of continental integration and cooperation.

General Sources
Aarim-Heriot, Najia. 2003. *Chinese Immigrants, African Americans, and Racial Anxiety in the United States, 1848-1882*. Urbana and Chicago, IL: U of Illinois P.

Abel, Kerry, and Ken S. Coates (eds.). 2001. *Northern Visions: New Perspectives on the North in Canadian History*. Peterborough, ON: Broadview Press.

Abu-Laban, Yasmeen, Radha Jhappan, and François Rocher (eds.). 2007. *Politics in North America: Redefining Continental Relations*. Peterborough, ON: Broadview Press.

Acuña, Rodolfo. 1988. *Occupied America: A History of Chicanos*. 3rd ed. New York, NY: Harper and Row.

Alamán, Lucas. 1849-52. *Historia de Méjico desde los primeros movimientos que preparon su independencia en el año de 1808 hasta la época presente*. 5 vols. Mexico City: J.M. Lara.

Alba, Victor. 1967. *The Mexicans: The Making of a Nation*. New York, NY: Pegasus.

Altman, Ida, and James Horn (eds.). 1991. *"To Make America:" European Emigration in the Early Modern Period*. Berkeley and Los Angeles, CA: U of California P.

Ambrose, Stephen E. 1988. *Rise to Globalism: American Foreign Policy Since 1938*. Rev. ed. New York, NY: Penguin.

Anderson, Fred. 2001. *Crucible of War: The Seven Years' War and the Fate of Empire in British North America*. New York, NY: Knopf.

Bailyn, Bernard. 1992. *The Ideological Origins of the American Revolution*. Rev. ed. Cambridge, MA: Belknap.

Bancroft, George. 1885-96. *History of the United States of America, from the Discovery of the Continent [to 1789]*. 6 vols. New York, NY: D. Appleton.

Bancroft, Hubert Howe. 1886-90. *The Works of Hubert Howe Bancroft*. 39 vols. San Francisco, CA: The History Company.

Bannister, Robert C. 1988. *Social Darwinism: Science and Myth in Anglo-American Social Thought*. Philadelphia, PA: Temple UP.

Barry, Tom (ed.). 1992. *Mexico: A Country Guide*. Albuquerque, NM: The Inter-Hemispheric Education Resource Center.

Bayly, C.A., *et al.* 2006. "On Transnational History." *American Historical Review* 111,5: 1441-64.

Bemis, Samuel Flagg. 1943. *The Latin American Policy of the United States*. New York, NY: Harcourt Brace.

Bender, Thomas. 2006. *A Nation Among Nations: America's Place in World History*. New York, NY: Hill and Wang.

Berger, Carl. 1986. *The Writing of Canadian History: Aspects of English-Canadian Historical Writing since 1900*. 2nd ed. Toronto, ON: U of Toronto P.

Bergeron, Gérard. 1990. *Quand Tocqueville et Siegfried nous observaient*. Quebec City, QC: Presses de l'Université du Québec.

Bergquist, Charles. 1996. *Labor and the Course of American Democracy: U.S. History in Latin American Perspective*. London, UK and New York, NY: Verso.

Berlin, Ira. 2000. *Many Thousands Gone: The First Two Centuries of Slavery in North America*. Cambridge, MA: Harvard UP.

Billington, Ray Allen, and Martin Ridge. 1982. *Westward Expansion: A History of the American Frontier*. New York, NY: Macmillan.

Bolton, Herbert Eugene. 1934. "The Epic of Greater America." In Lewis Hanke (ed.), *Do the Americas Have a Common History?* New York, NY: Knopf.

Bolton, Herbert Eugene, and Thomas Maitland Marshall. 1920. *The Colonization of North America, 1492-1783*. New York, NY: Macmillan.

Borneman, Walter R. 2006. *The French and Indian War: Deciding the Fate of North America*. New York, NY: HarperCollins.

Bothwell, Robert (ed.). 1998. *Canada and Quebec: One Country, Two Histories*. Vancouver, BC: U of British Columbia P.

Brebner, John Bartlett. 1968. *North Atlantic Triangle: The Interplay of Canada, the United States, and Great Britain*. Toronto, ON: Ryerson.

Brescia, Michael M. 1999. "Material and Cultural Dimensions of Episcopal

Authority: Tridentine Donation and the Biblioteca Palafoxiana in Seventeenth-Century Puebla de los Angeles, Mexico." *Colonial Latin American Historical Review* 8,2: 207-27.

Brinkley, Alan. 1997. *The Unfinished Nation: A Concise History of the American People*. New York, NY: McGraw-Hill.

Brooks, Stephen. 2006. *As Others See Us: The Causes and Consequences of Foreign Perceptions of America*. Peterborough, ON: Broadview Press.

Brown, Dee Alexander. 2001. *Bury My Heart at Wounded Knee: An Indian History of the American West*. New York, NY: Henry Holt and Company.

Bryce, James. 1923. *South America: Observations and Impressions*. New York, NY: Macmillan.

Bumstead, J.M. 1992. *The Peoples of Canada*. 2 vols. Toronto, ON: Oxford UP.

Burnham, John C. 1993. *Bad Habits: Drinking, Smoking, Taking Drugs, Gambling, Sexual Misbehavior, and Swearing in American History*. New York, NY: New York UP.

Calderón de la Barca, Frances Erskine Inglis. 1982. *Life in Mexico*. Berkeley and Los Angles, CA: U of California P.

Camp, Roderic A. 1993. *Politics in Mexico*. New York, NY: Oxford UP.

Caso, Alfonso. 1958. *Indigenismo*. Mexico City: Instituto Nacional Indigenista.

Chambers, Edward J., and Peter H. Smith (eds.). 2002. *NAFTA in the New Millennium*. La Jolla, CA, and Edmonton, AB: Center for U.S.-Mexican Studies and the U of Alberta P.

Chambers, Tom. 1996. *Canadian Politics*. Toronto, ON: Thompson Educational Publishing.

Chase, Stuart. 1933. *Mexico: A Study of Two Americas*. New York, NY: Macmillan.

Chennells, David. 2001. *The Politics of Nationalism in Canada: Cultural Conflict since 1760*. Toronto, ON: U of Toronto P.

Chevalier, François. 1963. *Land and Society in Colonial Mexico: The Great Hacienda*. Berkeley and Los Angeles, CA: U of California P.

Clemens, Samuel L. 1923. *Life on the Mississippi*. New York, NY: Harper and Brothers.

Clendinnen, Inga. 1991. *Aztecs: An Interpretation*. New York, NY: Cambridge UP.

Cline, Howard. 1966. *The United States and Mexico*. New York, NY: Atheneum.

Coatsworth, John H., and Carlos Rico (eds.). 1989. *Images of Mexico in the United States*. San Diego, CA: Center for U.S.-Mexican Studies and U of California P.

Cook, Sharon Anne, Lorna R. McLean, and Kate O'Rourke (eds.). 2001. *Framing Our Past: Canadian Women's History in the Twentieth Century*. Montreal, QC: McGill-Queen's UP.

Cooper Alarcón, Daniel. 1997. *The Aztec Palimpsest: Mexico in the Modern Imagination.* Tucson, AZ: U of Arizona P.

Cooper, William J. Jr., and Tom E. Terrill. 1991. *The American South: A History.* 2 vols. New York, NY: McGraw-Hill.

Cortés, Hernán. 1971. *Letters from Mexico.* Tr. Anthony Pagden. New York, NY: Grossman.

Cosío Villegas, Daniel. 1964. *American Extremes.* Tr. Américo Paredes. Austin, TX: U of Texas P.

Cramer, Zadok. 1966. *The Navigator, Containing Directions for Navigating the Monongahela, Allegheny, Ohio and Mississippi Rivers.* Ann Arbor, MI: University Microfilms.

Creighton, Donald Grant. 1956. *The Empire of the St. Lawrence.* Toronto, ON: Macmillan.

Daily Commercial News and Construction Record. 5 November 2007. Ontario, Canada.

Daniels, Roger. 1990. *Coming to America: A History of Immigration and Ethnicity in American Life.* New York, NY: Harper Collins.

Daudelin, Jean, and Edgar J. Dosman (eds.). 1995. *Beyond Mexico: Vol. 1, Changing Americas.* Ottawa, ON: Carleton UP.

DePalma, Anthony. 2001. *Here: A Biography of the New American Continent.* New York, NY: Public Affairs.

Desfor, Gene, and Roger Keil. 2004. *Nature and the City: Making Environmental Policy in Toronto and Los Angeles.* Tucson, AZ: U of Arizona P.

Díaz del Castillo, Bernal. 1966. *The True History of the Conquest of New Spain, 1517-1521.* Tr. A.P. Maudslay. New York, NY: Farrar, Strauss and Giroux.

Dinnerstein, Leonard, Roger L. Nichols, and David L. Reimers. 1990. *Natives and Strangers: Blacks, Indians, and Immigrants in America.* New York, NY: Oxford UP.

Douglass, Frederick. 1982. *Narrative of the Life of Frederick Douglass, an American Slave.* London, UK and New York, NY: Penguin.

Dunkerley, James. 2000. *Americana: The Americas in the World, around 1850.* London, UK and New York, NY: Verso.

Earle, Robert L., and John D. Wirth (eds.). 1995. *Identities in North America: The Search for Community.* Stanford, CA: Stanford UP.

Eccles, W.J. 1990. *France in America.* Rev. ed. Markham, ON: Fitzhenry and Whiteside.

Eden, Lorraine, and Maureen Appel Molot. 1993. "Canada's National Policies: Reflections on 125 Years." *Canadian Public Policy* 19,3: 232-51.

Englehart, Ronald F., Neil Nevitte, and Miguel Basañez. 1996. *North American Trajectory: Cultural, Economic, and Political Ties among the United States, Canada, and Mexico.* New York, NY: Aldine de Gruyter.

Fagan, Brian. 2005. *Ancient North America.* London, UK: Thames and Hudson.

Faludi, Susan. 2007. *The Terror Dream: Fear and Fantasy in Post-9/11 America*. New York, NY: Henry Holt and Company.

Ferguson, Will. 2005. *Canadian History for Dummies*. 2nd ed. Mississauga, ON: John Wiley and Sons.

Finkel, Alvin, Margaret Conrad, and Veronica Strong-Boag. 1993. *History of the Canadian Peoples*. 2 vols. Toronto, ON: Copp Clark Pitman.

Flannery, Tim. 2002. *The Eternal Frontier: An Ecological History of North America and Its People*. New York, NY: Grove Atlantic.

Foner, Philip Sheldon. 1947-92. *History of the Labor Movement in the United States*. 10 vols. New York, NY: International Publishers.

Fox, William T.R. 1985. *A Continent Apart: The United States and Canada in World Politics*. Toronto, ON: U of Toronto P.

Fox-Genovese, Elizabeth. 1988. *Within the Plantation Household: Black and White Women of the Old South*. Chapel Hill, NC: U of North Carolina P.

Franklin, John Hope, and Alfred A. Moss Jr. 1988. *From Slavery to Freedom: A History of Negro Americans*. 6th ed. New York, NY: Knopf.

Gagnon, Serge. 1985. *Quebec and its Historians*. 2 vols. Montreal, QC: Harvest House.

Galbraith, John Kenneth. 1988. *The Great Crash, 1929*. Boston, MA: Houghton-Mifflin.

Garneau, François-Xavier. 1866. *History of Canada from the Time of Its Discovery till the Union Years, 1840-41*. Tr. Andrew Bell. 2 vols. Montreal, QC: R. Worthington.

Garreau, Joel. 1981. *The Nine Nations of North America*. New York, NY: Avon Books.

Gaustad, Edwin S. 1987. *Faith of Our Fathers: Religion and the New Nation*. San Francisco, CA: Harper and Row.

Genovese, Eugene D. 1972. *Roll, Jordan, Roll: The World the Slaves Made*. New York, NY: Vintage Books.

Gibson, Charles. 1964. *The Aztecs Under Spanish Rule: A History of the Indians of the Valley of Mexico, 1519-1810*. Stanford, CA: Stanford UP.

Globe and Mail. [Toronto] 25 January 1995.

Goldberg, Michael A., and John Mercer. 1986. *The Myth of the North American City: Continentalism Challenged*. Vancouver, BC: U of British Columbia P.

Goldin, Liliana R. (ed.). 1999. *Identities on the Move: Transnational Processes in North America and the Caribbean Basin*. Albany, NY: Institute for Mesoamerican Studies.

González, Juan. 2000. *Harvest of Empire: A History of Latinos in America*. New York, NY: Penguin.

González y González, Luis J. 1983. *San José de Gracia: Mexican Village in Transition*. Tr. John Upton. Austin, TX: U of Texas P.

Gosner, Kevin. 1992. *Soldiers of the Virgin: The Moral Economy of a Colonial Maya Rebellion*. Tucson, AZ: U of Arizona P.

Grayson, George, M. 1992. *The Church in Contemporary Mexico*. Washington, DC: The Center for Strategic Studies, 1992.

Groulx, Lionel. 1958. *Notre grande aventure, l'empire français en Amérique du Nord, 1535-1760*. Montreal, QC: Fides.

Guinness, Paul Grattan, and Michael J. Bradshaw. 1985. *North America: A Human Geography*. Lanham, MD: Rowman and Littlefield.

Guy, Donna J., and Thomas E. Sheridan (eds.). 1998. *Contested Ground: Comparative Frontiers on the Northern and Southern Edges of the Spanish Empire*. Tucson, AZ: U of Arizona P.

Hale, Charles A. 1989. *The Transformation of Liberalism in Late Nineteenth-Century Mexico*. Princeton, NJ: Princeton UP.

Hamlin, Jean, and Jean Provencher. 1987. *Brève Histoire du Québec*. 5th ed. Montreal, QC: Boréal.

Handlin, Oscar. 1990. *The Uprooted: The Epic Story of the Great Migrations that Made the American People*. Boston, MA: Little, Brown.

Harrington, Michael. 1988. *The Other America: Poverty in America*. New York, NY: Penguin.

Harris, Charles H. III. 1975. *A Mexican Family Empire: The Latifundio of the Sánchez Navarro Family, 1765-1867*. Austin, TX: U of Texas P.

Hellman, Judith Adler. 1994. *Mexican Lives*. New York, NY: The New Press.

Hernández Chávez, Alicia. 1996. *¿Hacia un nuevo federalismo?* Mexico City: Fondo de Cultura Económica.

Hero, Alfred Olivier Jr., and Louis Balthazar. 1988. *Contemporary Quebec and the United States, 1960-1985*. Lanham, MD: UP of America.

Herzog, Lawrence A. (ed.). 1992. *Changing Boundaries in the Americas: New Perspectives on the U.S.-Mexican, Central American, and South American Borders*. San Diego, CA: Center for U.S.-Mexican Studies and U of California P.

Hinderaker, Eric, and Peter C. Mancall. 2003. *At the Edge of Empire: The Backcountry in British North America*. Baltimore, MD: The Johns Hopkins UP.

Hofstadter, Richard. 1979. *The Progressive Historians: Turner, Beard, Parrington*. Chicago, IL: U of Chicago P.

Innis, Harold A. 1954. *The Cod Fisheries: The History of an International Economy*. Toronto, ON: U of Toronto P.

Innis, Harold A. 1970. *The Fur Trade in Canada: An Introduction to Canadian Economic History*. Revised Edition. Toronto, ON: U of Toronto P.

Jackson, Hal. 2006. *Following the Royal Road: A Guide to the Historic*

Camino Real de Tierra Adentro. Albuquerque, NM: U of New Mexico P.

Jacobs, Wilbur R., John W. Caughey, and Joe B. Frantz. 1965. *Turner, Bolton, and Webb: Three Historians of the American Frontier*. Seattle, WA: U of Washington P.

Janelle, Donald G. (ed.). 1992. *Geographical Snapshots of North America*. New York, NY: Guilford Press.

Johns, Michael. 1997. *The City of Mexico in the Age of Díaz*. Austin, TX: U of Texas P.

Joseph, Gilbert M., and Timothy J. Henderson (eds.). 2002. *The Mexico Reader: History, Culture, Politics*. Durham, NC: Duke UP.

Katzenberger, Elaine (ed.). 1995. *First World, Ha Ha Ha! The Zapatista Challenge*. San Francisco, CA: City Lights Books.

Keegan, John. 1997. *Fields of Battle: The Wars for North America*. New York, NY: Knopf.

Kehoe, Alice B. 1992. *North American Indians: A Comprehensive Account*. Englewood Cliffs, NJ: Prentice Hall.

Kerouac, Jack. 1957. *On the Road*. New York, NY: Viking Press.

Ketcham, Ralph L. 1984. *Presidents Above Party: The First American Presidency, 1789-1829*. Chapel Hill, NC: U of North Carolina P.

Kicza, John E. 2003. *Resilient Cultures: America's Native Peoples Confront European Colonization, 1500-1800*. Upper Saddle River, NJ: Prentice-Hall.

Klepak, H.P. (ed.). 1996. *Natural Allies? Canadian and Mexican Perspectives on International Security, vol. 2: Changing Americas*. Ottawa, ON: Carleton UP.

Knight, Alan. 1986. *The Mexican Revolution*. 2 vols. Lincoln, NE: U of Nebraska P.

LaDow, Beth. 2002. *The Medicine Line: Life and Death on a North American Borderland*. New York, NY: Routledge.

LaFeber, Walter. 1989. *The American Age: United States Foreign Policy at Home and Abroad Since 1750*. New York, NY: W.W. Norton.

LaFeber, Walter. 1996. *The New Empire: An Interpretation of American Expansionism, 1860-1898*. 2nd ed. New York, NY: W.W. Norton.

Laforest, Guy. 1995. *Trudeau and the End of the Canadian Dream*. Montreal, QC: McGill-Queen's UP.

Langley, Lester D. 1991. *Mexico and the United States: The Fragile Relationship*. Boston, MA: Twayne Publishers.

Lanctot, Gustave. 1941. "Le Québec et les États-Unis, 1867-1937." In Gustave Lanctot (ed.), *Les Canadiens Français et Leurs Voisins du Sud*. Montreal, QC: Editions Bernard Valiquette.

Lawrence, D.H. 1930. *Mornings in Mexico*. London, UK: Martin Secker.

Lecker, Robert (ed.). 1991. *Borderlands: Essays in Canadian-American Relations*. Toronto, ON: ECW.

Legler, Thomas. 1995. *A Comparison of Canadian and Mexican Postwar Development (1845-1994): More than at First Meets the Eye.* Mexico City: Universidad Nacional Autónoma de México.

León-Portilla, Miguel. 1972. *The Broken Spears: The Aztec Account of the Conquest of Mexico.* Tr. Lysander Kemp. Boston, MA: Beacon Press.

León-Portilla, Miguel. 1990. *Endangered Cultures.* Tr. Julie Goodson-Lawes. Dallas, TX: Southern Methodist UP.

Linteau, Paul-André, *et al.* 1989. *Histoire du Québec contemporain.* 2 vols. Montreal, QC: Boréal.

Lipset, Seymour Martin. 1990. *Continental Divide: The Values and Institutions of the United States and Canada.* New York, NY: Routledge.

López Mateos, Adolfo. 1959. *The Voice of Mexico in the United States and Canada: Speeches by Adolfo López Mateos, President of Mexico, during his Visit to those Countries.* Mexico City: The Institutional Revolutionary Party.

MacLachlan, Colin M., and William H. Beezley. 1994. *El Gran Pueblo: A History of Greater Mexico.* Englewood Cliffs, NJ: Prentice-Hall.

McDougal, John. 2006. *Drifting Together: The Political Economy of Canada-U.S. Integration.* Peterborough, ON: Broadview Press.

McFaden, Fred, *et al.* 1993. *Canada: The Twentieth Century.* Rev. ed. Richmond Hill, ON: Fitzhenry and Whiteside.

McMillan, Alan D. 1995. *Native Peoples and Cultures of Canada: An Anthropological Overview.* 2nd ed. Vancouver, BC and Toronto, ON: Douglas and McIntyre.

McNaught, Kenneth. 1988. *The Penguin History of Canada.* London, UK: Penguin.

McWilliams, Carey. 1990. *North from Mexico: The Spanish-Speaking People of the United States.* Rev. ed. New York, NY: Greenwood and Praeger.

Mann, Charles C. 2006. *1491: New Revelations of the Americas before Columbus.* New York, NY: Knopf.

Martínez, Oscar J. 1988. *Troublesome Border.* Tucson, AZ: U of Arizona P.

Martínez Legorreta, Omar. 1990. *Relations between Mexico and Canada.* Mexico City: El Colegio de México.

May, Henry F. 1976. *The Enlightenment in America.* New York, NY: Oxford UP.

Metcalfe, William (ed.). 1982. *Understanding Canada: A Multidisciplinary Introduction to Canadian Studies.* New York, NY: New York UP.

Meyer, Michael C., and William H. Beezley (eds.). 2000. *The Oxford History of Mexico.* New York, NY: Oxford UP.

Meyer, Michael C., and Michael M. Brescia. 1998. "The Treaty of Guadalupe Hidalgo as a Living Document: Water and Land-Use Issues in Northern New Mexico." *New Mexico Historical Review* 73,4: 435-55.

Meyer, Michael C., William L. Sherman, and Susan M. Deeds. 2007. *The Course of Mexican History.* 8th ed. New York, NY: Oxford UP.

Milkis, Sidney M., and Michael Nelson. 1994. *The American Presidency: Origins and Development, 1776-1990.* Rev. ed. Washington, DC: Congressional Quarterly Press.

Mintz, Steven, and Susan Kellogg. 1988. *Domestic Revolution: A Social History of American Family Life.* New York, NY: The Free Press.

Morgan, Ted. 1993. *Wilderness at Dawn: The Settling of the North American Continent.* New York, NY: Simon and Schuster.

Morgenthaler, Jefferson. 2004. *The River Has Never Divided Us: A Border History of La Junta de los Ríos.* Austin, TX: U of Texas P.

Morton, W.L. 1964. *The Critical Years: The Union of British North America, 1857-1873.* Toronto, ON: McClelland and Stewart.

Nash, Gary B. 1992. *Red, White, and Black: The Peoples of Early North America.* Englewood Cliffs, NJ: Prentice-Hall.

The New York Times. 6 June 1892.

Nichols, Roger L. 1998. *Indians in the United States and Canada: A Comparative History.* Lincoln, NE: U of Nebraska P.

Noll, Mark A. 1992. *A History of Christianity in the United States and Canada.* Grand Rapids, MI: William B. Eerdmans.

Norrie, Kenneth, and Douglas Owram. 1996. *A History of the Canadian Economy.* 2nd ed. Toronto: Harcourt Brace and Company.

Oakes, James. 1990. *Slavery and Freedom: An Interpretation of the Old South.* New York, NY: Knopf.

Ogelsby, J.C.M. 1976. *Gringos from the Far North: Essays in the History of Canadian-Latin American Relations, 1866-1968.* Toronto, ON: Macmillan.

Paolino, Ernest N. 1973. *The Foundations of the American Empire: William Henry Seward and U.S. Foreign Policy.* Ithaca, NY: Cornell UP.

Papademetriou, Demetrios, *et al.* 2004. *NAFTA's Promises and Reality: Lessons from Mexico to the Hemisphere.* Washington, DC: Carnegie Endowment for International Peace.

Perry, Adele. 2001. *On the Edge of Empire: Gender, Race, and the Making of British Columbia, 1849-1871.* Toronto, ON: U of Toronto P.

Pirsig, Robert M. 1975. *Zen and the Art of Motorcycle Maintenance.* New York, NY: Bantam.

Quinn, David Beers. 1977. *North America from Earliest Discovery to First Settlements: The Norse Voyages to 1612.* New York, NY: Harper and Row.

Raat, W. Dirk. 2004. *Mexico and the United States: Ambivalent Vistas.* 3rd ed. Athens, GA: U of Georgia P.

Radway, Janice. 1999. "What's In a Name?" *American Quarterly* 51,1: 1-32.

Randall, Stephen J. (ed.). 1992. *North America without Borders? Integrating Canada, the United States, and Mexico.* Calgary, AB: U of Calgary P.

Reclus, Elisée. 1886-95. *The Earth and its Inhabitants.* 19 vols. New York, NY: D. Appelton.

Reed, Nelson. 1964. *The Caste War of Yucatán*. Stanford, CA: Stanford UP.

Rémond, René. 1986. *Histoire des États-Unis*. Paris: Presses Universitaires de France.

Richler, Mordecai. 1992. *O Canada, O Quebec*. New York, NY: Knopf.

Riding, Alan. 1986. *Distant Neighbors: A Portrait of the Mexicans*. New York, NY: Vintage Books.

Riendeau, Roger. 2000. *A Brief History of Canada*. Markham, ON: Fitzhenry and Whiteside.

Robertson, William. 1839. *The History of the Discovery and Settlement of America*. New York, NY: Harper and Brothers.

Robitaille, Georges. 1941. "L'éxpansion religieuse des Canadiens Français aux États-Unis." In Gustave Lanctot (ed.), *Les Canadiens Français et Leurs Voisins du Sud*. Montreal, QC: Editions Bernard Valiquette.

Rochlin, James. 1994. *Discovering the Americas: The Evolution of Canadian Foreign Policy towards Latin America*. Vancouver, BC: U of British Columbia P.

Ronda, James P. 1996. *Revealing America: Image and Imagination in the Exploration of North America*. Lexington, MA: D.C. Heath and Company.

Russell, James. W. 1994. *After the Fifth Sun: Class and Race in North America*. Englewood Cliffs, NJ: Prentice-Hall.

Schulzinger, Robert D. 1990. *American Diplomacy in the Twentieth Century*. 2nd ed. New York, NY: Oxford UP.

Shapiro, Henry D. 1986. *Appalachia on Our Mind: The Southern Mountains and Mountaineers in the American Consciousness, 1870-1920*. Chapel Hill, NC: U of North Carolina P.

Siegfried, André. 1968. *The Race Question in Canada*. Toronto, ON: McClelland and Stewart.

Seigel, Micol. 2005. "Beyond Compare: Comparative Method after the Transnational Turn." *Radical History Review* 91: 62-90.

Simeon, Richard, and Ian Robinson. 1990. *State, Society, and the Development of Canadian Federalism*. Toronto, ON: U of Toronto P.

Simonelli, Richard. 1992. "A Conversation with Native Flutist R. Carlos Nakai." *Winds of Change* 7,4: 16-26.

Sitkoff, Harvard. 1993. *The Struggle for Black Equality, 1954-1992*. Rev. ed. New York, NY: Hill and Wang.

Solberg, Carl E. 1987. *The Prairies and the Pampas: Agrarian Policy in Canada and Argentina, 1880-1930*. Stanford, CA: Stanford UP.

Spicer, Edward H. 1962. *Cycles of Conquest: The Impact of Spain, Mexico, and the United States on the Indians of the Southwest, 1533-1960*. Tucson, AZ: the U of Arizona P.

Smith, Allan. 1994. *Canada, an American Nation? Essays on Continentalism, Identity, and the Canadian Frame of Mind*. Montreal, QC: McGill-Queen's UP.

Smith, Neil. 2003. *American Empire: Roosevelt's Geographer and the Prelude to Globalization*. Berkeley and Los Angeles, CA: U of California P.

Stegner, Wallace. 1945. *One Nation*. Boston, MA: Houghton Mifflin.

Stegner, Wallace. 1990. *Wolf Willow: A History, a Story, and a Memory of the Last Plains Frontier*. New York, NY: Penguin.

Super, John C., and Briane K. Turley. 2005. *Religion in World History: The Persistence of Imperial Communion*. New York, NY: Routledge.

Takaki, Ronald (ed.). 1987. *From Different Shores: Perspectives on Race and Ethnicity in America*. New York, NY: Oxford UP.

Tannenbaum, Frank. 1929. *The Mexican Agrarian Revolution*. New York, NY: Macmillan.

Taylor, Alan. 2002. *American Colonies: The Settling of North America*. New York, NY: Penguin.

Thomas, David (ed.). 1993. *Canada and the United States: Differences that Count*. Peterborough, ON: Broadview Press.

Thomas, Hugh. 1993. *Conquest: Montezuma, Cortés, and the Fall of Old Mexico*. New York, NY: Simon and Schuster.

Thompson, Wayne C. 1997. *Canada, 1997*. Washington, DC: Stryker-Post Publications.

Tindall, George Brown, and David E. Shi. 1966. *America: A Narrative History*. New York, NY: W.W. Norton.

Tocqueville, Alexis de. 1966. *Democracy in America*. 2 vols. Tr. George Lawrence. Garden City, NY: Doubleday.

Trudel, Marcel. 1973. *The Beginnings of New France, 1524-1663*. 3 vols. Toronto, ON: McClelland and Stewart.

Turner, Frederick Jackson. 1920. *The Frontier in American History*. New York, NY: Henry Holt.

Tyrrell, Ian. 1991. "American Exceptionalism in an Age of International History." *American Historical Review* 96,4: 1031-55.

Utley, Robert M. 1984. *The Indian Frontier of the American West, 1846-1890*. Albuquerque, NM: U of New Mexico P.

Vasconcelos, José, and Manuel Gamio. 1926. *Aspects of Mexican Civilization*. Chicago, IL: U of Chicago P.

Verea Campos, Mónica (ed.). 1994. *50 años de relaciones México-Canadá: Encuentros y coincidencias*. Mexico City: Universidad Nacional Autónoma de México.

The Washington Post. 15 October 1995.

Watson, J. Wreford. 1967. *North America: Its Countries and Regions*. New York, NY: Frederick A. Praeger.

Weber, David J. 1992. *The Spanish Frontier in North America*. New Haven, CT: Yale UP.

Wilkie, James W. 1967. *The Mexican Revolution: Federal Expenditure and Social Change Since 1910.* Berkeley and Los Angeles, CA: U of California P.

Wilkie, James W., and Paul D. Wilkins (eds.). 1969. *Revolution in Mexico: Years of Upheaval, 1910-1940.* New York, NY: Alfred A. Knopf.

Winks, Robin. 1960. *Canada and the United States: The Civil War Years.* Montreal, QC: Harvest House.

Wolf, Eric R. 1982. *Europe and the People without History.* Berkeley and Los Angeles, CA: U of California P.

Womack, John. 1969. *Zapata and the Mexican Revolution.* New York, NY: Alfred Knopf.

Worster, Donald. 1985. *Rivers of Empire: Water, Aridity, and the Growth of the American West.* New York, NY: Pantheon.

Yeates, Maurice, and Barry Garner. 1976. *The North American City.* 2nd ed. New York, NY: Harper and Row.

Reference Sources

Asante, Molefi K., and Mark T. Mattson. 1991. *The Historical and Cultural Atlas of African Americans.* New York, NY: Macmillan.

Blazek, Ron, and Anna H. Perrault. 1994. *United States History: A Selective Guide to Information Sources.* Englewood, CO: Libraries Unlimited.

Canada. House of Commons. 2007. *Annual Report to Parliament on Immigration.* Ottawa, ON: Communications Branch, Citizenship and Immigration Canada.

Canada. Ministry of Foreign Affairs and International Trade. 2003. *NAFTA@10: A Preliminary Report.* Ottawa, ON: Ministry of Public Works and Government Services Canada.

The Canadian Encyclopedia. 1988. 2nd ed. 4 vols. Edmonton, AB: Hurtig.

Casanova, Rosa, and Adriana Konzevik. 2006. *Mexico: A Photographic History.* Mexico City: Consejo Nacional para la Cultura y las Artes and Instituto Nacional de Antropología e Historia.

Cordasco, Francesco (ed.). 1990. *The Dictionary of American Immigration History.* Metuchen, NJ: Scarecrow Press.

Diccionario Porrúa de historia, biografía y geografía de México. 1986. 3 vols. Mexico City: Editorial Porrúa.

Dictionary of American Biography. 1928-37. 20 vols. Republished 1943, 21 vols. Supplements, 1944-89. New York, NY: Scribner's.

Dictionary of Canadian Biography. 1966. 13 vols. Toronto, ON: U of Toronto P.

Elliot, Emory (ed.). 1988. *Columbia Literary History of the United States.* New York, NY: Columbia UP.

Enciclopedia de México. 1987-88. 14 vols. Mexico City: Secretaría de Educación Pública.

Energy Statistics Sourcebook. 1996. 11th ed. Tulsa, OK: PennWell Publishing.

Estadísticas históricas de México. 1990. 2 vols. Aguascalientes: Instituto Nacional de Estadística, Geografía e Informática.

The Europe Yearbook. 1997. London, UK: Europa Publications.

Foner, Eric, and John A. Garraty (eds.). 1991. *The Reader's Companion to American History.* Boston, MA: Houghton Mifflin.

Gallay, Allan (ed.). 1996. *Colonial Wars of North America, 1512-1763: An Encyclopedia.* New York, NY: Garland Press.

Gerhard, Peter. 1972. *A Guide to the Historical Geography of New Spain.* Cambridge, UK: Cambridge UP.

Gerhard, Peter. 1982. *The North Frontier of New Spain.* Princeton, NJ: Princeton UP.

Gerhard, Peter. 1979. *The Southeast Frontier of New Spain.* Princeton, NJ: Princeton UP.

Hall, Kermit L. (ed.). 1992. *The Oxford Companion to the Supreme Court of the United States.* New York, NY: Oxford UP.

Kurian, George Thomas. 1994. *Datapedia of the United States, 1790- 2000: America Year by Year.* Lanham, MD: Bernan Press.

Historical Atlas of the United States. 1988. Washington, DC: National Geographic Society.

Homberger, Eric. 1995. *The Penguin Historical Atlas of North America.* London, UK and New York, NY: Penguin.

Kanellos, Nicolás (ed.). 1994. *The Hispanic Almanac: From Columbus to Corporate America.* Detroit, MI: Visible Ink.

Magill, Frank N. (ed.). 1997. *Great Events from History: North American Series.* 4 vols. Rev. ed. Pasadena, CA: Salem Press.

Marlita, Reddy A. (ed.). 1994. *Statistical Abstract of the World.* Detroit, MI: Gale Research.

Mitchell, B.R. 1993. *International Historical Statistics: The Americas, 1750-1988.* New York, NY: Stockon Press.

Norton, Mary Beth (ed.). 1995. *The American Historical Association's Guide to Historical Literature.* 2 vols. 3rd ed. New York, NY: Oxford UP.

UNESCO Statistical Yearbook. 1994. Paris: UNESCO.

United States. Department of Commerce. 2004. *NAFTA: Ten Years Later.* Washington, DC: U.S. Government Printing Office.

United States. Department of Commerce, Bureau of the Census. 1993. *1990 Census of Population: Social and Economic Characteristics.* Washington, DC: U.S. Government Printing Office.

United States. Department of Commerce, Bureau of the Census. 1975. *Historical Statistics of the United States, Colonial Times to 1970.* Washington, DC: U.S. Government Printing Office.

United States. Department of Commerce, Bureau of the Census. *Statistical*

Abstract of the United States, yearly since 1878. Washington, DC: U.S. Government Printing Office.

Waldam, Carl. 1985. *Atlas of the North American Indian*. New York, NY: Facts on File.

Wilkie, James (ed.). 1995. *Statistical Abstract of Latin America*, vol. 31. Los Angeles, CA: UCLA Latin American Center Publications.

Wood, Jonina (ed.). 1996. *Canada Year Book 1997*. Ottawa, ON: Statistics Canada.

World Bank. 2003. *Lessons from NAFTA*. Washington, DC.

World Bank. 1995. *World Tables 1995*. Baltimore, MD and London, UK: The Johns Hopkins UP.

Zophy, Angela H. (ed.). 1990. *Handbook of American Women's History*. New York, NY: Garland Press.

World Wide Web
Official Government Websites

Canada: http://www.canada.gc.ca (all branches of government)
http://www.ainc-inac.gc.ca (Indian and Northern Affairs Canada)

Mexico: http://www.presidencia.gob.mx (executive branch)
http://www.cddhcu.gob.mx (Chamber of Deputies, lower house)
http://www.senado.gob.mx (Senate, upper house)
http:// www.scjn.gob.mx (Supreme Court)

United States: http://www.firstgov.gov (all branches of government)

Security and Prosperity Partnership of North America: http://www.spp.gov
The North American Institute: http://www.northamericaninstitute.org

INDEX

Aboriginal Peoples, xiii, 110
  (*See also* Indians)
Acadians, 46, 132, 139
Acapulco, 41
Acapulco-Manila connection,
  168
Act of Consolidation (1804),
  190
Adams, John Quincy, 76
Adams-Onís Treaty (1819), 93
aduanas secas, 172
Afghanistan, 106–7
AFL-CIO, 161
African Americans, 45, 77,
  86–87, 145, 147, 153 (*See
  also* blacks; slavery)
African immigrants, 137, 141
After the Fifth Sun (Russell),
  x, 147
agribusiness, 57, 185, 186
Agricultural Adjustment Act
  (1933) (US), 160
Al-Qaeda, 33, 107
Alabama, 152
Alamán, Lucas, 171
  Historia de Méjico, 3
Alaska, 38, 54, 97
Alaska Boundary dispute
  (1903), 99–100
Alaska Range, 40
Alberta, 59, 67, 80, 173
  BSE (mad cow disease), 34
  oil, 49
  settlement, 48
Alcatraz Island, 122
alcohol (*See* Prohibition;

Temperance Movement)
Alexander VI, Pope, 90
Alien and Sedition Acts, The
  (1798), 65
All-Canadian Congress of
  Labour, 157, 161
*Alternativa Social Demócrata
  Campesina*, 83
American Federation of
  Labor, 156, 161
American Indian Movement,
  122
American Indians, xiii, 109,
  145 (*See also* Indians)
American (Know-Nothing)
  Party, 133
Americanization, 58–59, 213
Amerindian (*See* Indians)
Anglican Church, 194
Anglo-Dutch rivalries in
  North America, 90
Anglo-French conflict, 91
  Seven Years' War, 23, 60,
  91–92, 114
anti-immigration groups (*See
  under* immigration)
anti-US sentiments, 100, 103,
  175, 177
Appalachia, 2, 44
Appalachians, 40, 46–47,
  51–52
Archaic Period, 16–17, 20
Argentina, 104
Arizona, 41, 43, 57, 96
Arkansas River, 42
Asian immigrants, 131, 141, 147

Chinese, 136–37, 143
  discrimination, 140 (*See
  also* race and racism)
  Japanese, 87, 136
Assembly of First Nations, 8,
  124
assimilation, 116–22, 144
Assiniboine River, 42
asymmetries, 2, 100, 104,
  163, 165, 167, 180
Atlanta, 51, 54
Atlantic fishery, 44
Atlantic seaboard colonies
  (*See* New England)
Atlantic trade patterns, 167–69
atomic bomb, 31
Austin, Moses, 134
Austin, Stephen F., 134
automobile industry, 48
Autopact, 179
Aztecs, 18, 150

Baja California Peninsula,
  54, 144
Baja California, 40, 81, 137
Baja California del Norte, 56
Baja California del Sur, 56
Balkanization, 4, 145
"Balkanization of North
  America, The," 10
Balsa River, 43
Baltimore, 41, 54
Bancroft, George, *History of
  the United States*, 3
Bancroft, Hubert Howe,
  Works, 3

Bank of the United States, 65
Baroque period (Mexico), 22
Barrios, Justo Rufino, 27
Battle of the Alamo, 94
Beezley, William H., *Gran Pueblo, El,* x
Bender, Thomas, 12
Bennett, Richard B., 30, 161
Biblioteca Palafoxiana, 22
Bissonette, Lise, 69
Black Hills of the Dakota Territory (reservation), 117
blacks, 151, 156 (*See also* African Americans; African immigrants)
Bloc Québécois, 80
Boer War (1899-1902), 101
Bolton, Herbert Eugene, *Colonization of North America, 1492-1783,* 6
"Do the Americas Have a Common History?", x
"Epic of Greater America, The," 5
"Bolton Theory," 5–6
Bonampak, 17
border culture. *See* "borderlands" sensibility
Border region, 56
"borderlands" sensibility, 12, 210
Boston, 41, 54
Bouchard, Lucién, 71, 80
Boundary Waters Treaty (1909), 100
Bourassa, Henri, 139
Bourbon Reforms, 22
braceros, 140, 160
Bravo, Nicolás, 73
Brazil, 104
Britain, 92, 132 (*See also* England)
retreat from the Americas, 98–99
British colonies (*See* Canada; New England)
British Columbia, 49, 53, 67, 80, 97, 173
British North America Act,

25, 67–68, 84, 97
Brooks Range, 40
Bryce, James, *South America,* 4
BSE (mad cow disease), 34
Bush, George H.W., 77, 180
Bush, George W., 77, 142, 212
friendship with Mexico, 105–6
push for grain-based fuel ethanol, 186
unilateralist foreign policy, 33–34, 213
war in Iraq (*See* Iraq, war with)

Calderón, Felipe, 34, 76, 83, 107, 186, 207
Calgary, 59
California, 40–41, 57, 65, 96, 138
growth, 53
Mexican gangs *(pachucos),* 140
Propositions, 187, 142
Calles, Plutarco Elías, 198
Calvin, John, 188
Camacho, Manuel Ávila, 159
Camino Real (Royal Highway), 174
Campeche, 55
campesino, 153, 159
Canada, 2 (*See also* New France)
allied with Britain, 24–25, 27, 29, 93
Anglican Church, 192
bicultural policy, 146
"Bill of Rights" (1960), 69
British North America Act, 25, 68, 84, 97, 118
Canada Act (1982), 68, 78, 124
Charlottetown Accord, 69, 71, 78, 124
Charter of Rights and Freedoms, 68
conscription legislation (World War I), 29
Constitution Act (1867),

25, 68–69, 110
Constitution Act (1982), 78
democracy, 85
Durham Report (1839), 25
export-driven economy, 85, 184
fear of US, 97, 99 (*See also* anti-US sentiments)
federal provincial power tensions (*See* federalism (Canada))
foreign investment, 9, 176
foreign policy (*See* Canadian foreign policy)
fusion of powers, 63
governor general, 67
group rights vs. individual rights, 84
immigration, 134, 136–37, 143–44 (*See also* Canadian immigration policies)
Indians (*See* Canadian Indian policies)
Loyalist supporters (*See* Loyalists)
Meech Lake Accord, 69, 71, 78, 124
Métis uprising, 26, 67, 117
monarchy, 67
multiculturalism, 146, 210
NAFTA's effect (*See* NAFTA)
National Energy Program, 49
National Policy, 68, 78, 136–37, 173
National Progressive Party, 28
nativism, 137
North-West Rebellion, 26
Official Languages Act (1969), 146
political culture, 25, 28, 84–85
population, 27, 31
population distribution, 38, 40
prime minister, 63

Privy Council Act 1003, 161
Progressive Party, 28
protectionism, 172
railway construction, 174–75
rebellions (1837), 25
Reciprocity Treaty (1854), 172
reform movements, 28, 209
religious plurality, 199
rich-poor gap, 163
Royal Commission on Bilingualism and Biculturalism, 146
Royal Commission on Canada's Economic Prospects, 178
Royal Commission on Dominion-Provincial Relations (1940), 68
secularization, 200
settlement of the west, 96–97
size, 38
slavery, 132
state-subsidized religious education, 195
support for union with US, 98
support for US led invasion of Afghanistan, 106
tariffs, 172–73
undocumented immigrants to US, 142
water resources, 43
welfare state, 30, 32
westward movement, 26
wheat economy, 173
World War I, 28–29
World War II, 31
Canada-Mexican relations, 105
economic, educational, and cultural exchanges, 104
North-South Conference (Cancún), 56, 104
Canada-Mexican trade, 176, 182 (*See also* NAFTA)
Canada and the Canadian

Question (Smith), 100
Canada Corn Act (1843), 172
Canada-United States Automotive Products Agreement (*See* Autopact)
Canada-US border, 94, 210 (*See also* Cascadia)
Convention of 1818, 94
49th parallel, 94, 96
Oregon Treaty, 96
Webster-Ashburton Treaty, 96
Canada-US trade relations, 172, 176, 178, 182 (*See also* Free Trade Agreement (FTA); NAFTA; tariffs)
Pacific trade, 168
Canadian Congress of Labour, 161
Canadian foreign policy, 9, 100
Commonwealth, 101
diplomatic relations with Cuba, 104
Francophonie, 101
Canadian Grange, 28
Canadian History for Dummies (Ferguson), x
Canadian immigration policies, 143
favoured white Protestants, 137
head tax on Chinese immigrants, 137
Immigration Act (1976), 143
interned Germans and Italians, 141
Japanese immigrants, 140
Canadian Indian policies, 118
alliances and treaties, 117
British North America Act, 118
Chrétien's proposal (1969), 123
enfranchisement, 123
Indian Act, 118, 123
"inherent right to self-government," 124
land claims, 124

Quebec, 124–25
reservations, 117–18
suppression of traditional rituals, 118
Canadian Labour Congress, 161, 180
Canadian-Mexican commonalities, 8–9
Canadian nationalism, 104, 177–78 (*See also* National Policy)
Canadian Pacific Railway, 48, 175
Canadian Shield, 38, 40, 47–48
Canadian-United States Defense Production Sharing Arrangement, 179
Cananea strike, 175
Cape Breton, 91
capitalism, 66, 164–65, 175
Cárdenas, Cuauhtémoc, 82
Cárdenas, Lázaro, 30, 81–82, 137, 158–59, 198
nationalization of oil industry, 30, 102
new direction to indigenismo, 120
patron of the campesino, 159
promoted well-being of Indians, 121
support for labor, 158–59
Carnegie Endowment for International Peace, 185
Carranza, Venustiano, 158
Carter, Jimmy, 51
Cartier, Jacques, 20
Casa de Contratación (Spain), 169
Casa del Obrero Mundial, 158
Cascade Mountains, 40, 58
Cascadia, 57–59
Caso, Alfonso, 121
Castro, Fidel, 103
Catholic Church, 85, 134, 157, 192, 197
missionary role, 189–90, 193

Catholic Church (Mexico), 189, 193, 198–99
  anti-clericalism, 74, 189–90, 194
  political voice, 201
Catholic Church (New Spain), missionary role, 189–90, 193
Catholic Church (Quebec), 209
  loss of power and influence, 198
  protection of Quebec culture, 191, 194, 206
Catholic Reformation, 22, 188
Central America, 37
Central American Confederation, 94
centralization and decentralization, 38, 63, 72 (See also federalism)
Chamizal, 103
Champlain, Samuel de, 20, 114
Chapultepec Conference, 177
Charest, Jean, 72
Charleston, 41
Charlottetown Accord, 71, 78, 124
Charter of Rights and Freedoms, 68
Chávez, César, 160
checks and balances (See under federalism)
Chesapeake Bay, 41, 51
Chesapeake Region, 131
Chiapas, 1–2, 9, 12, 55, 94
Chiapas-Guatemala border, 27
Chicago, 26, 52, 54
Chihuahua, 38, 41, 57
Chihuahuan desert, 41, 53
Chile, 104
China, 38, 59
Chinese Exclusion Act (US), 136–37
Chinese immigration, 136–37, 143
Chisholm Trail, 53
Chrétien, Jean, 79, 124
  anti-terrorist legislation (Bill C-36), 106

1969 proposal on Indians, 123
  promotion of federalism in Quebec, 71
  visit to Cuba (1998), 104
  on war in Iraq, 107
Christianity, 197–99
church and state, 74, 188, 191–94, 199 (See also Catholic Church)
Church of England, 188, 191–92
cimarrones, 132
Cincinnati, 54
civil rights, 209
Civil Rights movement, 86
Civil War (US), 25, 44, 60, 66, 96
  British support for Confederacy, 97
  causes, 52
  impact on Mexico's sovereignty, 97
Civilian Conservation Corps, 161
class, 150, 155, 162
Clinton, Bill, 51, 66, 77, 180
Clovis (11,000 BC), 16
Coahuila, 57
Coatzacoalcos River, 42
Colbert, Jean, 170
Colima, 56
Colonization of North America, 1492-1783 (Bolton), 6
Colorado, 96
Columbia, 96
Committee for Industrial Organization, 161
Commonwealth (British), 101
communal landholding of Indian villages (See ejidos)
Compagnie des Cent Associés, 23
Compromise of 1850, 65
Confederación de Trabajadores Mexicanos, 81, 158
Confederación Nacional de

Campesinos, 81, 159
Confederación Nacional de Organizaciones Populares, 81
Confederación Regional Obrera Mexicana, 158
Congregationalist Church, 192, 199
Congress of Industrial Organization, 161
conquistadores, 129, 150
Conservative Party (John A. Macdonald), 78
Conservative Party of Canada, 78, 80 (See also Progressive Conservative Party)
continental cooperation (See continentalism)
continental diplomacy, 89–108
  postwar trends, 103–8
Continental Divide (Lipset), x
continental features, 38–41
continental integration (See continentalism)
continental security, 11, 33 (See also post-9/11 security concerns)
continentalism, 9, 34, 63, 100–01, 213 (See also NAFTA)
  Mexican-US border and, 210
  Quebec nationalism and, 210
  suspicious response in US, 213
Convention of 1818, 94
convergence, 8–9, 11, 37, 209
  "Bolton Theory," 5–6
  Canadian-Mexican commonalities, 8–9
  continental (See continentalism)
convergence and divergence, 1–14, 35, 63, 203
  in Indian policies, 126
  religious beliefs, 187
Coolidge, Calvin, 102

Cooperative Commonwealth Federation (CCF), 79–80
cordillera, 40
Corn Laws (1660-1848), 170, 172
Cortés, Hernán, 7, 20
corvée, 151
Cosío Villegas, Daniel, 103
Costa Rica, 94
cotton, 51, 131, 152, 170
Council of Trent, 22, 188
coureurs de bois, 151
Cozumel, 56
Cree, 46, 113, 124
Cristero Rebellion, 198
crop-lien system, 154
Cruz, Sor Juana Inés de la (See Juana Ramírez de Asbaje)
Cuba, 27, 99, 103, 182
Cuban Refugee Program, 142
Cubans, 141–42
cuernavaca, 144
culture, 11, 58, 130, 139
    cultural distinctiveness, 10
    cultural pluralism, 145
    mestizaje, 120
    multiculturalism, 146, 210
    survival of, 18, 122

Dallas, 54
Dawes General Allotment (Severalty) Act (1887), 117, 119
De Gaulle, Charles, 70
debt, 104–5
debt peonage, 150
Delaware River, 42
democracy, 83–86, 105
Democracy in America (Tocqueville), 83
Democratic Party, 76–77
Democratic-Republicans, 76
Democratic Revolutionary Party (See PRD)
Denver, 54
DePalma, Anthony, Here, x
Departamento de Asuntos Indígenas, 121

"dependency theory," 206
Detroit, 52, 54
Devoir, Le, 70
Díaz, Porfirio, 27–28, 74–75, 137, 173, 194
    attacks on organized labor, 157
Díaz del Castillo, Bernal, True History of the Conquest of New Spain, 7
Díaz Ordaz, Gustavo, 159
Diego, Juan, 188, 201
Dion Stéphane, 71
District of Columbia, 65
divergence, 1–3, 9–10, 12, 37, 108 (See also convergence and divergence; regionalism)
"Do the Americas Have a Common History?" (Bolton), x
Dobbs, Lou, 213.
Dominicans, 188, 190
    las dos majestades, 188
draveur, 151
drug trade, 12, 104, 208, 210
Durango, 57
Dutch immigrants, 131

Earle, Robert, Identities in North America, x
Eastern European immigrants, 135, 137
economic integration, 104, 164 (See also NAFTA)
Ecotopia, 59
Edmonton, 59
education, 65–66, 68
    provincial power, 67, 195
    religious education, 194
    trinational programs, 8
Ejército Zapatista de Liberación Nacional (EZLN), 1, 82 (See also Zapatista uprising)
Ejército Popular Revolucionario, 82
ejidos, 30, 74, 119–20, 159
    breakup, 160

El Salvador, 94, 142, 144
El Salvadorans, 141–42
encomienda, 150
energy, 49, 66, 104 (See also oil)
Engel v. Vitale, 200
England (See also Britain)
    colonization of North America, 20–21, 90–92, 132
    mercantilism, 169–70, 172
English Canada (See Canada)
English Colonies (See Canada; New England)
"English-language only" movement, 145
environment, 8, 12, 57, 181, 209
"Epic of Greater America, The" (Bolton), 5
Eric the Red, 46
ethanol, 186
Eurocentrism, 6
export-driven economies, 9, 206
"Extra-Official Pact" (1923), 102
EZLN, 1, 82

Fallon, Michael Francis, 198
Far North, 50
farmers organizations, 154
federalism (Canada), 67–72, 97
    "Compact Theory of Confederation," 67
    constitutional issues, 68–69
    federal government powers, 30, 67–68
    fusion of powers, 63
    provincial powers, 67–68
    Quebec Question, 68–72
    Royal Commission on Dominion-Provincial Relations (1940), 68
federalism (Mexico), 72–75
    centralism, 30, 72
    regional animosities, 73
    separation of powers, 63
federalism (US)
    checks and balances, 64

federal powers, 64, 66
Great Society years, 66
separation of powers, 63, 65
state powers, 65, 97
Federalist Party, 76
Fenian raids, 97
Ferguson, Will, *Canadian History for Dummies*, x
Fernández de, Oviedo y Valdés, Gonzalo
Historia general y natural de las Indias, 2
filles du roi, 131
First Continental Congress, 23
"First International Congress of the Spanish Language," 147
First Nations, 110 (*See also* Indians)
Folsom (10,000 BC), 16
forced labor, 7, 150–52 (*See also* slavery)
foreign investment, 9, 102, 104–5, 176
Foreign Investment Review Agency (Canada), 178
Fort Duquesne, 92
Fort Worth, 54
Fox, Vicente, 34, 75, 81, 83, 105, 126, 186, 189, 201, 212–13
public opposition to Iraq war, 107
reaction to 9/11, 106
France
colonialism, 20–21, 23
colonization of North America, 89–90 (*See also* New France)
mercantilism, 170
franchise, 86–88
Franciscans, 188–90
Francophonie, 101
free trade, 170, 179–86 (*See also* NAFTA; Reciprocity Treaty (1854))
Free Trade Agreement (FTA), 180

French and Indian War (Seven Years' War), 23, 60, 91–92, 114
French language, 48, 68, 70, 101, 143
Bill 101, 71
frontier, 58
Frost, Robert, 215.

Gadsden Purchase, 96
Galt-Cayley Tariff (1859) (Canada), 172
Garneau, François-Xavier, *Histoire de Canada*, 3
Gaspé Peninsula, 91
Geneva Agreement of Tariffs and Trade 179–80
geography, 37, 54, 61
continental features, 38, 40–41
overlapping of national borders, 45
unity of North America, 4
Georgia, 23
German immigrants, 131, 135, 137, 147
Gettysburg, 60
Globe and Mail, 59
gold, 45, 50, 96–97, 174
Gompers, Samuel, 156
"Good Neighbor Policy," 102
Goodnight-Loving Trail, 53
Gore, Al, 77
governor general, 67
Graham, Billy, 199
Gran Pueblo, El (Beezley), x
grand narrative tradition, ix, 89
grandeur of America theme, 3
Grange, the, 155
Grangers, 154
Grapes of Wrath, The (Steinbeck), 53
Great Awakening, 195–96, 208
Great Basin, 40, 54
Great Bear Lake, 41, 50
Great Depression, 29–30, 66, 68, 77, 79–80, 160–61, 176–77

labor and, 158
repatriation of Acadians and Mexicans, 139
Great Lakes, 41, 48
Great Plains, 40–41, 52–53
Great Slave Lake, 41, 50
"Great Society," 32, 66
Greenland, 6, 49
Groulx, Lionel, 41
Gu, Wulong, 184
Guadalajara, 56, 144
Guatemala, 17, 27, 144
guest-worker programs, 58, 105, 107 (*See also* US immigration policies)
Gulf Coast, 57, 131
Gulf of California, 56
Gulf of Campeche, 17, 56
Gulf of Mexico, 41, 55

habitants, 151, 153
Haiti, 142
Halibut Fisheries Treaty, 100
Halifax, 41, 46
Hamilton, Alexander, 65, 76–77
Report on Manufactures, 171
Harper, Stephen, 34, 78–79, 107
pro-US leanings, 213
recognition of Quebec as nation, 72, 209
Hawley-Smoot Tariff (1930) (US), 176
Hay-Pauncefote Treaties, 99
Haymarket Square Strike (Chicago), 156
Helms Burton Bill (US), 182
Here (DePalma), x
Hidalgo y Costilla, Miguel, 24, 189, 193
Hispanic immigrants, 138, 141 (*See also latino*; Mexican immigrants)
emphasis on cultural distinctiveness and preservation, 145
fear of, 103

largest ethnic minority in
US, 142
Hispanic water law in the
US, 43
Histoire de Canada
(Garneau), 3
Historia de Méjico (Alamán), 3
*Historia general y natural de
las Indias*, 2
historical periods, 15–35
Archaic Period, 16–17, 20
Classic Periods, 17–18
colonialism, 21–23
contact and conquest, 20
early North American his-
tory, 16
growth (second half of
19th C.), 26
imperialism (US), 27
making of nations, 23–25
mid-century (19th) chal-
lenges, 25–26
1920s, Great Depression
and World War II, 29–31
Post Classic, 18
postwar trends, 31–35
reform and revolution
(late 19th/early 20th C.),
27–29
*History of the Discovery and
Settlement of America,
The* (Robertson), 3
History of the United States
(Bancroft), 3
HMS *Trent*, 97
Holland, 20–21
Hollywood, 60–61
homeland security (*See* post-
9/11 security concerns)
Homestead Strike, 156
Honduras, 17, 94, 144
Hoover, Herbert, 176
House of Burgesses, 84–85
House of the Workers of the
World (*See Casa del
Obrero Mundial*)
Houston, 54
Hudson Bay region, 23
Hudson River, 42

Hudson's Bay Company, 91, 96
Huronia, 114
Hurons, 114, 190
Hussein, Saddam, 107, 212
Hydro-Québec, 70

icons of place, 59–60
Idaho, 54
Identities in North America
(Earle), x
Iglesias Law, 74
Illinois, 52
immigrants and immigration,
7, 12, 26, 104–5, 129–48,
156
anti-immigration groups,
209
first wave (1830s-1850s),
133–35
illegal immigrants, 163,
181 (*See also* Mexican
immigrants; undocu-
mented immigrants)
immigration debate,
143–44
immigration reform, 60
literacy requirement, 136
perceived threat to way of
life, 135-36
repatriation, 139–40, 211
second wave, 135–37
third wave, 141, 143–44,
147
*Immigration Reform and Con-
trol Act* (1968) (US), 142
Imperial Oil, 175
import-substitution, 177–78
indentured servants, 131, 152
Indian, xiii, 109–11
Canadian definition and
usage, xiii, 110–11
Mexican definition of, 110
US defintion of, 110
Indian-European interaction,
6, 91, 109–27 (*See also*
Seven Years' War (French
and Indian War))
assimilation, 116–22
colonization stage, 111–15

commercial relations, 115
intermarriage, 114
land issues, 114–15, 119
(*See also ejidos*)
population size and, 111
Indiana, 52
Indians, 67, 84 (*See also*
Canadian Indian policies;
Mexican Indian policies;
US Indian policies)
in cities, 126
conversion to Christianity,
189–90
cultures, 116, 118, 125,
146, 187
European diseases, 111
franchise, 87
Indian-owned casinos,
123, 125
Indian pueblo (village),
113, 119
inferior position, 112–13,
151
interpreters and traders,
111, 114
labor source, 111, 149–50
(*See also* slavery)
migration of, 45
poverty, 125–26
resilience, 7, 109, 125-27
self-determination goals,
125
separation and isolation,
114–15
size of population, 149, 204
sovereignty, 115, 125
syncretic religion, 190
*Indians in the United States
and Canada* (Nichols),
125–26
indígena. (*See* Indian)
indigenismo, 120
Indigenous peoples (*See also*
Indians)
disregard for, 37
movement as way of life,
6, 116
national boundaries and,
109

indigo, 51
"indio" (*See* Indian)
industrial unionism (*See* organized labor)
Industrial Workers of the World, 156–57
Institutional Revolutionary Part (*See* PRI)
Instituto Indigenista Interamericano, 121
Instituto Nacional Indigenista, 110, 121
Inter-American Conference on Problems of War and Peace (*See* Chapultepec Conference)
International Joint Commission, 100
Inuit, 46, 50, 124
Inuit Committee on National Issues, 124
Investment Canada, 179
Iraq, war with, 104, 211
    Canada's opposition, 2, 107, 212
    continental diplomacy and, 105
    Mexico's opposition, 2, 107, 212
Irish immigrants, 131, 133–34
Iroquois, 91, 115
Isthmus of Tehuantepec, 54–55
Iturbide, Augustín, 24, 73, 193
    Plan of Iguala, 73
Iztaccíhuatl (Sleeping Woman), 18, 40

Jalisco, 56
James Bay hydroelectic project, 47, 124
Jamestown, 20, 51, 84, 114, 131
Japan, 59
Jefferson, Thomas, 65, 76–77, 93, 116, 153
Jesuits, 188–90
Jews, 137, 192
John Paul II, Pope, 200

Johnson, Lyndon, 103
    "Great Society," 32
Juárez, Benito, 98
Juárez Law, 74
Juárez-Payne Tariff (1856) (Mexico), 172

Kansas City, 26
Kansas-Nebraska Act (1854), 65, 76
Kennedy, John F., 103
Kentucky, 52
Kerouac, Jack, *On the Road*, 7
King, Martin Luther, 200
King, William Lyon Mackenzie, 30, 78
King Philip's War, 115
Knights of Labor, 157
Korean immigrants, 143
Korean War refugees, 141

La Salle, René-Robert, 23
Labastida, Francisco, 105
labor, 181 (*See also* organized labor; slavery)
    braceros, 140, 160
    colonial period, 149–53
    rural, 2, 152–54, 160
    temporary, 162
    urban, 158, 160
Labrador, 46 (*See also* Newfoundland and Labrador)
Lake Athabasca, 41
Lake Winnipeg, 41
land, 30 (*See also ejidos*; private property)
    agrarian reforms (1992), 120
    campesino access to, 159
    reserves, 117–18
land bridge theory, 16
latino, 141
Laurentian Highlands, 47
Laurentian Shield (*See* Canadian Shield)
Laurier, Wilfrid, 78, 176
Lawrence, D.H., *Mornings in Mexico*, x

League of Nations, 29
Lerdo Law, 74
Lerma River, 43
Lesage, Jean, 70
Lévesque, René, 70
Lewis, John L., 161
Liberal Party, 68, 78–79
Life on the Mississippi (Twain), 42
Lincoln, Abraham, 60, 76
Lipset, Seymour Martin, 86
    Continental Divide, x
López Mateos, Adolfo, 103
López Obrador, Manuel, 83
Los Angeles, 41, 53–54
Louis XIV, King, 85
Louisbourg, 91
Louisianna, 152
Louisianna Territory purchase, 93
Loyalists, 24, 93, 133
Luther, Martin, 187
Lutherans, 192

Macdonald, John A., 67, 78, 97, 156, 173
Mackenzie, Alexander, 78
Mackenzie River, 42, 50
MacLachlan, Colin M., x
Madero, Francisco, 99
Madison, James, 65
Madrazo, Roberto, 83
Maine, 46–47, 65, 96
Manifest Destiny, 4–5, 94–97
Manitoba, 48, 67, 87, 173
Manitoba Act (1870), 68
maquiladoras, 163, 165, 179, 210
Maritime provinces, 2, 44, 46, 173
Martin, Paul, 72, 78–79, 212
Maryland, 23, 52
Massachusetts Bay Company, 192
"Massacre of Tlateloco," 32
Massacre of Wounded Knee, 117
Maximilian, Ferdinand, 25, 98
Maya, 17, 55

McKinley Tariff Act (1890)
(US), 175
mechanization of agriculture,
160 (*See also* agribusiness)
Meech Lake Accord, 69, 71,
78, 124
"melting pot," 144–45
Mercado, Patricia, 83
mercantilism, 167, 169–70,
172
Mercredi, Ovide, 8
meseta central, 56
Mesoamerica, 17–18
mestizaje (racial and cultural
mixing), 120–21
mestizos, 60, 84, 146–47,
151, 205
Methodist Church, 199
Métis, 114
Métis National Council, 124
Métis uprising, 26, 67, 117
Mexican-American
Commission of
Continental Defense, 8
Mexican-American General
Agreement, 102
Mexican-American War
(1846-48), 96, 207
Mexican Border Region (*See
also maquiladoras;*
Mexico-US border)
new culture, 58, 139
social and environmental
problems, 57
Mexican foreign policy, 9
control of foreign investment, 104
non-intervention, 103
relations with Cuba, 103
self-determination, 103
Mexican immigrants, 8,
138–39, 141–42, 147 (*See
also* guest-worker pro-
grams; undocumented
workers)
"Operation Wetback," 140
Mexican immigration policy,
140–41
deportation of Central

American population,
144
Mexican Independence
(1810-21), 24, 94, 171
Mexican Indian policies (*See
also indigenismo;* Mexican
Revolution (1910))
agrarian reform (1992), 119
assimilation, 119–21
Indian rights bill, 126
*Instituto Nacional
Indigenista*, 121
Mexican migration north of
border, 11, 45, 211
"Mexican Miracle, the," 178
Mexican nationalism,
100–04, 175, 177
Mexican Northwestern
Railway Company, 176
Mexican Revolution (1910),
74, 119, 158, 194
Mexican southern border, 96
"Mexicanization," 58
Mexico, 2, 17, 37, 204–5
agriculture, 43, 54, 57,
168, 181, 185–86, 207
anti-clericalism (not anti-
Catholicism), 189–90,
194
anti-foreign sentiment, 137
anti-US sentiment, 3, 27,
96, 99–100, 175, 177
Baroque period, 22
birth rate, 211
Border Industrialization
Program, 179
Catholicism (*See* Catholic
Church (Mexico))
central government power
(*See* federalism
(Mexico))
central highlands, 55
civil war (*See* War of the
Reform)
commitment to industrial-
ization, 177–78
Constitution (1824), 73
Constitution (1857), 74, 119
Constitution (1917), 28,

30, 74, 102, 119, 158–59,
194, 198, 208
debt crisis, 104–5
democracy, 83, 86, 105
drug-trafficking culture,
12, 104, 208, 210
effect of NAFTA (*See*
NAFTA)
expanding role of military
and police, 76, 208
export-driven economy, 9
factionalism, 73, 207
foreign investment, 102,
104, 171, 173–74, 176
foreign relations (*See*
Mexican foreign policy)
free trade, 173 (*See also*
NAFTA)
freedom of religion, 194
French invasion, 25, 74,
98, 207
icons of place, 59
ideological and regional
conflicts, 24
immigration, 129, 134,
137, 144
import licenses, 178
independence 24, 130, 189
language politics, 147
loss of Texas, 44, 94, 96,
135, 207
"Massacre of Tlateloco,"
32
mestizaje (racial and cultural mixing), 120–21
mestizos, 60, 84, 146–47,
151, 205
Mexican-American War
(1846-48), 96, 207
mineral resources, 57,
168, 174
monarchy, 73
"multi-ethnic" nation, 121
multiculturalism, 146
Pacific trade, 168
peso devaluation, 163, 182
petroleum industry, 56,
159, 174, 181
political culture, 84–85

political feminism, 83
political (in)stability, 7, 27, 73
population, 26–27, 31
poverty, 1, 32, 55
protectionism, 178
railway construction, 174–75
revolt against Spanish rule (1810), 24, 94, 171
revolution (1910) (See Mexican Revolution (1910))
rivers, 42–43
separation of powers (See federalism (Mexico))
settlement, 41
silver, 168, 174
size, 38, 96
slavery, 132
social and economic inequalities, 28, 32, 85, 163
survival of Indian culture, 18, 112
tariffs, 171–73, 178
tourism, 55–56
Tropic of Cancer, 54
urbanization, 31
weakness of reform movements, 207–8
women's suffrage, 87
World War I, 29
World War II, 31, 102
Mexico City, 31, 55, 60–61, 82, 89
Diocese of, 190
growth, 75
Mexico City Light and Power Company, 176
"Mexico for Mexicans," 102
Mexico-US border, 48, 96, 105, 107, 142, 181, 210
Operation Centinela, 107
pollution, 8
settlement patterns, 5
wall, 142, 148
Mexico-US Reciprocal Trade Agreement (1942-50), 177

Mexico-US relations, 104
George W. Bush and, 105–7
1920s and 30s, 101–2
US intervention, 95, 99, 175
Mexico-US trade, 177–78
post NAFTA, 182
Miami, 54
Midwest, 52
Minnesota, 52
Mississippi, 152
Mississippi River, 52, 93
French settlers, 42, 90–91
Missouri Compromise (1820), 65–66
Missouri Plateau, 52
Missouri River, 42
Moctezuma I and II, 18
modernization, 26, 74
Monongahela River, 42
Monroe Doctrine, 94, 98
Montagnais, 46, 113
Monte Albán, 17
Monterrey, 26, 57–58
Montreal, 41, 47, 152, 197
Moral Majority, 200
Moravians, 193
Morelos, José María, 193
Mornings in Mexico (Lawrence), x
Morones, Luis, 158
Morril Tariff (1861) (US), 172
Morrow, Dwight, 102
Mt. Logan, 40
Mt. McKinley, 40
Mulroney, Brian, 78–79, 180
multiculturalism, 145–46, 210

NAFTA, 1, 8, 104–5, 180–82, 184–85
effect on labor, 164–65
effect on Mexican peasants, 164
environmental critics, 181
tenth anniversary reports, 182, 184
Nakai, R. Carlos, 127
nation state, 3, 7, 15, 203
artificial creation, 37

Indigenous peoples, 127
National Action Party (See PAN)
national defense, 8 (See also post-9/11 security concerns)
National Origins Act (US), 136
National Petroleum Workers Syndicate, 102
National Policy (Canada), 68, 78, 136–37, 173
National Progressive Party, 28
nationalism, 9, 97 (See also Canadian nationalism; Manifest Destiny; Mexican nationalism; Quebec nationalism)
"Native American," xiii, 109 (See also Indian)
Native American Association (1837), 133
Native American Church, 200
Native American Free Exercise of Religion Act, 200
Native American Grave Protection and Repatriation Act I (NAGPRA), 122–23
Native American Party (1845), 133
Native Council of Canada, 124
nativism, 133–34, 137, 211
Navigation Act (Britain), 169–70, 172
Navigator, The, 42
Nayarit, 56
Near North, 50
Neolithic Age, 16
Nevada, 54, 96
New Amsterdam, 90
New Brunswick, 42, 46, 67, 96, 192, 196
New Deal, 30, 77, 208
increased federal power, 66
Wagner Act, 160
New Democratic Party, 80
New England, 23, 41, 52
Catholic Church, 192
Congregationalist Church, 192

French Canadian migration, 45, 139
immigration, 131
opportunities, 206
religious pluralism, 191
New France, 23 (*See also* Quebec)
Catholic Church as instrument of colonization, 190
centralization of authority, 85
immigrants, 130–31
Indians as guides, trappers, traders, 113–15
opposed to union with US, 98
New Hampshire, 23, 47
New Jersey, 52
New Mexico, 21, 43, 57, 65, 96, 138
New Orleans, 23, 42, 91, 93, 174
New Spain, 150, 190 (*See also* Mexico)
African slaves, 130
conquistadores, 129–30
debt peonage, 150
encomienda, 150
hierarchy based on race and culture, 130
immigration, 129–30
labor pool (Indians), 149–50
promise of seigneurial life, 130
repartimiento, 150
"New World," 3, 6
New York, 41–42, 47, 52, 54, 96
New York Times, 139
Newfoundland, 6, 23, 67
Atlantic fishery and, 44
cod banks, 46, 168
English land bases, 91
Newfoundland and Labrador, 46–47
Nicaragua, 94
Nicaraguans, 141–42

Nichols, Roger, *Indians in the United States and Canada*, 125–26
9/11, 11, 33, 106, 210
Nixon, Richard, 88, 122
Noble Order of the Knights of Labor, 156
North American Air Defense Agreement, 8
North American common market, 211–12
North American Competitiveness Council, 212
North American continental features, 38–41
North (Canada), 49–50
North (Mexico), 57, 205
meseta central, 56
North-South Conference (Cancún, Mexico), 104
North (US), 10, 51–52
North-West Rebellion, 26
Northwest Territories, 38, 49–50, 67
Nova Scotia, 23, 46, 67, 192
Nuevo León, 57–58
Nunavut, 49–50, 124

Oaxaca, 55
Oaxaca (protests, 2006), 75–76
Official Languages Act (1969), 146
Ohio, 42, 52
Ohio River Valley, 92
oil, 50, 158
Mexico, 56
off-shore oil, 46
Petro-Canada, 49
Petróleos Mexicanos (PEMEX), 159, 181
Oklahoma land Rush, 53
Oklahoma Territory (reservation), 117
Olmec, 17
Olympics, 51, 60
On the Road (Kerouac), 7
Ontario, 2, 30, 48, 67

industry, 48, 207
opposition to NAFTA, 180
SARS outbreak, 33
Ontario Superior Court of Justice, 196
Operation Centinela, 107
"Operation Hold the Line," 144
"Operation Wetback," 140
Oregon, 53
Oregon Treaty, 96
Organization of American States, 103
organized labor, 155–56
Canada, 156–57, 161–62
Mexico, 158–60
strikes, 156–58
unsympathetic cultural and political climate, 157, 162
US, 160–61, 164
Ottawa Agreements (1932), 176–77

Pacific trade, 168
Palafox y Mendoza, Juan de, 22
Palenque, 17, 55
Paleo-Indian Period, 16
PAN, 81–83, 198
Pan Indian movement, 122
Panama, 96
Panama Canal, 99
Parc des Laurentides, 47
Parizeau, Jacques, 71
parliamentary systems
fusion of power, 63
majority rule, 63–64
Parti Québécois, 70–72
Partido de Acción Nacional (*See* PAN)
Partido Revolucionario Democrático (*See* PRD)
Partido Revolucionario Institucional (*See* PRI)
Passion of the Christ, The (film), 201
patrias chicas, 54
Patrons of Husbandry, 154
Pax Porfiriana, 74

Payne-Aldrich Tariff (1909), 176
Pearl Harbor, 31, 140
Pearson, Lester, 70
Penn, William, 192
Pennsylvania, 42, 52, 192
People's Party of the USA (See Populist Party)
Pequot War (1637), 114
periodization schemes (See historical periods)
Perot, Ross, 77, 180–81
Pershing, John J., 99
Petro-Canada, 49
Petróleos Mexicanos (PEMEX), 159, 181
peyote in religious ceremonies, 200
Philadelphia, 41, 54
Philippine immigrants, 143
Philippines, 27, 99
Pico de Orizaba, 40
Pinckney's Treaty (See Treaty of San Lorenzo (1795))
Pinkerton Detective Agency, 156
Pirsig, Robert M., Zen and the Art of Motorcycle Maintenance, 8
Pittsburgh, 52, 54
Plains of Abraham, 60
Plan of Iguala, 73
plantation societies, 51, 131
Platte River, 42
Plaza de las Tres Culturas, 59–60
Pleistocene Age, 16
Plymouth, 20, 51, 191
police powers, 65, 76, 106, 208
political culture, 83–86
political feminism, 83
political parties
  farmers parties, 154–55
political parties (Canada)
  Bloc Québécois, 80
  Canadian Alliance, 80
  Conservative Party, 78
  Conservative Party of Canada, 78–80

Cooperative Commonwealth Federation (CCF), 79–80
Liberal-Conservative Party, 78
Liberal Party, 78–79
New Democrati Party, 80
Progressive Conservative Party, 78
Reform Party, 80
Social Credit, 79–80
third parties, 79–80
political parties (Mexico), 80–83
  Alternativa Social Demó-crata Campesina, 83
  PAN, 81, 83
  party patronage networks, 75
  PRD, 82–83
  PRI, 75, 80–83
political parties (US), 76–77
  centralist tendencies, 77
  Democratic Party, 77
  Democratic-Republicans, 76
  Democratics, 76
  Federalist Party, 76
  National Republicans, 76
  nativists, 133
  Republican Party, 76–77
  third parties, 77
  Whig Party, 76
Popocatépetl (Smoking Mountain), 18, 40
popular sovereignty, 65–66
populism, 84, 211
Populist movement, 208
Populist Party, 27, 154
porous borders, 11
Portland, 59
Portland-Seattle corridor, 53
Portugal, 3, 90
post-9/11 security concerns, 58, 104, 106–7
  immigration debate and, 34, 142, 148
  US preoccupation with, 105

potlatch, 118
poverty, 214–15 (See also rich-poor gap)
Prairie provinces (See also names of individual Prairie provinces)
  settlement, 96–97, 173
  wheat economy, 48
prayer in public schools, 200
PRD, 82–83
Precambrian Shield (See Canadian Shield)
predestination, 188
Presbyterians, 192, 199
president, 64, 66, 72, 75
PRI, 75, 82–83, 181
prime minister, 63–64, 67
Prince Edward Island, 46, 67
private property, 117, 119
Progressive Conservative Party, 68, 78 (See also Conservative Party)
Progressive movement, 66, 208
Progressive Party, 28, 155
prohibition, 196–97
protectionism, 172–73, 177 (See also tariffs)
Protestant Reformation, 22
provincial powers (See under federalism (Canada))
Puebla, 22
Puerto Ricans, 141–42
Puerto Rico, 99
Puritans, 20, 51, 114, 191–93

Quakers, 192
Quebec, 2, 9, 30, 47, 67, 101, 169
  biculturalism, 146
  Catholic Church, 194, 198, 206, 209
  De Gaulle's visit (1967), 70
  diversified economy, 48
  fear of Americanization, 139
  French language, 48, 71, 143
  James Bay hydroelectic project, 47

opposition to conscription, 29, 68
opposition to prohibition, 197
power-sharing arrangements, 70
public employees unions, 162
Quiet Revolution (*révolution tranquille*), 32, 70, 209
reform movements, 209
secularization, 198–200, 202
size, 38
sovereignty-association, 70
women's right to vote, 87
Quebec Act (1774), 23, 69, 92, 191, 195
Quebec City, 20, 41, 47, 60, 92, 152
Quebec Department for Immigration, 143
Quebec Liberal Party, 70
Quebec nationalism, 3, 12, 44, 69–70, 210
Quebec referendum (1980), 32, 71
Quebec referendum (1995), 1, 32, 71, 78
Quebec secession reference, 71
Queen Anne's War (*See* War of the Spanish Succession)
Queen's Privy Council of Canada, 67
Quiet Revolution *(révolution tranquille)*, 32, 70, 209
Quintana Roo, 55

race and racism, 3, 32, 66, 138, 151, 205–6
mestizaje, 120–21
Rae, Bob, 180
railroads, 48, 67, 138, 173–75
Chinese immigrants, 136
rivers and, 42
Ramírez de Asbaje, Juana, 22
Sátira filosófica (Philos-

ophical Satire), 22
ranchero (small farmer), 153
ranching, 48, 53
ranchos, 56
Reagan, Ronald, 66
Reciprocal Trade Act (1936), 177
Reciprocal Trade Agreements Act (1934) (US), 177
reciprocity, 78, 176
Reciprocity Treaty (1854), 172
Récollets, 190
Red River, 42
reform movements, 196–97, 207–9
Reformation, 188
Refugee Relief Act (1953), 141
Regina Manifesto, 79
Regional Confederation of Mexican Workers (*See Confederación Regional Obrera Mexicana)*
regionalism, 12, 37, 43–44, 147, 173
binational, 57–59
Chiapas, 9
Mexico, 72–75
Puerto Rico, 10
Quebec, 9
US, 10
regions of Canada, 45–49
regions of Mexico, 54–57
regions of US, 50–54
Reglamento para el Comercio libre (Spain), 170
religion, 187 (*See also* names of individual churches)
Christianity, 197–99
emergence of religious right, 209
importance in US, 197, 202
religious education, 195
religious pluralism, 191
religious revivalism, 195
religious toleration, 192–93
secularization, 199–200
social reform and, 196
repartimiento, 150

Report on Manufactures (Hamilton), 171
Republican Party, 66, 76–77, 105
republican systems of government,
checks and balances, 64
divided government, 64
president (head of state and government), 64
révolution tranquille (See Quiet Revolution)
Rhode Island, 192
rich-poor gap, 162–63, 167
Riel, Louis, 26, 117
Río Blanco strike, 158
Río del Fuerte, 43
Rio Grande or Río Bravo, 45, 57, 96, 103
political boundary, 42
Rio Grande Valley, 138, 181
Río Sonora, 43
Río Yaqui, 43
Rivera, Norberto, 201
"Roaring Twenties," 29
"Robber Barons," 155
Robertson, William, *History of the Discovery and Settlement of America, The*, 3
Rockies, 40
Roe v. Wade, 200
Romero Tariff (1872) (Mexico), 173
Roosevelt, Franklin Delano, 30, 66, 102
Roosevelt, Theodore, 99
Royal North-West Mounted Police, 157
Royal Proclamation of 1763, 115
Rush-Bagot Agreement (1817), 94
Russell, James W., *After the Fifth Sun*, x, 147

Salinas de Gortari, Carlos, 82, 181
agrarian reforms (1992), 120

neo-liberal model of economic development, 105
private ownership of land, 159
restored diplomatic relations with Vatican, 201
San Antonio, 58
San Diego, 41, 53–54
San Francisco, 41, 168
San Miguel de Allende, 144
San Pedro Mártir, 40
San Xavier del Bac (Tucson, Arizona), 189
Santa Fe, 21
Santa Fe Trail, 174
Santiago Tlatelolco church, 60
SARS, 11, 33–34
Saskatchewan, 48, 67, 173
Savannah, 41
school curricula, 12, 15 (See also education)
science, rise of, 199
"Scopes monkey trial," 197
Sea of Cortés, 56
Seattle, 41, 53, 59
Second Continental Congress, 23
Second Great Awakening, 195, 208
sectionalism, 52, 66
secularization, 199–200
Security and Prosperity Partnership of North America (2006) (SPP), 34, 212–13
Seigel, Micol, 11, 14
self-determination (Indian tribes), 121
September 11, 11, 33, 106, 210
Seven Years' War (French and Indian War), 23, 60, 91–92, 114
Severe Acute Respiratory Syndrome (See SARS)
Seward, William Henry, 97
Sheen, Fulton J., 200
Siegfried, André, 4
Sierra Madre Occidental, 40, 56

Sierra Madre Oriental, 56
Sierra Nevada range, 40
"Significance of the Frontier in American History, The" (Turner), 53
silver, 45, 168, 174
Sinaloa, 56
sinarquistas, 198
slavery, 51, 65–66, 86, 96, 130
cimarrones, 132
Indian, 132
plantation agriculture, 131, 152
Underground Railroad, 132
Smith, Adam, Wealth of Nations, 170
Smith, Donald, 174
Smith, Goldwin, Canada and the Canadian Question, 100
Social Credit, 80
Social Democratic and Peasant Alternative, 83
Social Gospel, 197, 208
social welfare, 32, 66
Sociedad México-Tejano, 139
Society for the Propagation of the Gospel, 193
Sonora, 41, 56, 137
Sonora Dynasty, 74
Sonoran desert, 41, 53
Sons of Temperance Union, 196
South America (Bryce), 4
South (of Mexico), 55–56
South (of US), 12, 51, 77, 154
slavery, 131, 152
Southern League, 10
Spain, 3
colonization of North America, 85, 89–90
mercantilism, 169–70
Spanish absolutism, 75
Spanish American War (1898), 27, 99
Spanish colonialism, 21, 93
conversion of Indian population, 188
Hispanization of Indians, 112

ideal of seigneurial lord, 204
Indian labor, 112, 115, 204
Spanish conquest, 19–20, 112
Spanish language, 146–47
sponsorship scandal, 72, 79
St. John River, 42
St. Lawrence River, 42, 89
St. Lawrence River valley, 47–48
St. Lawrence Seaway, 47
St. Louis, 54
Standard Oil, 175
"staples theory," 206–7
states' rights (See federalism (US))
Statue of Liberty, 60
Statute of Westminster (1931), 100
Ste. Marie among the Hurons, 190
Stegner, Wallace, 144
Wolf Willow, 8
Steinbeck, John, Grapes of Wrath, The, 53
stock market crash (1929), 29
Stronach, Belinda, 79
Suffrage Movement, 208
Sugar and Stamp Acts, 23
Sun Dance, 118
Supreme Court (Canada), 71
Supreme Court (Mexico), 75, 102
Susquehanna River, 42

Tabasco, 55
Taft, William H., 176
Taliban, 107
Talon, Jean, 170
Tamaulipas, 57
Tampico, 174
Tariff Act (1789), 171
Tariff Act (1837), 172
tariffs, 171–72, 175–76, 178
Temperance Movement, 208
Tennessee, 52
Tenochtitlán, 18, 20, 55, 113, 150

Teotihuacán, 17
tequila, 56
Termination Laws (1953-62), 122
tierra fría, 54
Territorial Grain Grower's Association, 155
terrorism, 11, 33
    anti-terrorist legislation, 106
Texas, 41, 51, 53, 94, 96, 138
    colonization, 134
    immigrants, 135
    Lone Star Republic, 73, 94
    reputation for mistreating Mexicans, 140
    slavery, 131
    twenty-eighth state (1845), 94
Three Years' War, 25
tierra caliente, 54
tierra templada, 54
Tohono O'Odham nation, 11, 125, 189
Toledano, Vicente Lombardo, 158
Toleration Act (1649), 192
Toltec culture, 18
Tocqueville, Alexis de, 84–87
    Democracy in America, 83
Toronto, 34, 47
Toronto printers' strike (1872), 156
tourism, 46, 55, 75
trade, 104 (*See also* Free Trade Agreement (FTA); NAFTA)
    early patterns of, 167–69
    liberalization of trade, 172 (*See also* free trade)
    protectionism, 172–73, 177
    transportation and, 174
Trade Unions Act (Canada), 156
Trades and Labor Congress of Canada, 157, 161
transnational history, 11, 14
transportation, 38, 52, 66
    railways, 136, 174–75

water, 42, 47
Welland Canal, 207
Treaty of Fontainebleau (1762), 92
Treaty of Guadalupe Hidalgo, 43, 96
Treaty of Madrid (1670), 90
Treaty of Paris (1763), 92
Treaty of San Lorenzo (1795), 93
Treaty of Tordesillas (1494), 90
Treaty of Utrecht (1713), 91, 132
Treaty of Versailles (1783), 92
Treaty of Washington (1871), 97
tri-national cooperation, 63 (*See also* continentalism)
Tropic of Cancer, 54
Trudeau, Pierre, 68, 78, 124
True History of the Conquest of New Spain (Díaz del Castillo), 7
Turner, Frederick Jackson "Significance of the Frontier in American History, The," 53
Twain, Mark, *Life on the Mississippi*, 42
Tyrrell, Ian, 14

Underground Railroad, 132
undocumented immigrants, 34, 58, 142
undocumented workers, 142–43, 148, 213
unemployment, 162–63
unemployment insurance, 30, 161
Union Saint-Jean-Baptiste d'Amérique, 139
unions, 155–56, 162, 164 (*See also* organized labor)
    Catholic Church and, 157
    Industry vs. craft based, 161
    opposition to NAFTA, 181

United Auto Workers, 161
United Church of Canada, 199
United Farm Worker's Union, 160
United Mine Workers, 161
United Nations, 29
United Nations International Security Assistance Force (ISAF), 107
United Nations Security Council, 107
United Steel Workers, 161
Université du Québec, 70
urbanization, 26, 31, 45
US (United States), 2
    annexation of West Florida, 93
    belief in opportunity and social mobility, 60
    "Bill of Rights," 65
    Civil War, 25, 44, 52, 66, 69, 96–97
    Constitutional Act (1791), 24, 133
    control of Cuba, Puerto Rico, and the Philippines, 99
    Declaration of Independence, 23–24, 86, 92, 170
    democracy, 84–85
    diversity, 131
    economic and political hegemony, 27, 29, 175, 178
    economy, 207
    Eighteenth Amendment (1919), 196
    Episcopalian Church, 192
    expansion, 94, 96–98
    exports, 170–71
    farmers organizations, 154
    federal powers (*See* federalism (US))
    Fifteenth Amendment (1870), 86
    foreign capital, 170, 175
    foreign policy (*See* US foreign policy)

Fourteenth Amendment (1868), 86
franchise, 86–87
immigration, 103, 133–38, 140–42
immigration debate, 60, 144
immigration policies (*See* US immigration policies)
imperialism, 27
international investment, 175–76
involvement in Venezuela/British Guiana boundary dispute, 99
isolationism, 29, 211
loss of jobs to Mexico and Asia, 164
Manifest Destiny, 4–5, 94–97
Monroe Doctrine, 94
multiculturalism, 145
NAFTA (*See under* NAFTA)
National Industrial Recovery Act (1933), 160
National Labor Relations Act (1935), 160 (*See also Wagner Act*)
nativism, 133–34
Nineteenth Amendment (1920), 87
Patriot Act, 106
percentage of white people, 145
political culture, 84–86
political equality, 84–85
population, 26–27, 31
populism, 84
Progressive movement, 28
purchase of Alaska, 97
racial conflict, 32, 66
railway construction, 26, 174
Reciprocity Treaty (1854), 172
Reconstruction, 25

reform movements, 27–28, 208–9
regionalism, 54
religious plurality, 199
revival of the South, 10
rich-poor gap, 163
sectionalism, 52
separation of church and state, 199
separation of powers (*See* federalism (US))
settlement, 51
size, 38, 93, 96
slavery, 65
social mobility, 206
student activism, 32
tariffs, 171–72, 175
Thirteenth Amendment (1865), 86
Vietnam War, 32, 104, 141
War of 1812, 24, 93
war with Mexico, 53
World War I, 29
World War II, 31
US-Canada border (*See* Canada-US border)
US foreign policy, 33
"Big Stick" diplomacy, 98–99
"Good Neighbor Policy," 102
unilateral, 34, 103
US immigration policies
Chinese Exclusion Act (US), 136–37
deportation of Mexicans (1930s), 139–40, 211
Emergency Quota Act, 136
Immigration Act (1924), 136
Immigration Act (1990), 141
Immigration and Nationality Act (1965), 141
Japanese retention camps, 140
National Origins Act, 136
"Operation Hold The

Line," 144
"Operation Wetback," 140
US Indian policies
American Indian Citizenship Act, 87
assimilation, 116–17, 122
Dawes General Allotment (Severalty) Act (1887), 117, 119
"dependent sovereign nations" recognition, 125
expulsion of Indians (1830s), 116
franchise (1924), 121
Indian Appropriations Act (1871), 117
Indian Civil Rights Act (1968), 122
Indian-owned casinos and, 123
Indian Reorganization Act (1934), 121
Native American Grave Protection and Repatriation Act (NAGPRA), 122–23
policy of "concentration," 116
policy of "confinement" (reservations), 117
special status for Indians, 122
Termination Laws (1953-62), 122
treaties, 116
war, 116–17
US invasion of Iraq (*See* Iraq, war with)
US-Mexico border (*See* Mexico-US border)
US-Mexico relations (*See* Mexico-US relations)
US nationalism, 94 (*See also* Manifest Destiny)
Utah, 54, 65
Uxmal, 17, 55

Valley of Mexico, 55

Vancouver, 34, 41, 49, 59, 168
Vancouver Island, 96
Vasconcelos, José, 147
Veracruz, 41, 174
Vermont, 47, 96
Victoria, Guadalupe, 73
Vietnam War, opposition to,
    32, 104
Vietnam War refugees, 141
Vietnamese immigrants, 143
Villa, Pancho, 99
Virgin of Guadalupe, 189, 201
Virginia, 23, 192
voyageurs, 151

wages, 2, 30, 163, 185
Wagner Act, 160
War Measures Act, 69
War of 1812, 24, 93
War of the Reform (1858-
    61), 25, 74, 194, 207
War of the Spanish
    Succession, 91
Washington, 40, 53, 59
Washington, George, 92, 116
Washington Post, 10
water, 41–43
Wealth of Nations (Smith), 170
Webster-Ashburton Treaty, 96
Welland Canal, 207
west (Mexico), 56
west (US), 53–54
West Virginia, 42
Western Trail, 53
wheat economy, 48, 173
Whewell, Lori, 184
Wilson, Henry Lane, 99, 102
Wilson, Woodrow, 29, 176
Winnipeg, 26, 48, 173
Winnipeg General Strike
    (1919), 157
Wirth, John, x
Wisconsin, 52
Wolf Willow (Stegner), 8
women, 129–31
    organized labor and, 156,
        164
    preferred in *maquiladoras*,
        163

Women's Christian Temp-
    erance Union, 196
women's rights, 209
women's suffrage, 87
Works Project
    Administration, 161
World Bank, 185
World War I, 28–29, 68, 101
    immigrants from enemy
        nations, 136–37
World War II, 31, 53, 68,
    101–2, 140
Wounded Knee, 122
Wyoming, 53, 96

Yellowknife, 50
yeoman farmer, romanticized
    image of, 153
Yucatán, 55, 73
Yucatán Peninsula, 17, 41,
    54–55
Yucatán Power Company, 176
Yukon Territory, 49, 67

Zacatecas, 56
Zapata, Emiliano, 119
Zapatista uprising, 1, 8, 82,
    126
Zedillo, Ernesto, 82, 105, 159
*Zen and the Art of
    Motorcycle Maintenance*
    (Pirsig), 8